Law's Environment: Critical Legal Perspectives

Law's Environment: Critical Legal Perspectives

Ubaldus de Vries and Lyana Francot (eds.)

eleven international publishing

Published, sold and distributed by Eleven International Publishing
P.O. Box 85576
2508 CG Den Haag
Tel.: +31 70 330 7033
Fax: +31 70-330 7030
e-mail: verkoop@budh.nl
www.elevenpub.com

Sold and distributed in USA and Canada
International Specialized Book Services
920 NE 58th Avenue, Suite 300
Portland, OR 97213-3786, USA
Tel: 1-800-944-6190 (toll-free)
Fax: +1 503 280-8832
orders@isbs.com
www.isbs.com

Printed on acid-free paper.

ISBN: 978-94-90947-22-4

Printed in The Netherlands

Morpheus: The Matrix is a system, Neo. That system is our enemy. But when you're inside, you look around, what do you see? Businessmen, teachers, lawyers, carpenters. The very minds of the people we are trying to save. But until we do, these people are still a part of that system and that makes them our enemy. You have to understand, most of these people are not ready to be unplugged. And many of them are so inured, so hopelessly dependent on the system, that they will fight to protect it.

The Matrix (Warner Bros., Australian Village Roadshow Pictures, 1999). Quote from: <www.imdb.com/title/tt0133093/quotes> (14 June 2011)

Preface

This book of essays follows from and adds to the presentations, discussions and debates – the exchanges of ideas – of the Critical Legal Conference 2010, held in Utrecht 10-12 September at the Department of Legal Theory of the Faculty of Law (Utrecht University).

The Critical Legal Conference is an annual gathering of legal scholars that share a critical outlook on law and legal scholarship. This year's conference focused, as a main theme, on exposing the normative abuse of law against the background of 'multiple modernities', i.e. the idea that modernity is not a single encompassing, Western concept but entails different traditions and ways of thought about contemporary society.

We would like to thanks all the author contributors to this book of essays and the manner in which they were able to deal with our deadlines and other requests. Our thanks also goes out to the staff at Eleven publishers.

Utrecht, June 2011

Ubaldus de Vries and Lyana Francot

Table of Contents

Introduction

Law's environment is characterized by socio-structural developments that demand, now more than ever, a critical perspective, not only on law but also on legal scholarship. The environment of law refers to society in the widest sense of the word. Of course, one may refer to the environment of law in territorial terms: the environment of law is that what is under the authority of the state, limiting society to national society. Indeed, modern lines of thought took the nation state as point of departure for analysis and some contemporary thinkers, also in legal theory and philosophy, still adhere to, what is termed, methodological nationalism in their field of study. [1] Although this may still be a legitimate starting point for analysis, it does not allow accounting for developments that transcend the nation state. Our understanding of law's environment in this book of essays is not limited to this perspective. Rather, we believe it to be more adequate to refer to law's environment as the totality of processes that law seeks to regulate through communication – for better, for worse and sometimes in vain.

The environment is not constituted and defined by territory solely but also by social, psychological and biological processes that take place in and outside territory, then, now and in the future, here and there. What is shared with modern thought is the idea of a functional differentiation of the social processes, distinguishing between politics, economy, religion, morality, culture, art, ecology, love, law itself, etc. The notion of law's environment implies a relationship between law and *its entire* environment. This relationship is one of interplay: the environment with all its noise and turbulence determines the role and position of law while at the same time law seeks to address developments and phenomena in its environment. This interplay comes about in and through communication and constitutes an inter-relationship.

At the same time, the inter-relationship is limited, in both ways. The environment with its typical quirks and wilfulness limits the possibilities of law's function, while at the same time law seeks to limit or at least: to define the possibilities of the environment. Although the limitation is double-sided, the inter-relationship is not fully symmetrical. It is if and when structural changes in the environment occur, that law's regulatory and limiting function reveals its own limited capacities. Law is capable to respond to the demands of

1 For an overview of the concept, see D. Chernilo, 'Methodological Nationalism: Theory and History', paper presented at the Annual Conference of the International Association of Critical Realism, King's College, London, July 2008. See also: <www.kcl.ac.uk/depsta/law/events/0708/iacr/papers/Chernilo_Methodological_Nationalism.pdf> (last accessed: 18 May 2011).

the environment as long as these demands fit within the structure of law as it is, here and now. Or to put it differently: as long as these demands are voiced in such a way that it connects with the existing legal structures. But if the demands derive from structural changes that are paradigmatic, law shows its limitations and shortcomings. These limitations and shortcomings are an inherent part of the existing law, disclosing the side effects of its application and, as a consequence, the inability to come up with 'new' law to address that what causes these side effects and if it addresses the side-effects, only haphazardly and belatedly. The law on pharmaceutical patents is perhaps illustrative. Patents on medicines exist to promote pharmaceutical innovation as they guarantee an exclusive property right in the new medicine. It allows the possibility of a return on investment and a decent profit for shareholders. Patent law, and its focus on exclusive property rights and profit generation, fits within the overall scheme of modern private law and its focus on individual property, regulated and protected within the nation state and among states. The side effect of this regulatory framework is that millions of people are devoid of life-saving or life-prolonging medicine, for example, those suffering from AIDS – a problem that transcends states and is a truly global problem. It shows law's limited function and the side effects it produces, which can only be addressed when *re*considering law's function at a structural level both in terms of the environment it serves and what it serves.[2]

Developments and events, as the patents example illustrates, show that changes of a structural nature unavoidably take place within law's environment. These developments become manifest in phenomena such as the financial and economic crisis, the ongoing humanitarian wars, civil unrest, ecological disasters (whether caused by man or nature), and the increasing intolerance towards 'others'. These developments, and the phenomena with which they are represented, can be encapsulated as symptoms of the contemporary processes of globalization. These processes are interdependent and illustrate that globalization is multidimensional. The last decades or so have seen a seismic transformation in the way we can communicate, enabled by information technology; we have seen the emergence of a global economy and shifts in the organization of trade and finance enabled by deregulation of state control; travel has become more easy (and cheap); we have seen the formation of state-transcending political entities – both governmental and non-governmental,

---

2 There are many causes to the AIDS crisis in Africa and elsewhere. Te point is to show that law's function creates side effects in its application that demands reconsideration of the function if we want to take these effects seriously. And only outside the law changes are slowly taking place, for example, in respect of the Access to Medicine Index (<www.accesstomedicineindex.org/> (last accessed: 29 May 2011)). On patents and property rights, see WIPO, *Patent Protection and Access to HIV/AIDS Pharmaceuticals in Sub-Saharan Africa*, The International Intellectual Property Institute, Washington 2000. But also: Lawrence Lessig, *Free Culture: How Big Media Uses Technology and the Law to Lock Down Culture and Control Creativity*, 2004, published under the creative commons license; see <www.free-culture.cc/> (last accessed: 18 May 2011). Less radical: Th. Pogge, *World Poverty and Human Rights*, Polity Press, Cambridge 2008 (2nd ed.), Chapter 9.

and with it instances of global law though often still masquerading as international law and in the last decade or so presented as 'transnational law'.[3]

All these developments and processes suggest that we live in a world society, changing for ever the customary ways of understanding our life world. Indeed, they have an impact on how we live our lives as individuals, both enabled and forced to make life choices and develop our identities: IPod IPhone IPad Iam.[4]

Modernization is not longer only characterized by processes of industrialization and democratization, safely anchored within the confinement of the nation state. These processes are incorporated, so to speak, in the wider and encompassing processes of globalization and individualization. These processes characterize contemporary modernization. Contemporary modernization theories provide us with analyses as to how society evolves, changes, develops, and more in particular: progresses. There is not a single modernity, nor one uniform theory. Rather, one could speak of 'multiple modernities', as proposed by Eisenstadt. According to this Israeli sociologist, the notion of multiple modernities:

> goes against the views long prevalent in scholarly and general discourse. It goes against the view of the 'classical' theories of modernization and of the convergence of industrial societies prevalent in the 1950s.[5]

It suggests an approach that does not take as its point of departure the idea that the Western programme of modernization would result in a universal and homogeneous (world) society. On the contrary. The long-held view that globalization entailed global modernization; *viz.* the global victory march of Western democracy, values and norms is now eroded by the side-effects of this victory march. It is these side-effects that form the object of analysis of contemporary modernization theories, and allows, depending on the focus, modernity to be described as a reflexive modernity, a liquid modernity, a second modernity, a post-modernity, etc. and to observe anti-modern developments as well, which become visible in the re-emergence of a nationalist sentiment of the dangerous kind across Europe – a sentiment that thrives on the explicit exclusion of the physical 'other' within our midst, shaping politics and hijacking public debate with freedom of speech as the highest democratic value to silence the other.[6]

---

3 See also Eugene McNamee's contribution in this book.

4 After: <www.mobilemac.nl/iphone/kijktip-ipod-i-phone-i-am/> (last accessed: 17 May 2011).

5 S.N. Eisenstadt, 'Multiple Modernities', *in*: S.N. Eisenstadt (ed.), *Multiple Modernities*, Transaction Publishers, New Brunswick/London 2002, p. 1-30.

6 See also: U. de Vries, 'Anger and Courage: Fitna and the Politics of Disengagement', Sfera Politicii, Vol. 10, Nr. 4, 2010, p. 165-170.

Theories on modernization constitute a suitable and effective point of departure to make sense of society and, we believe, to frame and analyze the relationship between law, politics and other systems in a critical way. These theories can contribute to understanding law's function *vis-à-vis* these side-effects. A critical understanding, then, allows us to take issue with law and confronts law with its limitations, as to how it shapes fundamental values, or organizing principles, with which we are accustomed to describe Western society. This critical understanding would also demand a constant evaluation or re-evaluation of these values or principles and how they relate to the ongoing process of modernization and, by implication, a new perception of justice.[7]

It is this perspective that ties the essays in this book together. Critique implies a method of observation, analysis, interpretation and argumentation, representing a point of view on what is wrong with law in contemporary society. The perspective is shaped by the argument that there is *something* wrong with law. This is how critical legal theory distinguishes itself from mainstream legal theory. What is wrong with law is its actual and potential normative abuse (unintentional and intentional), and made visible in the side-effects of modernization. Social developments demand a critical perspective on law and legal scholarship to lay bare this abuse. The various contributions to this book all address law's environment in a particular way in order to address the relationship between law and society and how this relationship changes under the influence of societal developments. In effect, the contributions, in critically exploring the side-effects of Western modernization (theoretically and empirically), offer the possibility of alternative ways of understanding contemporary law and scholarship, and their manifestations in different legal systems. In doing so, some contributions take a meta-perspective (legal pluralism and legal theory, 'critical autopoiesis', cosmopolitanism), while others focus on either structural developments (torture and human rights, modern risks and the problem of distribution), organizations (Rwanda tribunal, the French commercial court)) or the work of other scholars as object of analysis (Grotius, Vitoria, Benjamin, Schmitt).

Taking the normative abuse of law as a central theme, the obvious question is how we must understand 'law'. Does the notion allow for a state-centred view on (positive) law only or does it include, by necessity, considering the globalized social order, notions that transcend this state-centred perspective, and if so, what does this mean for legal theory and its object of study? It is this fundamental question that is explored in Mariano Croce's contribution. Croce argues that apparently incommensurable approaches to the legal phenomenon – such as analytical jurisprudence, legal anthropology and legal sociology –

---

7 L.M.A. Francot and U.R.M.T. de Vries, 'Normativity in the Second Modernity', *Rechtstheorie*, Vol. 39, No. 4, 2008, p. 477-494.

do not exclude each other. Indeed, he suggests that they can fruitfully be integrated in order to outline a pluralist theory of law. In Croce's view, law is a composite phenomenon, but characterized by certain specific properties that distinguish it from other social practices and institutions. Legal theory can help determining whether new transnational negotiated orders are suited to play the function we ascribe to law.

Another meta-perspective on law's environment is taken by Andreas Philippopoulos-Mihalopoulos, in which he continues the exploration of Luhmann's work on the relationship between law and (its) environment. This relationship is presented as a connection of disrupted continuum. Philippopoulos-Mihalopoulos considers that the recent 'turns' in law towards spatiality, corporeality and materiality at large disconnect the usual distance between law and its environment and enhance the continuum between the two. Law is no longer abstract but spatially emplaced, corporeally felt, materially present. The environment destabilizes the system, rendering it more precarious and more distant from its usual self-description. Building on Luhmann's theory of autopoiesis, Philippopoulos-Mihalopoulos presents his 'critical autopoiesis' – the autopoietics of materiality, spatiality and corporeality as they emerge from contemporary legal theory.[8] In doing so, he employs Deleuze and Guattari in connection to Luhmann in order to multiply and indeed fractally explode the Luhmannian boundaries between law and its environment.

Taking serious the processes of globalization implies addressing the concept of cosmopolitanism. Cosmopolitanism, here, can be understood, in the broadest sense, as how to deal, normatively, with the process of globalization. In particular, the question that arises is how to understand law in this process. Is there a cosmopolitanism that befits the world of today and goes beyond traditional notions of it and, if so, can we speak of cosmopolitan law? Peter Fitzpatrick addresses this question in his contribution. Going beyond the state as focal point of a Kantian understanding cosmopolitanism, Fitzpatrick reaches towards the other and seeks a notion of cosmopolitan law in the 'transaction' of a 'law of unconditional hospitality' (Derrida), and conditional hospitality, circumscribed by law, politics, economy, giving the unconditional 'determinate effect'. With Mignolo, Fitzpatrick advances the perspective of a 'critical cosmopolitanism' generated by those included yet excluded by cosmopolitanism as a universalist arrogation.[9]

Can Öztaş' contribution illustrates the Western, state-centred, cosmopolitan notion – 'to rule as universal through the particular' (in Fitzpatrick's words), addressing in more detail

8 A. Philippopoulos-Mihalopoulos, *Niklas Luhmann: Law, Justice, Society*, Routledge, London 2009.

9 W.D. Mignolo, 'The Many Faces of Cosmo-polis: Border Thinking and Critical Cosmopolitanism', *Public-Culture*, Vol.12, No. 3, 2000, p. 728-731.

Vitoria's and Grotius' self-serving view on the world, imposing a legal structure that remains fundamental to understanding modern international law. Both scholars spoke of a *universal* system of law that included all while excluding the other who failed to share the underlying values of this universal system – right to property, free trade, etc. – legitimizing a just war. Understanding Vitoria's and Grotius' construction of their system helps us understanding contemporary (international) law as essentially self-serving, escaping or circumventing a more encompassing responsibility towards the others.

Such an understanding of law is also visible in Eugene McNamee's contribution. McNamee develops the argument that the meaning structure employed at the International Criminal Tribunal for Rwanda provides an insulation from wider considerations of long term (colonial) historical responsibility, while the meaning structure within Rwanda itself, is entirely based on this wider responsibility as a means to provide a unity of position to differently identified internal groups. The result, suggests McNamee, is an inevitable clash of meaning which brings to the fore important questions about the nature of international criminal justice, and the interests and ends that it serves.

We can understand Costas Douzinas' contribution in a similar vein, critiquing the way we understand human rights as the new secular, cosmopolitan ideology, when he addresses Luhmann's stance on torture. Douzinas' critique is twofold, first aimed at (and shared with Luhmann) on the rhetoric of human rights, where self-evidently good norms have political usefulness but no philosophical value. Second, the critique is aimed at, in Douzinas' view, the inability of systems theory to improve society, as it is unable to deal with the social order and the power relations that constitute it. We need more, he says, if we are to resist the brutality of our times and this 'more' lies in reversing the priority of knowledge over action.

Marc de Wilde analyzes Benjamin's *Critique of Violence*,[10] as essentially a critique of *legal* violence, the kind of violence which the state yields through coercively binding its subjects to law. In emphasizing law's structural dependence on violence, Benjamin's essay is a deeply troubling text and De Wilde suggests that it radically questions those aspects of law which we may find most valuable, indeed essential to liberal legal systems and the rule of law. Rather than violence, Benjamin takes responsibility as an alternative basis for another law. De Wilde suggests that it prevents us from hiding behind 'the rules or behind some supposed objectivity of the legal text' but warns that it entails a new risk of coercion when the law is abandoned and responsibility ignored.

---

10 W. Benjamin, 'Critique of Violence', *in* M. Bullock and M.W. Jennings (Eds.), *Walter Benjamin: Selected Writings, Volume 1, 1913-1926*, Harvard University Press, Cambridge (Mass.)/London 1999, p. 236.

Jeroen Kiewiet contributes to the newly ignited interest, among critical scholars, in the work of Carl Schmitt. At first perhaps counter-intuitive, Kiewiet suggests that Schmitt's anti-liberal stance coincides with that of critical legal studies. They share the idea of the unavoidability of the political, while modern liberal society obscures by moulding society's conflicts into economic terms or translating them into the human rights vocabulary. In particular, Schmitt's critique on the neutrality of legal positivism, understood as rule formalism comes very close to the critique of critical legal studies on liberalism and legal positivism. Kiewiet analyzes the question how far and in what sense the legal indeterminacy theses of Schmitt and critical legal studies are in fact related.

Emmanuel Lazega examines the main characteristics of the French *régime consulaire* of social control of markets by describing and analyzing features of the organization and operation of the Commercial Court of Paris in which judges are voluntary, lay business people. Its pragmatic legal reasoning is considered in relation to Richard Posner's individual 'experiential pragmatism' or 'everyday pragmatism', showing that behind the individual pragmatism of French commercial court judges, there is a collective, neo-corporatist pragmatism and institutional capture mainly by the financial sector. Given the spread of this 'consular' model, reflecting the State's increasing readiness to delegate management of its core functions to private actors, Lazega raises the issue of alternative ways of protecting the public interest in market society.

In the final contribution, Lyana Francot and Ubaldus de Vries argue that if contemporary law is to deal with world society problems effectively, it can do so only if it can take issue with its changing environment and the meta-rules of justice that can be deduced from within this global environment. The environment of contemporary law is global now and no longer limited to the nation state or international and supranational alliances. De authors focus upon those problems that are conceptualized, in the social theoretical literature, as 'modern risks' and analyze how these modern risks confront contemporary law with unexpected problems. Western society has been preoccupied, throughout its modern development, with the problem of the just distribution of wealth. This distribution problem is compounded now by a second problem: modern risks. It necessitates legal-theoretical considerations, about a possible just distribution of these risks. Is it possible to devise a just distribution key that can deal with the *responsibility* for these risks, as a meta-rule of justice, which allows for the formulation of enforceable legal rules?

Ubaldus de Vries and Lyana Francot,

Utrecht 2011

Is There Any Place for Legal Theory Today?

The Distinctiveness of Law in the Age of Pluralism

Mariano Croce[*]

Introduction

The backdrop of the present writing is the relationship between concepts and reality. I will explore this multifaceted relation from a particular vantage point. I will question if and how legal theory and its conceptual framework allow understanding a social reality that today is undergoing several key transformations. The phenomena denoted by the generic label of 'globalization' seem to be so radical that many scholars are tempted to dispose of the whole set of conceptual tools developed in the last centuries, in which the pre-eminence of state law was a taken-for-granted point of reference. In the last decades many theoreticians and practitioners in various areas of the legal domain have felt the need to distance themselves from any state-centred, Western-oriented, neo-colonial and neo-imperialist vision of law in order to embrace sounder and open-minded conceptual schemes. In their view, these new schemes have to capture the dynamics of a social reality that is characterized by the rise of alternative normative sources and hybrid regulatory phenomena. What a few decades ago would have been simply regarded as a *non-legal* normative entity hierarchically subjected to the normative pre-eminence of state law nowadays is regarded as a kind of *non-state law* that brings into question all normative hierarchies. As a result, the legal domain is noticeably expanding and the borders separating the legal from the social are progressively disappearing. This new state of affairs seems to make the traditional instruments of legal theory incapable of understanding how the legal domain is changing. This is why, as I will show below, some authors have even claimed that legal theory should be seen as but a branch of social analysis, which in turn should be based on empirical data more than on speculative reason.

---

* I want to thank all the participants to the Critical Legal Conference 2010 and in particular the organizers, Lyana Francot and Bald de Vries. I am grateful to Lyana and Bald for their precious comments on this contribution.

In the present work I aim to question two basic assumptions that underlie this broad shift. On the one hand, I will show that the issue of pluralism did not emerge out of recent changes, but rather is a state of things that can potentially take place in any geo-historical context. On the other hand, I will contend that today, more than ever before, we need theoretical guidelines precisely because the pluralism of normative orders is increasingly challenging the configuration of law along with our perception of it. In doing so, I will also try to bridge the divide between positivist jurisprudence and legal pluralism by showing that they should be integrated. To do this, in section two I will trace the paradoxical trajectory of legal positivism by showing how the attempt at drawing the borders of law, and of the science that studies it, induced legal positivism to erode its own basis and *raison d'être*. In section three I will prove that, already at the beginning of the twentieth century, some scholars in the fields of legal theory, legal sociology and legal anthropology strove to enlarge the domain of law in order to include both non-state social orderings and the normative repertoires of non-Western populations. Subsequently, since the 1970s, many legal scholars picked up this legacy and carried it forward so far as to create the brand new field of 'legal pluralism'. In sections four and five I will canvass some conceptual and pragmatic problems arising out of legal pluralism in order to verify if it can really be a more thorough approach to legal reality. In section six I will defend a particular view of legal pluralism as a basic theoretical approach providing us with conceptual tools that can well carry out the function that legal positivists assigned to legal theory. In doing so, I will also try to defend the idea that law is a composite phenomenon, which however has certain specific properties that distinguish it from other social practices and institutions.

Jurisprudence and the Distinctiveness of Law

Most of the advocates of analytical jurisprudence have been obsessed with the *differentia specifica* of law, or rather, the feature that distinguishes law from other normative systems, such as morality or religion. This tendency is significantly epitomized by John Austin, one of the acknowledged fathers of early positivist jurisprudence, and his project to outline *scientifically* the borders of jurisprudence. [1] Although he was not so popular among his contemporaries both as a teacher and as a reformer, his project to rebuild the fundamentals of legal theory met with great success. Austin "was determined to map out a rational, scientific approach to legal understanding – a modern view of law which would replace archaic, confused, tradition-bound common law thought". [2] To do this, he strove to

1 See J. Austin, *The Province of Jurisprudence Determined* (1832), Cambridge University Press, Cambridge 1995.

2 R. Cotterrell, *The Politics of Jurisprudence: A Critical Introduction to Legal Philosophy*, University of Pennsylvania Press, Philadelphia 1992.

identify precisely the subject-matter of jurisprudence and to differentiate it from others, which only bear some resemblances to it. Austin clearly asserted that "the appropriate matter of general and particular jurisprudence" is positive law – i.e. a set of commands issued by "a sovereign person, or a sovereign body of persons, to a member or members of the independent political society wherein that person or body is sovereign or supreme"[3] – while the term 'law' has to be clearly distinguished by similar uses, such as the 'law of God' or the 'moral law'. This idea of law was particularly instrumental in defining the borders of jurisprudence: if legal theorists are called upon to determine whether something is legal or not, there are clear-cut guidelines. Austin's belief is that legal theorists must simply ascertain that what is under scrutiny is the command of someone who is habitually obeyed by the bulk of the population and which has no habit to obey anybody else.

Austin 's goal to set the borders of jurisprudence was highly prized by one of the most relevant exponents of twentieth century legal positivism, Hans Kelsen. Nevertheless, Kelsen comments that Austin fell short of his goal, in that the latter contaminated the *pureness* of legal science with the *impurity* of factual reality. In effect, Austin asserted that it is the "the chance of incurring *evil*" that *obliges* law-bearers to comply with the commands of the sovereign.[4] Kelsen objects that then, were it to be true, the obligatory character of a legal rule would turn out to be entirely dependent on a factual circumstance, that is to say, the concrete possibility of applying sanctions by the sovereign.[5] Consequently, legal scientists should do nothing but scrutinize effectual reality in order to verify if such commands are socially efficacious. In this reading, legal scientists would merely act as social observers required to record facts in order to attest to the efficacy of the legal system. Quite the opposite, Kelsen is intent on freeing completely "the science of law from alien elements",[6] i.e. from psychology, sociology, ethics, and political theory. His *purified* theory of law is meant to provide a description of law as it really is, regardless of the fact whether it is actually obeyed. In Kelsen's view, legal theorists have to carry out a strictly *cognitive* task: "The science of law endeavors to comprehend its object 'legally', namely from the point of view of the law",[7] that is to say, by adopting the legal norm as a "scheme of interpretation",[8] in the light of which it makes sense to define something that happens in concrete reality as legal or non-legal.

3 Austin 1995, p. 16.
4 *Id.*, p. 24.
5 See H. Kelsen, *General Theory of Law and State*, Harvard University Press, Cambridge (Mass). 1949, p. 171-172.
6 H. Kelsen, *Pure Theory of Law* (1967), The Lawbook Exchange, Clark (N.J.) 2007, p. 1.
7 *Id.*, p. 70.
8 *Id.*, p. 3.

Therefore, Kelsen proposes a sort of 'division of labour' between officials and legal theorists: the former apply valid laws while the latter are called upon to determine what properties laws must exhibit in order to be legitimately considered as part of the legal system. Consequently, the subject-matter of jurisprudence is neither the psychological will of the sovereign nor the actual behaviour of citizens, but the 'ought-to' quality of legal rules. This quality is independent from any factual circumstance and can be known by way of a pure theoretical inquiry. Actually, what makes a given norm legal is the fact that a competent norm-maker has assigned a sanction to a given fact-type (*Tatbestand*), which is described in the normative statement. The fact-type is the condition that explains when a sanction *ought to be applied*. The sanction is the *primary legal norm*, which makes legal the norm at issue. Without sanction being present, there is no legal norm. It is worth noting that, in the wake of Kelsen's scientific amendment of positivism, the addressee of legal norms changes. While in Austin's view commands are conveyed to citizens, in Kelsen's view legal norms are indications addressed to those who are called upon to apply them, i.e. to officials. In Kelsen's view, this shift from citizens to officials is inevitable, unless we want the *differentia specifica* of law to vanish. In this abstract and artificial portrayal, the law is a system of norms, in which any inferior norm is validated by a superior one, until we reach the peak of the system, i.e. the *basic norm*. This latter norm, he argues, does not exist concretely; for it is a mere presupposition that makes the legal system and the activity of officials intelligible. The basic norm must be presupposed if the discourse about law has to make sense in any way. In reality, such a particular norm is "determined by facts",[9] and is only expressed in the words of legal theorists who account for the way in which a given order works.

It is well known that this is one of the points of departure of Herbert L.A. Hart in his seminal book *The Concept of Law*,[10] where he denies that the basic norm may be a mere presupposition. Quite the opposite, what he calls the 'rule of recognition' is an actual rule inscribed in the practice of law carried out by legal officials (and in particular by judges). This fundamental rule provides officials with shared criteria that guide them in determining which rules are valid rules of the legal system. Although Hart does not clarify whether such a rule is a duty-imposing rule or a mere epistemic indication,[11] he fiercely claims that it

9 Kelsen 1949, p. 120.

10 This is clearly expressed in A. Marmor, *Philosophy of Law*, Princeton University Press, Princeton/Oxford 2011, Ch. 2.

11 Michael Bayles, who carefully deals with this issue, addresses and comments on the hypothesis of some renowned interpreters. Then he concludes that the rule of recognition is neither a power-conferring nor a duty-imposing rule, but only a standard that operates *epistemically* (M. Bayles, *Hart's Legal Philosophy. An Examination*, Kluwer, Dordrecht 1992, p. 65-67). Moreover, he contends that, if there were a duty-imposing social rule obligating judges to follow the rule of recognition, it would be a different rule than the rule of recognition. Bayle's view on the epistemic nature of the rule of recognition is close to that of many significant

exists and governs the practice of law. It is well known that Hart insists that the rule of recognition is a standard that officials accept from an 'internal point of view' as a reason for action and a standard for criticism. Although there has been a great deal of debate about the proper meaning of 'internal', [12] Hart, as Scott Shapiro suggests, does not conceive of "the internal point of view simply as the perspective of a legal insider; rather, he meant it to refer to the perspective of an insider who accepts the law's legitimacy". [13] In other words, the point of view is internal when the rule guides the conduct as a reason for action and as a standard for criticism.

But Hart's concept of law has a Janus-face, which, as I will soon demonstrate, is deeply tied to the very status of legal theory. On the one hand, Hart engages himself in a fierce battle with some prominent exponents of jurisprudence, such as Austin, Holmes, Kelsen, and Ross, who, according to the English thinker, reach extreme conclusions about what law is. In particular, Hart denies both that legal rules are mere commands backed by the threat of sanctions and that any legal rule must be accompanied by a sanction designed to instruct judges. His main concern is with how the law "is used to control, to guide, and to plan life out of court". [14] Hart argues that rules are valid not because they are backed by sanctions (sanctions either addressed to private individual as motivational factor or to officials as indications on how to apply rules); nor are they valid because of some widespread feeling of obligation. On the contrary, people in everyday life adopt legal rules from an internal point of view, i.e. as duty-imposing rules setting standards for criticism and as power-conferring rules designed to render citizens into private legislators. Yet, on the other hand, by thoroughly analysing the arguments deployed in *The Concept of Law*, we can easily realize that Hart is unable to solve an ambiguity stressed by both supporters and critics. For example, Jules Coleman claims that an oscillation affects the first edition of Hart's book. [15] Here Hart sometimes seems to portray all *legal rules as social rules* that are adopted from an internal point of view both by officials and by private individuals. Yet,

interpreters, such as Bulygin, MacCormick, and Raz. Other authors, such as Jules L. Coleman and Scott Shapiro, propose a conventionalist reading of the rule of recognition. See for instance, J.L. Coleman, *The Practice of Principle. In Defence of a Pragmatist Approach to Legal Theory*, Oxford University Press, Oxford 2001.

12 In particular, the internal/external dichotomy seems to pertain to two different levels: that of rule-bearers and that of those who aim to account for the actions of rule-bearers. The first level concerns the relation of rule-bearers to rules and the way the latter affect the practical reasoning of the former, while the second level relates to the very possibility of providing a theoretical account of rule-following. See for instance H. Rottleuthner, *A Treatise of Legal Philosophy and General Jurisprudence. Vol. 2: Foundations of Law*, Springer, Dordrecht 2005, pp. 12-17.

13 S. Shapiro, The Bad Man and the Internal Point of View, *in* S.J. Burton (ed.), *The Path of the Law and its Influence. The Legacy of Oliver Wendell Holmes*, Cambridge University Press, Cambridge 2000, p. 200.

14 H.L.A. Hart, *The Concept of Law*, Oxford University Press, Oxford 1994 (2nd ed.), p. 40.

15 J.L. Coleman, Authority and Reason, *in* R.P. George (ed.), *The Autonomy of Law: Essays on Legal Positivism*, Oxford University Press, Oxford 1999, p. 298.

most of the time Hart treats the rule of recognition as the sole *social* rule, constituted by the convergent behaviour of *legal officials*, that confers validity on the remainder of non-social legal rules. This oscillation is not present in Hart's last writing, his *Postscript* in the second edition of *The Concept of Law*,[16] in which he refers solely to the convergent conducts of officials as the social rule supporting the practice of law. His analysis of the core structure of social rules in general and of their being binding on social agents seems to be primarily instrumental in showing the core structure of the rule of recognition and its being binding on legal officials. In this view, the sole *genuinely social* rule of the law is the rule of recognition that claims to guide the conduct of officials and must be accepted by them from an internal point of view.

If this is true, then under a conceptual point of view, non-officials do not have to adopt the rule of recognition and rules in general as reasons for action, although they obviously are free to do it. But, as some critics have remarked, [17] this latter conceptual argument paradoxically leads Hart to defend an Austinian image of law: for a legal system to exist, the minimum condition is that officials accept secondary rules from an internal point of view, while private individuals can simply look at primary rules as coercive constraints. Based on this reading, Peter Fitzpatrick observes:

> Hart erases the element of the popular and reaffirms the positivist equation of law with official authority and with formal, pre-set meaning. The populace is thus excluded from law and relegated to a state of Austinian inertness. [...] In short, what counts as law becomes exclusively and comprehensively determined by officials and the positivist enterprise is preserved. [18]

It is worth understanding why Hart arrives at this paradoxical conclusion. In my view, the origin of the problem is precisely Hart's intent to justify the law – and the science that studies it – as a self-sufficient and free-standing domain. In fact, Hart's declared goal is "to further the understanding of law, coercion, and morality as different but related social phenomena".[19] He is convinced that those who see law as a set of coercive rules misconceive legal phenomena as much as those who claim that the sole valid law is just law. [20] Hart aims to show that coercion is an ancillary aspect of legal rules and that, despite this, law is by no means dependent on conventional morality. According to Hart, a sound conceptual

16 H.L.A. Hart, Postscript, *in* Hart 1994.

17 See for instance M. Payne, 'Hart's concept of a legal system', *William & Mary Law Review*, Vol. 18, 1976, p. 287-319.

18 P. Fitzpatrick, *The Mythology Of Modern Law*, Routledge, London/New York 1992, p. 4.

19 Hart 1994, p. vi.

20 See also A. Schiavello, *Perché obbedire al diritto? La risposta convenzionalista e i suoi limiti*, ETS, Pisa 2010.

inquiry proves that the law is a social practice with certain distinctive properties, among which the most relevant is the existence of secondary rules for recognizing, applying and modifying rules, which instruct officials on how to administer primary rules. In the *Postscript*, he clarifies this view by saying that "the distinctive features of law are the provisions it makes by the secondary rules for the identification, change, and enforcement of its standards".[21] Needless to say, this view lays great emphasis on officials, as secondary rules can only be addressed to them.

Yet, somehow, Hart represents the celebration of the positivist paradigm. Actually, the role of legal theory as a specific discipline is solidly vindicated, whereas, at the same time, the law is freed from the narrow image of imperatives accompanied or even validated by sanctions. The law as such is no longer inspired to criminal law: the legal practice is a complex practice in which there are different bodies of persons with different kinds of powers, able to yield entirely new states of things. At the same time, Hart's theory depicts law as a self-sufficient field, in that its properties are truly distinctive. The law can be recognized and distinguished in the light of two characteristics. The first is the presence of two different kinds of rules: *primary rules*, which provide binding models for conduct and prescribe how to perform certain actions in order that they may be recognized as valid, and *secondary rules*, which indicate how primary rules must be issued, applied, or amended. The second characteristic is the clear distinction between a delimited group of authorized rule-creating and rule-applying officials, who are the genuine addressees of secondary rules, and the generality of ordinary citizens, who are the real addressees of primary rules.[22]

Nonetheless, according to some interpreters, this portrayal disposes too hastily of the connection between law and force. With the intent to distinguish the law both from morality and coercion, Hart willy-nilly obliterates features that were traditionally deemed as hallmarks of law and equates it to many organizations that populate social reality. According to Frederick Schauer, this paradoxical outcome is mainly due to Hart's central intent to demonstrate that coercion is ancillary or even superfluous to a sound definition of legal obligation.[23] Schauer argues that Hart supports a notion of 'role obligation' by which roles precede and create obligations: those who occupy a given role, who recognize that they do occupy it, and who conceive of themselves as someone for whom the rules of

21 Hart 1994, p. 249.

22 This view is associated with many thinkers in the field of analytical jurisprudence, such as Jules L. Coleman, Neil MacCormick, Andrei Marmor, Gerard Postema, Scott Shapiro, and others. For an analysis of this type, see R.E.S. Brigido, *Groups, Rules and Legal Practice*, Springer, Dordrecht 2010.

23 F. Schauer, 'Was Austin Right After All? On the Role of Sanctions in a Theory of Law', *Ratio Juris*, Vol. 23, No. 1, 2010, pp. 1-21.

the role provide reasons for action, have an inherent obligation to comply with the rules which their role prescribe. Then, Schauer concludes that:

> once we see that this analysis applies as straightforwardly to football and religious duties as to legal duties, we have not made much progress in trying to understand the institution of law, other than it being just one more system of rules. [24]

In effect, this outcome is quite surprising: just while pursuing the goal of discovering law's distinctive feature, legal theory erodes its own peculiarities and removes the borderline separating the legal from the social. Incredibly, Hart, one of the most prominent exponents of legal positivism, seems to have certified that law, once it is freed from any ties with morality and coercion, exhibits no particular difference with, say, religious or sporting organizations, in which there are secondary rules prescribing how to administer primary rules and bodies of officials designed to identify, apply and change rules of conduct.

However, I would like to make the claim that the inner tension between the two faces of Hart's concept of law does not merely stem from any contradictions in his theoretical premises. On the contrary, they symbolize a key problem that crosses the entire Western legal theory: Can the dividing line between law and non-law be truly justified under a conceptual point of view? As we have seen, the positivist solution was to connect the law to the exercise of political power and thus to the monopoly of force on the part of the state apparatus. But this account of law only takes into consideration a small portion of the history of legal practice, i.e. the legal order as an emanation of the state, and put aside centuries of history in which the law was by no means a sheer technique of social control in the hands of political rulers. [25] In the end, this relation of law to sanction is what Neil MacCormick defines as "one of the perennial and persistent fallacies in legal philosophy". [26]

Hart's paradoxical outcome, in light of which the barriers separating the legal from the social break down, has led some interpreters to understand Hart as a 'reluctant' pluralist, who offers cogent arguments for showing that state law is a normative system among other similar systems, while he himself is finally incapable of abandoning legal centralism. [27] In

---

24 *Id.*, p. 16.

25 See P. Grossi, *L'ordine giuridico medievale*, Laterza, Roma/Bari 2006.

26 N. MacCormick, 'Legal Obligation and the Imperative Fallacy', *in* A.W.B. Simpson (ed.), *Oxford Essays in Jurisprudence. Second Series*, Clarendon, Oxford 1973, p. 101.

27 See e.g. W.F. Menski, *Comparative Law in a Global Context. The Legal Systems of Asia and Africa*, Cambridge University Press, Cambridge 2006, pp. 98-103. For an opposite reading – which, in my view, underestimates the force of Hart's conceptual tools, despite his plain adhesion to legal centralism – see S. Roberts, 'After

the next section I will argue that the conclusion reached by Hart is considerably similar to those of some scholars who, in other fields of legal theory, have been trying to disprove the identity between state legal orders and *the* law.

Legal Pluralism and the Vanishing of Legal Borders

As I said earlier, the pluralism of legal orders is not a recent effect of globalization.[28] Already at the beginning of the twentieth century – when the state was exceptionally strong and was enhancing its own competences – some authors start criticizing the identification of law in general with state law under a both pragmatic and conceptual point of view. In 1913 Eugen Ehrlich claims that "[t]he inner order of the associations of human beings is not only the original, but also, down to the present time, the basic form of law".[29] He points out that there is always a gap between '*Rechtssatz*' (legal proposition) and '*Rechtsleben*' (the legal life), and that this gap risks being widened by the myopic tendency of state centralism. In fact, more often than not, legal propositions of state law, issued by state officials, are largely insensitive to the actual requirements of social parties, and, for this reason, official law becomes inert and useless just like the "water that is put in the pond is no longer a living stream but a stagnant poll".[30] Nevertheless, Kelsen rebuts such criticism by contending that legal sociologists do a different kind of job than that of legal scientists.[31] Kelsen claims that Ehrlich is right when he asserts that social life is governed by a vast array of normative orderings that are even more compelling than official legal norms. However, this does not prove that legal orders are either conceptually or pragmatically identical to social orderings. Thus, a legal order is a special technique of social control, tied to the legitimate use of force, which has nothing to do with the rules of everyday life.

A far stronger criticism to the jurisprudential celebration of state law was levelled by the Italian jurist Santi Romano. In his influential book, *L'ordinamento giuridico*,[32] he explicitly

Government? On Representing Law without the State', *The Modern Law Review*, Vol. 68, No. 1, 2005, p. 1-24, at p. 10-11.

28 For a striking example of this, which transports us back to a very ancient past, see W.F. Menski, 'Sanskrit Law: Excavating Vedic Legal Pluralism', in *SOAS* School of Law Legal Studies Research Paper, No. 5, 2010.

29 E. Ehrlich, *Fundamental Principles of the Sociology of Law* (1913), Transaction Publishers, New Brunswick (N.J.) 2009, p. 37.

30 Ehrlich 2009, p. 488.

31 See Kelsen 1949, p. 24-29.

32 See S. Romano, *L'ordinamento giuridico* (1918), Sansoni, Firenze 1977 (3rd ed.). Romano's book has been translated into French (1975), German (1975), and Spanish (1963). See also my own reconstruction of Romano's theory in M. Croce, 'Does Legal Institutionalism Rule out Legal Pluralism? Schmitt's Institutional Theory and the Problem of the Concrete Order', *Utrecht Law Review*, Vol. 7, No. 2, 2011, p. 42-59; and M. Croce & A. Salvatore, 'Ethical Substance and the Coexistence of Normative Orders. Carl Schmitt, Santi Romano, and Critical Institutionalism', *Journal of Legal Pluralism*, Vol. 56, 2007, p. 1-32.

says that his work is a contribution to the field of legal theory, not to that of legal sociology. His institutional theory of law is aimed at proving the conceptual and ontological identity between legal order and institution: any institution is a legal order and vice versa. [33] But what is the meaning of an institution? He believes it to be an *organized social practice*, in which a given set of rules creates a set of roles and attaches to them specific stocks of knowledge. Thus, an institution is a normative device meant to assure that a given practice may outlive its original creators by issuing rules and defining roles. In this reading, it is not coercion that qualifies the legal, but the capacity to self-organize. 'Legal' is an attribution that legitimately pertains to every organized context or practice, no matter how it coerces compliance and exerts jurisdiction. If this is true, then the legal order of the state is an institution among others, such as churches, sporting organizations, and even criminal gangs: each of them has an inner order made up of rules and roles. Confronted with this, Romano paid much heed to a dilemma stemming from his thought: Once we have reached the conclusion that state law is an order among others, how then can we justify its pre-eminence? And once we have recognized that any organization has its own inner order, how then can we deny that the mafia has the same right to maintain its order as a religious or as an ethnic group? Romano dwells on the relationship of the various legal orders to the state legal order, so as to determine whether the supremacy of the state is a matter of brute force or else the state legal order has some peculiar quality that makes it a special order. Unfortunately, Romano provides us with unconvincing answers.

This dilemma has also characterized the recent debate on legal pluralism. What happens to law when its ties with the state and its monopoly of legitimate violence are severed? In the middle of the nineteenth century, this issue compellingly re-emerged in the field of legal anthropology, where scholars dealing with non-state law were particularly interested in the question as to whether or not it makes sense to claim that a law is present even when the state is absent.

There was no full agreement among the leading figures of legal anthropology. In particular, we can single out two main streams of thought: that of Alfred Radcliffe-Brown and Adamson Hoebel, as opposed to that of Bronislaw Malinowski. In following Roscoe Pound's definition, Radcliffe-Brown describes law as "social control through the systematic application of the force of politically organized society". [34] In his view, coercion and political

33 Along with Maurice Hauriou, Romano is one of the founding fathers of classic institutionalism, which is significantly different from what today is known as new institutionalism. See M. La Torre, *Law as Institution*, Springer, Dordrecht 2010. See also the comparison between two kinds of classic institutionalism – i.e. those of Romano and Carl Schmitt – which I make in Croce 2011.

34 A.R. Radcliffe-Brown, *Structure and Function in Primitive Society. Essays and Addresses*, The Free Press Glencoe, Illinois 1952, p. 212. The Chapter XII ("Primitive Law") that I quote here was already published in *Encyclopaedia of the Social Sciences*, Macmillan, New York 1933, Vol. IX, pp. 202-206.

power have to be part of any sound definition of law. In this reading, it makes no sense to say that all societies possess what Westerners call 'law'; let alone that the law is a plural phenomenon. Hoebel is less attached to classic jurisprudential definitions of law, but in his celebrated book, *The Law of Primitive Man*, he also refers to coercion and power as essential features of the legal phenomenon. For, he admits that there can be many groups with their inner norms, but the sole norms that can be meaningfully defined as legal are those whose "neglect or infraction is regularly met, in threat or in fact, by the application of physical force by an individual or group possessing the socially recognized privilege of so acting".[35] It is evident that this first anthropological stream of thought makes the law depend on there being an organized political centre – although not necessarily a state – with the capacity to coerce compliance. There is no room for pluralism of legal orders.

In contrast, Malinowski offers a view of law that opens the door to what Brian Tamanaha will define "the folly" of legal pluralism.[36] In fact, in *Crime and Custom in Savage Society*, Malinowski aims to represent non-Western law in such a way to show that the definition of most anthropologists is rooted in the conceptual framework of Western jurisprudence and thus tends to concentrate only on the criminal side of the law of non-Western populations. Quite the opposite, with regard to Trobriand Islanders, Malinowski stresses that, however inappropriate the label may be, their law can be compared to Western 'civil law', in that it is mainly based on a set of obligations, seen as "a right of one party and acknowledged as a duty by the other, kept in force by a specific mechanism of reciprocity and publicity inherent to the structure of their society".[37] Not only does such a definition of legal phenomena underrate coercion as an essential feature, given that the mechanism designed to assure compliance is the publicity of rules and the reciprocity among the members of a given collectivity. But this definition also states that every collectivity possesses what we call 'law'. By this definition, law is actually identified with a spontaneous and intrinsic instrument of social control, inscribed in the relational web deployed by the agents in everyday interaction.

Although Malinowski is not a legal pluralist,[38] Tamanaha argues that his heterodox definition of law was one of the main impulses to the rise of what today we know as legal plu-

35 E.A. Hoebel, *The Law of Primitive Man. A Study of Comparative Legal Dynamics*, Harvard University Press, Cambridge (Mass). 1954, p. 28.

36 B. Tamanaha, 'The Folly of the "Social Scientific" Concept of Legal Pluralism', *Journal of Law & Society*, Vol. 20, No. 2, 1993, p. 192-217.

37 B. Malinowski, *Crime and Custom in Savage Society. An Anthropological Study of Savagery*, Routledge & Kegan Paul, London 1926, p. 58.

38 Malinowski is often cited among the founders of legal pluralism (see e.g. Tamanaha 1993), but in reality he is not a pluralist at all (for a similar interpretation, see F. von Benda-Beckmann, 'Who is Afraid of Legal Pluralism?', *Journal of Legal Pluralism*, Vol. 47, 2002, p. 37-83, where the author mentions Ehrlich and Max

ralism.[39] With a high level of approximation, I can say that pluralist authors put forward two theses. The first is that the law of the state is a type of law among many others, such as customary, indigenous, folk, or generally unnamed laws. In fact, many sectors of social life – what Sally Falk Moore calls "semi-autonomous social fields"[40] – produce their own rules, possess their own mechanisms for coercing compliance, and develop dispute-settling procedures. The second thesis is that pluralism is a phenomenon that does not only concern post-colonial or generally non-Western countries, but also affects the legal orders of Western national states, which have to confront with many semi-autonomous sub-sectors of society.[41] In doing so, legal pluralists pick up the legacy of both Malinowski and Ehrlich. By following Malinowski, pluralists dispose of biased Western jurisprudential categories that are unable to capture the life of the law outside of Western countries. By following Ehrlich, pluralists claim that Western state legal systems possess a patchwork character, in that they are composite frameworks encompassing a vast array of social regulations that arise out of smaller sectors of society and interact in different ways with official law.

Unfortunately, these conclusions bring with them many conceptual and pragmatic problems. In the next section I will first tackle the conceptual ones, and in particular the effects that they exert on legal theory. More precisely, if state law is presented as but a particular type of law, if the label 'law' cannot be limited to it, and if, as a consequence, every collectivity, group, or association is regarded as having its own inner legal order, what should legal theorists investigate? Do they become mere sociologists, as Kelsen already observed

---

Weber as genuine ancestors of legal pluralism). In effect, Malinowski clearly states that the law is but one aspect of the tribal life, one side of the overall tribal structure, as "the specific result of the configuration of obligations, which makes it impossible for the native to shrink his responsibility without suffering for it in the future" (Malinowski 1926, p. 59). Therefore, he thinks of law in terms of a set of rights and duties that allow social interaction, while it is for the broad machinery of social control to assure that duties are fulfilled and rights exercised.

39 This wide-ranging movement officially entered the theatre of the international debate in 1978, when the International Union of Anthropological and Ethnological Sciences instituted the Commission on Folk Law and Legal Pluralism. This is a work group comprised of scholars belonging to various fields of study, such as Franz and Keebet von Benda-Beckmann, Mark Galanter, John Gilissen, John Griffiths, Sally Engle Merry, Gordon R. Woodman and many others. Their primary goal is to "further knowledge and understanding of legal pluralism, with a focus upon theoretical and practical problems resulting from the interaction of different legal order" (<www.commission-on-legal-pluralism.com/our-constitution>). In addition to this group, other significant authors have contributed to the rise of legal pluralism as a general field of study, such as Antony Allott, Masaji Chiba, Peter Fitzpatrick, John Gilissen, Barry Hooker, Werner Menski, Sally Falk Moore, Leopold Pospisil, Boaventura de Sousa Santos, Rodolfo Sacco, Gunther Teubner, Jacques Vanderlinden. However, in this article I will be concerned neither with the history of legal pluralism nor with the articulated composition. On the contrary, my chief interest is in understanding the way in which the status of legal theory and its tasks change under the pressure of the pluralist challenge.

40 S.F. Moore, 'Law and Social Change: The Semi-Autonomous Social Field as an Appropriate Subject of Study', *Law & Society Review*, Vol. 7, No. 4, 1973, p. 719-746.

41 This is one of the main arguments developed in the influential article J. Griffiths, 'What is Legal Pluralism?', *Journal of Legal Pluralism*, Vol. 24, 1986, p. 1-55.

while arguing against Ehrlich? And, what counts more, should the positivist aim to discover the line separating the law from social orderings be regarded as straightforwardly utopian? What happens when this distinctive line is simply deemed to be a matter of degree, law covering "a continuum which runs from the clearest form of state law through to the vaguest forms of informal social control"? [42]

CONCEPTUAL IMPASSES: 'MALINOWSKI PROBLEM' AND 'ROMANO'S DILEMMA'

Some critics have argued that raising questions like those mentioned above proves that the concept of legal pluralism is neither definable nor useful. [43] In particular, despite the considerable differences among its various advocates, legal pluralism seems to be trapped into two distinct but related impasses, namely what Tamanaha calls the 'Malinowski problem' and what I call 'Romano's dilemma'. In what follows, I will argue that, while the former does not jeopardize the general project of legal pluralism, the latter urges it to be amended in some respects.

According to Tamanaha, the concept of law offered by Malinowski and picked up by most legal pluralists is so broad that it is indistinguishable from social relationships in general. Such a compromising legacy yields a theoretical problem that can be split into two lines of argument. The first line states that, once law and social order in general are conflated, legal theory becomes social theory and the problem of how law works in society becomes the problem of how society can be integrated by means of social rules and mutual relationships. The second line of argument claims that, if law is an inner mechanism of social integration, the validity of *legal* rules is confused with the effectiveness of *social* rules. But in doing so, legal pluralists ignore that, unlike social rules, legal rules continue to be valid even if they are not effective, or rather, even though they are not supported by widespread social observance. It is evident that Tamanaha's criticisms are very close to those conveyed by Kelsen to legal sociology.

It should be noted that the first line of argument draws on the observations of two pioneers of legal pluralism, i.e. Sally Falk Moore and Sally Engle Merry. This is evidence that, since the beginning, legal pluralists have paid due heed to this conundrum. Moore maintains that Malinowski's over-extensive definition of law "made it difficult to separate out or

42 G.R. Woodman, 'Ideological Combat and Social Observation. Recent Debate about Legal Pluralism', *Journal of Legal Pluralism*, Vol. 42, 1998, p. 21-59, at p. 45.

43 In this section I will mainly refer to Tamanaha 1993, but see also S. Roberts, 'Against Legal Pluralism. Some Reflections on the Contemporary Enlargement of the Legal Domain', *Journal of Legal Pluralism*, Vol. 42, p. 95-106.

define as law any special province of study".[44] Moreover, she notices that, although one cannot deny the common character of binding rules at all levels, "it may be of importance to distinguish the sources of the rules and the sources of effective inducement and coercion".[45] Some years later, Merry contends that it is pointless to use the term 'law' for denoting all forms of ordering that are not state law.[46] Merry claims that an overextension of the meaning of law may reduce the heuristic value of the concept, since it becomes too wide and turns out to comprise anything, to the extent that certain crucial discrepancies between different modes of ordering risk disappearing. Yet, Moore and Merry do not offer precise indications on how to find this dividing line and where it is located.

In his seminal contribution, 'Justice in Many Rooms',[47] Mark Galanter suggests a more workable solution. He argues that, beneath the shadow of official law, there is a plethora of indigenous orderings that regulate many aspects of social life. More often than not, official law does not intervene directly in social life, but provides a 'bargaining endowment'.[48] Law provides a set of rules and procedures used by indigenous orderings as a background for regulation and negotiations. But this state of affairs cannot be described in a dichotomous way, as if official law and indigenous orderings were ontologically distinct. On the contrary, Galanter suggests that we should imagine a *normative continuum* with pure types at the ends. Official 'exogenous' law is composed of formal written rules, remote from everyday understandings, enunciated and enforced by officials. At its 'indigenous' end there are rules applied by non-officials and enforced by social pressure. In between these two basic prototypes there are multiple forms of law that approximate to them to a smaller or greater degree. Therefore, Galanter argues that a neater distinction among types of law could be obtained by employing the following criterion: "The differentium is the introduction of a second layer of control – of norms about application of norms".[49] In fact, he goes on by saying, exogenous law can count on more explicit standards, more deliberation about their application, and more precise rule-making and rule-applying procedures. In contrast, indigenous laws are all those rule-governed practices that make social life a vast web of overlapping and reinforcing regulations, where the means to coerce compliance are not governed by a secondary type of rules and there are no specialized

44 S.F. Moore, *Law as Process: An Anthropological Approach* (1978), new Introduction by M. Chanock, LIT Verlag, Hamburg 2000, p. 220.

45 Moore 1973, p. 745.

46 See S.E. Merry, 'Legal Pluralism', *Law & Society Review*, Vol. 22, No. 5, 1988, p. 869-896,

47 M. Galanter, 'Justice in Many Rooms: Courts, Private Ordering, and Indigenous Law', *Journal of Legal Pluralism*, Vol. 19, 1981, p. 1-47.

48 This is an expression that Galanter takes from Robert Mnookin and Lewis Kornhauser, who speak of "bargaining in the shadow of the law" (R.H. Mnookin & L. Kornhauser, 'Bargaining in the Shadow of the Law: The Case of Divorce', *Yale Law Journal*, Vol. 88, 1979, p. 950-997).

49 Galanter 1981, p. 19. It is worth noting that, to this end, Galanter draws on two leading representatives of legal philosophy and legal anthropology, i.e. Herbert Hart and Paul Bohannan.

body which is endowed with special powers. Surprisingly, in a more empirical field of analysis, Galanter reaches the same conclusion that in 1961 Hart had reached with conceptual instruments.

This is the main reason why legal pluralists can be said to reach the same conclusion as Hart does. As I said above, Schauer remarks – although with critical intent – that Hart's thoughts turn out to conceal the distinguishing line separating the law from the ordering of other organizations. Likewise, in the field of legal pluralism there are scholars who conclude that both empirical and conceptual analysis attest to the nonexistence of this line. In many of his writings Gordon R. Woodman shows how legal anthropological research provides ground for holding that "there is not a clear dividing line on the spectrum which runs from the state legal rules forbidding murder to the rules of etiquette and good manners."[50] However, even accepting this, the Malinowski problem could be overcome by saying that legal scholars are not mere social observers, in that they must develop and employ sound conceptual tools that may help to inspect the normative continuum. It is up to them to determine whether a given normative repertoire is closer to the exogenous or to the indigenous end. Thus, even if law is no longer seen as a clear-cut and unmistakably recognizable set of rules, but as a comprehensive family of phenomena, the function of legal theory and its set of conceptual categories are preserved.[51]

This reply, however, does not overcome what I call 'Romano's dilemma'. As I explained in the previous section, Romano equates law to an institution, that is, an organized social practice: every social body that is structured by a set of rules and roles can be said to possess a legal order. His solution, therefore, is rather close to that of Hart and Galanter. And also in Romano's view, although the label 'legal' loses a lot of heuristic value, legal theory is not dismissed. In fact, Romano shows that legal theory must serve the task of investigating the function that rules and roles play in the construction and maintenance of legal bodies. Legal theoreticians must not dwell on existing forces, transient social activities, or factual historical happenings, but they are called upon to explain how it is possible that a social body exists by virtue of its internal order. That is, legal theory must account for the way

50 G.R. Woodman, 'Diritto consuetudinario e diritti consuetudinari: una considerazione comparativa sulla loro natura e sulle relazioni tra tipi di diritto', *Politica & Società*, Nr. 2, 2009, p. 91-107, at p. 100.

51 I cannot deal here with Tamanaha's second line of argument, concerning the conflation of validity and efficacy. Suffice it to say that not only do most legal pluralists recognize that legal rules can be valid even though they are not backed by widespread observance. In addition, I contend that the problem validity/efficacy affects many non-legal spheres of reality, and above all certain social orderings – such as syntax or sports – in which many rules remain valid even though they are not followed, and in which, at the same time, there are broadly followed rules that are at odds with official guidelines. In sum, the second side of the Malinowski problem represents more a general conundrum of practical philosophy and social theory than an argument against legal pluralism.

in which legal orders carry out certain specific functions that are instrumental in the ordering of society.

But, as I have already written, Romano is incapable of solving a further and even serious dilemma: Can or should legal theory say something about the relation between state and non-state institutions? Whilst legal pluralism originally was borne out of the challenge to the overpowering dominance of the state over self-organizing spheres of society that demanded a higher degree of autonomy, whilst legal pluralism in the middle of the nineteenth century re-emerged so as to unmask and demystify the state hegemony that misrecognized the local law of politically subjugated communities, then what happens if the revenge of *the social* over the state turns out to harm the traditional instruments of national legal orders and to cause havoc in national political communities? [52] In other words, Romano's dilemma appears to be not only a conceptual issue. Or better, its appearance reveals how much theoretical premises can effect relevant consequences at a pragmatic level. Hence Romano's dilemma throws some light on the relationship between concepts and practices: the way in which we conceive of a practice noticeably affects the very same practice to such an extent that, in changing the conceptual categories we use to account for it, the practice in question may be transformed and become something else. I will discuss this problem in the next section.

Pragmatic Risks of Extending the Legal Domain

We have so far seen how a sound conceptualization of the legal phenomenon, as separated from the state and its monopoly of power, leads to a very broad notion of law. The signifier 'law' comes to refer to a vast range of signified orderings, extending from large-scale sub-state orderings to small-scale supra-state ones. Romano, Hart, and Galanter seem to converge on a basic criterion that may be used to determine what is legal and what is not: if an ordering is made up not only of primary rules meant to govern conduct, but also of standardized procedures and secondary rules addressed to specialized bodies, such an ordering must be considered as a legal order. This allows pluralists to discard any essentialist view of law, [53] and to look at the normative world through the lens of conceptual categories with no centralist prejudice. To use Moore's celebrated label, many sectors of reality – and the state among them – are seen as semi-autonomous social fields, in which rules are produced autonomously, compliance is coerced in some sort of way (agreement,

52 See D. Kennedy, 'Two Globalizations of Law & Legal Thought: 1850-1968', *Suffolk Law Review*, Vol. 36, No. 3, 2003, p. 631-679.

53 Obviously, the 'degree of essentialism' varies from author to author. Romano advances a thicker notion of institution, which inevitably makes his theory more essentialist than that of Galanter, Moore, or Woodman.

cooptation, shame, blame, exclusion, ostracism, excommunication, and/or force) and there are specialized groups of persons called upon to administer primary rules.[54]

For a long time – roughly until the 1980s – this unconventional portrayal of legal phenomena was endorsed by a small number of legal theorists, in that mainstream scholars paid scant attention to non-state law. Nonetheless, in the global scenario that emerges out of the fall of the Berlin Wall, in which alternative sources of law proliferate and non-state regimes of justice multiply, legal pluralism seems to provide a more suitable scheme for understanding the life of the law in social reality. The pureness of positivist theory has started to be seen as the expression of an ideology, or rather, as a game that sets its own goals and draws its own boundaries in order to justify an alleged objectivity.[55] Many critics, but also many past and current advocates, today acknowledge that the centralism with which traditional jurisprudence is imbued was used as a powerful ideological weapon meant to justify colonial exploitation and technocratic modernization. In contrast, the pluralist paradigm appears to account for sub-state, state and supra-state legal phenomena better than alternative paradigms for two main reasons.[56] First, the flexible and de-substantialized idea of semi-autonomous social fields is able to capture and scrutinize the numerous and articulated interplays between legal orders, that positivist pyramidal schemes presented as a vertical relationship between the legal and the non-legal. Secondly, legal pluralism deploys useful analytical instruments for analyzing situations of legal pluralism in which the state may be involved, and therefore to develop appropriate policies that may be adopted by the state towards non-state laws.[57]

Nonetheless, some scholars have expressed strong discomfort with this sort of 'new orthodoxy'. They claim that the process of re-labelling it involves not only yields a loss of heuristic value. In addition to that, the erosion of the traditional line separating the legal from the social could even serve as a battering ram for knocking down the walls of national democratic politics and for severing the link that, despite their despotic and colonial inclination, modern states created between law and justice. Let me examine this argument in more detail.

The prominent anthropologist Simon Roberts expresses such concerns in his recent article 'After Government?' He had long since declared his scepticism about the use of the label 'law' for denoting normative repertoires of non-Western entities. In a small article devoted

54 Notice that this third characteristic is not advanced by Moore.

55 See V. Kerruish, *Jurisprudence as Ideology*, Routledge, London/New York 1991.

56 See also P.S. Berman, 'The New Legal Pluralism', *Annu. Rev. Law Soc. Sci.*, Vol. 5, 2009, p. 225-242.

57 See Woodman 2009, where the author singles out four types of possible relations between state law and non-state law, i.e. concurrence, conflict, agglomeration and integration.

to bringing into question the theoretical status of legal anthropology, he contended that "however the map [of anthropological studies] may be drawn there is little case for a territory labelled 'law'".[58] Roberts is also one of the fiercest critics of legal pluralism, which he defined as "a creature of the law school: it is something that academic lawyers do; a lawyerly way of looking at the social world".[59] But in 'After Government?' Roberts conveys some important criticisms to the overextension of the notion of law that deserve to be examined closer.

He laments that the new orthodoxy of legal pluralism strives to represent law as existing beyond and above the state. In this view, law has nothing to do with governing. In his opinion, views of this kind "leave us with a diminishing sense of what law 'is'".[60] But while, in the past decades, the vexed question of the borderline between the legal and the social could merely be seen as an academic quarrel exerting sheer theoretical effects, today it has acquired a pragmatic significance. In fact, nowadays what Roberts calls 'essentially negotiated orders', whether at local or global level, are to be distinguished from legal orders not only in order to eschew a loss of understanding. A much more serious pragmatic worry is that an undue overextension may harm the relation between law and justice. He contends that negotiated orders, and above all transactional social orderings that pervade the global constellation, have their own rationalities, which involve a different orientation to rules from those of state law; in addition, their decision-making is based on agreement, rather than the decision of a third party.[61] By drawing on Laura Nader, he hints at the fact that a widespread 'harmony ideology' tends to present conflict as intrinsically bad and agreement as intrinsically good, in that the former harms community and the latter has a high survival value.[62] Roberts concludes that the overextension of the notion of law, at one and the same time, may turn out to erode the state competencies, to pervert the nature of essentially negotiated orders and to promote surreptitiously structural adjustment programmes.

The actuality of this danger is well illustrated by the sociologist Wolf Heydebrand.[63] According to him, economic globalization is promoting a general shift from procedural formalism, typical of national state apparatuses, to a *procedural informalism*, typical of

58 S. Roberts, 'Do We Need an Anthropology of Law?', *RAIN*, Nr. 25, 1978, 4-7, at p. 4.

59 Roberts 1998, p. 97.

60 Roberts 2005, p. 3.

61 *Id.*, p. 23.

62 See L. Nader, *The Life of the Law*, University of California Press, Berkeley (Ca.) 2002. See also L. Rose, *The Politics of Harmony: Land Dispute Strategies in Swaziland*, Cambridge University Press, Cambridge 1992, in which the author explains how harmony ideologies can be used by foreign development agents or indigenous new elites for downplaying land disputes and implementing land tenure changes.

63 W. Heydebrand, 'Globalization and the Rise of Procedural Informalism in Europe and America', *in* V. Gessner & D. Nelken (eds.), *European Ways of Law: Towards a European Sociology of Law*, Hart Publishing, Oxford 2007.

global informal social networks. He accounts for this shift as the rise of alternative forms of dispute resolution, such as arbitration, mediation and negotiation. In his opinion, these forms of dispute-settlement are weakening the traditional modes of judicial adjudication. He explains that this spread of informalism is in many ways connected to the growth of the so-called 'soft law', soft procedure, soft regulation, and self-regulation, emerged since the 1980s and 1990s. Heydebrand's arguments are close to those of Roberts insofar as both of them underline that the way in which states and social networks administer justice is intrinsically different: agreement, negotiation, and mediation can integrate but never replace adjudication. Yet, Heydebrand expresses more serious doubts than Roberts does about the nature of the emerging global negotiated orders. They are generally "shielded from the so-called 'discipline of the market' insofar as they can engage in oligopolistic or monopolistic practices with contractual impunity and, indeed, with relative immunity."[64] Furthermore, informal social networks are less accountable and "may imperceptibly shade over into collusion and corruption".[65]

But the deepest concern Heydebrand voices, is that procedural informalism is often at odds with equality:

> A crucial and highly problematic aspect of this informal process is that just as members of informal circles, webs and networks are not automatically 'equals', the partners in process often have unequal bargaining power and thus may disregard or circumvent typical conventions such as the norm of reciprocity or mutual social obligations. [...] In view of the tacitly assumed 'equality' among partners in exchange relations, it is this lacuna of theorising power that leads one to be sceptical about the putative 'democratic' and 'participatory' character of informal network processes.[66]

This is why Heydebrand concludes that legal pluralism must be carefully assessed in all of its instances. Pluralism can be highly seductive as an alternative to legal centralism; it can even help to counter cases of exploitation and domination. Yet, legal pluralism is by no means "identical to democracy".[67]

Still, I believe that legal pluralists have never regarded their theorizing as a plea for democracy. Quite the reverse, they have been cautious in providing too much an idyllic vision of social orderings. For instance, Moore suggests that semi-autonomous social fields

64 *Id.*, p. 101.
65 *Id.*
66 *Id.*, p. 101-102.
67 *Id.*, p. 108.

should not be thought of as perfectly and functionally organized contexts. Within them, not always people follow rules spontaneously and voluntarily; let alone common good and self-interest coincide. In most semi-autonomous social fields many conflicts between rules and individual purposes occur. In brief, social fields can well be sites where many forms of power and oppression are at work. Also Mark Galanter expressly departs from any irenic understanding of indigenous laws, which are not "either more virtuous or more efficient than official law".[68] They often reflect narrow and parochial concerns, are based on power differentials, may be harshly and indiscriminately coercive and may significantly harm weak subjects.

All in all, in my view, considerations of this kind only attest that legal pluralism is first and foremost a *scheme of comprehension*, and not a moral or political theory. In fact, one thing is to investigate the features that make an order legal, another is to acknowledge that this inquiry, as every scientific enterprise, has many pragmatic bearings. In the next section I will argue that a pluralist legal theory has above all to carry out a theoretical task, and that, in particular, it must offer analytical tools for discovering potential circumstances of *legal* pluralism.

THE DISTINCTIVENESS OF LAW AND THE NEED FOR A PLURALIST LEGAL THEORY

It was not my intention to suggest a simple divide between two clearly distinguished factions: anti-state law and pro-society supporters as opposed to pro-state law and anti-society ones. Theories can seldom be submitted to rigid taxonomies. My main concern was with the potential outcomes of theoretical premises on both a conceptual and a pragmatic level, especially in an age in which, as Carol Greenhouse observes, the chief problem "is the contested nature of states' claims regarding the legitimacy of official law".[69] In this final section I will stress two points. On the one hand, I will argue that the original project of legal positivism should be preserved in order that *legal* pluralism may be distinguished from *social* pluralism. On the other hand, I will contend that, just to this end, legal theory must adopt a pluralist approach. My final goal is to show that legal theory can serve as a scheme of comprehension and as a guideline both for empirical research and for actual policies insofar as it is able to develop conceptual tools that may allow recognizing, assessing and coping with circumstances of legal pluralism.

---

68 Galanter 1981, p. 25.

69 C.J. Greenhouse, 'Legal Pluralism and Cultural Difference. What is the difference? A Response to Professor Woodman', *Journal of Legal Pluralism*, Vol. 42, 1998, p. 61-72.

Legal pluralists advance cogent reasons for dismissing the identification of state law with law in general. This identification was promoted by the rise of the modern Western state government as the sole, or at least the chief, source of law, with an indisputable jurisdictional supremacy. An unbiased look at social reality shows that there is a myriad of social practices to which state law tends to attribute secondary importance, whereas, on the contrary, they constitute the framework of highly organized and partially self-sufficient social sectors. It may *prima facie* seem that most centralists could easily accept this view, as Kelsen himself does. Yet, legal pluralists manage to demonstrate that Kelsen's objection to sociology of law does not stand close scrutiny. It is meaningless to posit that legal theory and social analysis must be *logically* distinguished because of a previous *ontological* distinction between state law and social orderings. In fact, the law of the state does not exhibit any peculiar feature that differentiates it from the inner order of many social fields.[70] In addition, as I showed in the first section, such a conclusion need not necessarily be proved with recourse to the 'impurity' of social observation; for, as (a particular interpretation of) Hart's theory of law shows, it can be validated by means of a thorough conceptual analysis, which does not take for granted the positivist mantra of law as the legitimate use of organized violence.

At the same time, I think that we should differentiate between *legal* and *social* pluralism, as they are two different states of things. Obviously, the possibility of doing this is tied to the very same possibility of portraying law as different from other kinds of social ordering. Now, if it is true that today it is highly complicated to draw precise boundaries around distinct normative orders, as they overlap in many sectors of social life,[71] it is also true that this factual difficulty does not prevent us from differentiating between the legal and non-legal conceptually, by formulating criteria for this conceptual differentiation. Indeed, the task that legal positivists attribute to jurisprudence can well be carried out by a *pluralist theory of law*. This is also the opinion of Franz von Benda-Beckmann, who develops a solid and consistent idea of legal pluralism as a theoretical arena more than as a well-defined theory of law. In the article 'Who's Afraid of Legal Pluralism?' he faces some of the questions I have so far tackled. He asks: "How far can we get with the concept of law? Which criteria should give social phenomena the quality of being 'legal', and how do we distinguish such legal phenomena from other, non-legal ones?"[72]

---

70 See in particular Woodman 2009.

71 On this issue see M. Bavinck & G.R. Woodman, 'Can There be Maps of Law?', *in* F. von Benda-Beckmann, K. von Benda-Beckmann & A. Griffiths (eds.), *Spatializing Law: An Anthropological Geography of Law in Society*, Ashgate, Farnham 2009. See also W. Twining, *General Jurisprudence. Understanding Law from a Global Perspective*, Cambridge University Press, Cambridge 2009, Ch. 3.

72 F. von Benda-Beckmann, 'Who is Afraid From Legal Pluralism?', *Journal of Legal Pluralism*, Vol. 47, 2002, p. 37-83.

Von Benda-Beckmann stresses the importance of concepts that may help to discover *similarities* and *differences* in diachronic and cross-societal comparison. He believes legal pluralism to be an 'analytical tool' that allows to understand better a multifaceted set of phenomena – the legal – by way of comparison. Different phenomena can be defined similar insofar as their empirical manifestations exhibit some properties of the category outlined by means of analytical tools. Thus, legal pluralism is not an unquestionable *factual reality* but a *theoretical possibility* that must be conceptually postulated and be empirically tested. As von Benda-Beckmann rightly notices, this is a convincing solution to the Malinowski problem. It dispels the doubts of Moore and Merry as to a concept of law so wide that it may comprise anything. Actually, it is up to legal theory to pinpoint reliable (though always provisional, fallible and revisable) criteria that may help the observers to recognize similarities and differences. Needless to say, this is not a *substantial* solution, in that it does not claim to determine *in advance* any possible occurrences of legal pluralism. This is only a consistent starting point for theoretical discussion and empirical investigation. In sum, von Benda-Beckmann has the merit of stressing the need for legal theory *above all* in an age of increasing pluralism.

By adopting this starting point, I can conclude my contribution by concisely formulating some hypothesis as to what are the criteria that may help to determine whether or not something is legal. First of all, let me distinguish between law's *formal structure* and law's *functions*. On the one hand, under the vantage point of its formal structure, law is an organized practice among others, made up of distinct kinds of rules and differentiated roles. On the other hand – and this is the solution to the Romano's dilemma – law can claim to exert a normative supremacy not only because it serves certain basic functions (given that, as some critic remarks, many practices fulfil similar functions[73]) but by virtue of the particular way law serves them. Let me explore these two points in more detail.

As far as the formal structure is concerned, I have nothing to add to what I said above while discussing Galanter, Hart and Romano. Law is characterized by two fundamental aspects. First, the presence of two distinct kinds of rules: *primary rules* providing standards for conduct and *secondary rules* indicating how the former must be issued, applied, or changed. Second, the clear distinction between a delimited group of authorized rule-creating and rule-applying officials (who are the principal addressees of secondary rules) and the generality of ordinary subjects (who are the principal addressees of primary rules). The main advantages in portraying law in these terms are two. First, the combination of these

---

73 For a critique of functionalist approaches to law, see B. Tamanaha, 'A Non-Essentialist Version of Legal Pluralism', *Journal of Law & Society*, Vol. 27, No. 2, 2001, p. 296-321. See also Twining 2009, p. 109-112, which is a reply to Tamanaha's criticisms by defending a 'thin functionalism'.

two aspects allows distinguishing the legal practice from other less organized practices: for instance, religious precepts, moral principles or social manners cannot be defined as instances of law simply because they provide rules of conduct meant to regulate the activity of those who adopt them as standards. In order for religion, morality or etiquette to be defined as genuine laws, they must develop and stabilize a complex structure in terms of secondary rules and differentiated groups (although secondary rules may be more or less reflective and formal and although groups may be more or less rigid and sealed-off). The second advantage is that law is no longer characterized by its connection to either coercion or political power, which, however relevant they might be in concrete reality, turn out to be ancillary at a conceptual level.

Nevertheless, as I have repeatedly said, this conceptualization fails to distinguish law from some other complex institutions that also exhibit the two aspects mentioned above. Should all the institutions comprised of secondary rules and differentiated groups be considered as having a law? I think not. Or better, it depends. For my contention to be convincingly justified, it would require a comprehensive argumentation, which I cannot develop here. I will just set forth some theoretical considerations, also based on historical and anthropological studies.

A first move for grasping the distinctiveness of law is 'thin functionalism'.[74] It is my opinion that Hoebel and Karl Llewellyn are right when they introduce the notion of "law-jobs",[75] that is to say, certain basic functions that are indispensable for there being a social collectivity. First, law *defines relationships* among the members of a society, so as to assure integration among the activities of individuals and groups. This is a key function of law, in that it establishes the possible types of relation among subjects and defines the rights, duties, privileges, powers, immunities, and liabilities pertinent to each position in the composite relational web. Second, law allocates authority, establishes authoritative procedures for decision-making and trans-personalizes power by defining offices and social statuses. Third, law *settles trouble cases* as they arise, in order to discourage unlawful behaviours and to bring the relations of the disputants back into balance. In brief, law has to solve trouble cases in order that social life may resume its normal course. Fourth, law *redefines relations between individuals and groups* as the conditions of life undergo transformations, i.e. law has to accommodate social change.

---

74 See *supra*, note 73.

75 Hoebel 1954, Ch. 2. He develops this notion in collaboration with Karl Llewellyn while working on Cheyenne law (see K.N. Llewellyn & E.A. Hoebel, *The Cheyenne Way: Conflict and Case Law in Primitive Jurisprudence*, University of Oklahoma Press, Norman 1941). See also K.N. Llewellyn, 'The Normative, the Legal and the Law-jobs: The Problem of Juristic Method', *Yale Law Journal*, Vol. 49, No. 8, 1940, p. 1355-1400.

Nonetheless, thin functionalism does not still manage to distinguish the law from the inner order of some complex organizations, which also fulfil very similar functions.[76] The last crucial aspect to be considered is the special way in which law carries out law-jobs. This way is special because the law opens up *a trans-sectional and insulated venue, neatly separated from everyday life, in which everyday reality can be renegotiated and rephrased by means of a special knowledge (usually mastered by legal experts) and a rigid set of conceptual categories*. The basic variables involved in this definition are: trans-sectionality, professionalization, separateness from everyday life, self-sufficient knowledge, rigid conceptual categories, and formulaic language. No single variable is peculiar to law. Physics can be trans-sectional and separated from everyday life, a church can be highly professionalized and can adopt formulaic languages, theology or economics are insulated forms of knowledge and deploy special sets of conceptual categories. But it is in the conjunction of all or most of these variables – along with the formal structure of organization examined above – that law is unique. Obviously, different conjunctions among these variables produce remarkably different configurations of law, also in relation to the socio-historical context in which law operates and to the requirements of those who inhabit that context. But it is my contention that this broad definition manages to capture the core nature and the way of functioning of this special trans-sectional venue – the legal field – which is meant to assure that the multiple array of social orderings – that govern the everyday life of social subjects more closely than the law – may coexist. Let me briefly explore how law operates by examining the variable identified above.

As I have already said, law serves as a trans-sectional venue in which everyday reality is renegotiated and rephrased by means of a special set of categories. Those categories are nothing but the legal normative repertoire, made up of rules that *define things*, *establish the possible types of relation among subjects* and *prescribe binding procedures* in order that actions and transactions may be recognized as valid. Importantly, legal categories also define *what falls inside and what outside the legal domain*. The borders of the legal field correspond to the borders of its insulated stock of knowledge. In addition, knowledge and categories are often, although not always, mastered by a restricted group of persons, such as elders, wises, *iuris periti*, professors, officials. The discussions that take place in the field of law, and the decisions made in the light of them have a *restorative effect* on social reality precisely because the stock of knowledge employed in the legal field is autonomous, self-sufficient and transcends sectional interests. Obviously, law's being trans-sectional depends on its being based on a self-sufficient knowledge, which is equally distant from the various

76 This is also one of the reasons why Hoebel resorted to include in his definition the application of physical force and why Llewellyn always refused to provide a general conception of law that could be precisely distinguished from other social institutions and practices.

entities that comprise the context in which the legal field serves as a neutral field and legal experts figure as third parties.[77]

The separateness of legal knowledge from everyday knowledge and its being mastered by a well-defined group of persons are instrumental in the custody and maintenance of this trans-sectional bedrock. Insofar as it remains separated from everyday reality, the legal field offers a set of tools that are able to mend the tears produced by the disputes arising among the different parties of a collectivity. Conversely, these tools work as a source of efficient means for dispute-settlement just because they are located in a sealed-off and self-sufficient field, left to the care of personalities that are perceived and recognized as neutral and dependable. Hence, it is crucial that law may claim, or at least may pretend, to be trans-sectional in that it requires social agents to abandon the language of everyday life, and the rules of the social ordering that they usually obey. Within the legal field, both officials and ordinary subjects are required to adopt the special language of the law and to apply the categories it entails.[78] By providing the plaintiff and the defendant with a special language and with special categories that belong neither only to the former nor only to the latter, the law induces the conflicting parties to reframe the events that were at the origin of the conflict and to give them an entirely new form.

In conclusion, the distinctiveness of law rests on its unique *productive circularity*, which is triggered by the employment of its special categories on the part of all those who situate themselves in the legal field. Even when recognizable experts lack (as some anthropologist has insisted[79]), law acts as a venue in which there takes place a constant and circular interplay between categories and facts: categories allow to describe facts in a certain manner, while in turn facts, described in a certain manner, allow to overcome potential conflicts between categories. In other words, the typical circularity of law – that does differentiate it from every other institution or practice – is *the double way in which categories are used to elucidate facts* and *in which these facts*, elucidated in such and such a way, *retroact on categories*. This productive circularity is made possible by the separateness of legal

77 See P. Bourdieu, 'La force du droit', *Actes de la recherche en sciences sociales*, Vol. 64, 1986, p. 3-19. Needless to say, law's being trans-sectional and self-sufficient, and also its being perceived that way, depend on factors that cannot be anticipated theoretically, but must be discovered empirically.

78 Many historical, anthropological and socio-linguistic studies attests that in most Western and non-Western countries, while discussing in reference to a legal normative repertoire, both the conflicting parties and those who act as a third party adopt a *formal code*, marked by *stylistic formality, reliance on metaphors, and impersonal and authoritative quality*. See for instance B. Danet, 'Language in the Legal Process', *Law & Society Review*, Vol. 14, No. 3, 1980, p. 445-564; J.L. Comaroff & S. Roberts, *Rules and Processes. The Cultural Logic of Dispute in an African Context*, The University of Chicago Press, Chicago/London 1981; A. Schiavone, *Ius. L'invenzione del diritto in Occidente*, Einaudi, Torino 2005.

79 See e.g. P.H. Gulliver, 'Dispute Settlement without Courts: The Ndendeuli of Southern Tanzania', *in* L. Nader (ed.), *Law in Culture and Society*, University of California Press, Berkeley/Los Angeles 1997 (2nd ed.).

knowledge, by the formulaic rigidity of its language, by the inflexibility of its categories. These characteristics permit the law to bind the parties to comply with a restricted and fixed set of categories that allow them to provide *entirely new account of events*. Those accounts are able *to affect perfomatively* their representations and *to retroact* on their perception of events.

As a final point, a last question may be asked: How can such an understanding of law help us to cope with circumstances of legal pluralism? A quick, and therefore altogether unsatisfactory, answer is due. As far as the issues explored in this contribution are concerned, legal theory can help to determine whether or not the new transnational negotiated orders, which end up affecting significantly our daily life,[80] are really suited to play the function pertaining to law. In other words, legal theory has to take up the following questions: Can negotiated orders really operate as a trans-sectional bedrock? Do their categories allow social subjects to revise, renegotiate and rebuild their everyday reality? Or, rather, are Roberts and Heydebrand right when they argue that transnational negotiated orders are structurally different from law, to such an extent that their being adopted as part of our legal repertoire may bring about serious problems and deficiencies?

80 One only has to consider the incidence of certain supra-state sets of rules that regulate specific sectors of reality, such as WTO law, transnational labour law, merchant law, copyright law or internet law.

Critical Autopoiesis: The Environment of the Law

Andreas Philippopoulos-Mihalopoulos

The Environment Literally

A special responsibility is being handed out when, by editorial decree, contributions to a volume are required to deal with the environment of the law. Perhaps the standard way to deal with the concept of the environment is in some generic, contextual way, like something that surrounds without touching the law. If, however, one wants to be radical about the environment, one is expected to plunge headlong into the vicissitudes of what this environment may be, how to understand it without colonizing it, how to employ its appearance without forcing its presence. The environment must be taken literally. By this I mean that no representation of the environment should be offered, conveniently packaged for the law to ingest, instrumentalize and use. Instead, the environment must be understood as a disturbance for the law, as a space of unsettling whispering or even stentorious arguing, of unresolved conflict, of intense questioning. The environment of the law is the law's worst fears and, at the same time, law's avenue of potentially becoming more just.

Bringing the environment of the law into the law is our chance and indeed our responsibility to revolt against the law as regime and deal with the law as a site of expectations of justice. By bringing the law in touch with its environment, that is by contextualizing the law in the field of velocity in which the law swims, we aim at rethinking of the law as one amongst several mechanisms of social justice, and indeed employing the law as a way of dealing with a pressing and unsettled reality. This is because environment for the law is not just external to law but significantly law's externalization, that is law's graveyard of otherness. Environment for the law is the locus of law's haunted, repressed memory, as well as its various becomings that the law often disavows. This makes the environment more than mere contingency for the law. It is a space filled with awe and miscomprehension for the law, a beloved symptom at the same time invited by the law *and* kept at a safe distance. Environment is the *heart* of the legal paradox, and as such appropriately located *outside* the law. But this paradox will have to be introduced into the law, with all the potentially unsettling consequences.

The purpose of this contribution, therefore, is to interrupt this symmetry of law inside/environment outside. I plan to do this by redefining the concept of law's environment and by moving it from mere context to actualized materiality. Indeed, the main point of the text is an urge for the law to engage further with its environment – but environment taken literally: I consider the environment of the law to be pure matter, pulsating tissue and bricks and elements that the law habitually locks up in dry concepts and processes. Law's environment is space, bodies and structures that surround and indeed constitute the law. Such a call to law, however, reveals the complex topology of the concept of the environment. No more a thing 'around' the law, a safety blanket of opt-in/opt-out relevance, the environment floods in the law and consumes its edifices. Like a city lost in the jungle, the law is taking a risk by dealing with its environment in its materiality. At stake is nothing less than law's self-description as a *systematic* system, namely the understanding of the law propagated, within at least some legal circles, as a totality of at least some regular coherence and reliability. This new perspective on the environment, in short, demands an ethico-political re-articulation of the law, away from a historicized, abstracted and systematic understanding of power, and towards an embodied, spatial and multiple element that couples with other materialities and produces constantly new combinations.

The most appropriate way to show this passage of the environment from context to matter is by employing a rather heady methodological combination of Niklas Luhmann's sociological jurisprudence and Gilles Deleuze's material jurisprudence. While neither of the two theorists was explicitly a jurist, they both have something relevant to offer to the discussion. Luhmann has dedicated a great deal of his writings to law and has revisited his understanding of the legal system more often that he has with other systems, such as the economic, the political, etc.[1] Deleuze, on the other hand, has been right from the outset allergic to the law.[2] His co-authoring with Felix Guattari only enhanced this tendency, to the point that the various attempts at rereading Deleuze as a legal theorist require considerable acrobatics. But these do pay off since one can come up with an embodied understanding of normativity and an enhanced sense of the environment in which the law is operating.[3] What I try to elicit from this combination is a notion of what I have elsewhere called *Critical Autopoiesis*,[4] namely a novel reading of autopoietic theory that departs

1 Law is the one topic to which Luhmann has dedicated two different books: N. Luhmann, *A Sociological Theory of Law*, E. King & M. Albrow (Trans.), Routledge & Kegan Paul, Boston 1985; and N. Luhmann, *Law as a Social System*, (K. Ziegert, Trans.; F. Kastner, R. Nobles, D. Schiff & R. Ziegert (Eds.), Oxford University Press, Oxford 2004.

2 See his comments on the law and its limitations in G. Deleuze, *Difference and Repetition*, P. Patton (Trans.), Continuum, London 2004.

3 See for example, R. Braidotti, C. Colebrook & P. Hanafin (Eds.), *Deleuze and the Law: Forensic Futures*, Palgrave Macmillan, Basingstoke 2009.

4 A. Philippopoulos-Mihalopoulos, *Niklas Luhmann: Law, Justice, Society*, Routledge, London 2009.

from systems theory as it had been envisaged by the early Luhmann and dwells more on Luhmann's later writings of the autopoietic turn. Even so, however, critical autopoiesis increasingly picks up speed and moves beyond the confines of the original theory, enabling corporeality and spatiality to put in a full appearance, thus converting a traditional understanding of autopoiesis into a sensory experience.

LEGAL SYSTEM, LEGAL ENVIRONMENT

In the majority of the received readings of Niklas Luhmann's theory of autopoiesis and its application to law, the environment is the negative constitutive of the law, namely the thing that law is not and through which the law forms its systemic consistency, its identity. In other words, the law *needs* the environment to be left out of the law, in order for the law to carry on with its function. At best, the environment is where the other side of closure rests. Thus, the famous adage "the open rests on the close",[5] that puts together normative closure with cognitive openness simultaneously makes the one a precondition of the other, and risks demoting the environment into an opportunity for cognitive evolution – an exotic space of infinite, unexplored (yet!) possibilities that may or may not eventually become part of the great legal empire. It is the space of cognitive expedition, the forest into which the law ventures when in need of food, but not the place in which the law would ever be found lingering. It is a quick in and out.[6] Because of its normative closure, the law cannot observe the environment, only itself. The environment remains a resource, unobservable yet intensely used by the law. The process is unstoppable, the expansion in fact almost begged for by the colonized-to-be environment:[7] the environment needs the law in order to 'exist', to acquire some epistemological status. Of course at some points, the law learns from its environment, indeed the law integrates into its own legal language environmental issues that heretofore were not relevant to the law but at some point became precisely that. This is how cognitive openness works and how it relies on contingency – thus, some things may claim the attention of the law faster than others, or indeed escape law's attention altogether. Interestingly, as soon as the environment becomes part of the law, that is, as soon as the law deals with new issues that until that moment were not deemed worthy of legal enlightenment, these issues stop being part of the legal environment and automatically occupy a place in the legal system. This is of course the case with every

5 *"L'ouvert s'appuie sur le fermé"*, E. Morin, *La Méthode II: La Connaissance de la Connaissance*, Seuil, Paris 1986, p. 203.

6 This is a metaphor that only barely works for autopoietic systems, since the system hardly has access to its environment. It denotes, however, a rather predatory nature of a system towards its environment and, for my purposes, it is apposite.

7 This is the process of colonial narcissism described by H. Bhabha, *The Location of Culture*, Routledge Classics, London 2005.

issue that, when first appearing as a social phenomenon, is not yet dealt with by the law. These issues include technological innovations, geopolitical movements, natural disasters or oppressive practices within the jurisdictional practice of a state. In all such cases, the law contingently might or might not wake up to them, and even if it does, it might be just national rather than international law, or regulation rather than law, or even just regulation of insurance policies rather than legal prevention. Regardless of what kind of normativity becomes alerted to the issues, the latter remain unregistered by the law until the point that, well, they become registered by the law. From that point onwards, however, these issues stop being in the environment of the law and become part of the law. Topologically, therefore, something can never be in the environment of the law. The moment something of the environment is recognized as relevant to law, then the thing itself is no longer of the environment but of the legal system.

This is not mere technicality. The environment of the law – and at this stage we can think of it as social context – is radically deprioritized to the point of non-existence unless and until it becomes law. And then, it is no longer environment. Traditionally the environment is the *grand manqué*, the unobservable, the Nothing that guards and legitimizes the boundaries of the system. Inside the law is all light and knowledge, outside is all complex noise and impenetrability. This means that the law focuses only on its processes and ignores its environment. Things become acutely political when legitimacy is brought into the discussion. Thus, while law is self-legitimizing,[8] in that its use of force is justified by its very conditions of use,[9] it relies on political legitimacy in order to carry on its self-legitimizing day-dreaming. But political legitimacy, just like anything else beyond the control of the law, lies outside the law, namely in law's environment. The paradox is that the law *must* ignore political legitimacy for otherwise the law would be dependent on short-term political instrumentalities. At the same time, however, law's deliberate ignoring of its environment (namely, its social context that includes its narrower political context) is also the cause of law's inability to promise the delivery of justice.[10]

To advance towards the announced introduction of materiality, let me compare the above symmetry law/environment to the gendered form. Recall how Hélène Cixous and Catherine Clément have put it: "shut out of his system's space, she is the repressed that ensures the system's function".[11] Law and its environment are arranged in some macho

8 Luhmann 2004.

9 J. Derrida, 'Force of Law: The Mystical Foundation of Authority', M. Quaintance (Trans.), *in* D. Cornell, M. Rosenfeld & D. Gray Carlson (Eds.), *Deconstruction and the Possibility of Justice*, Routledge, New York 1992.

10 Philippopoulos-Mihalopoulos 2009.

11 H. Cixous & C. Clément, *The Newly Born Woman*, B. Wing (Trans.), Manchester University Press, Manchester 1986, p. 67.

unidirectionality that chops up binary impasses. This is the risk of a facile reading of autopoiesis: for, as Iris Marion Young reminds us albeit from a different perspective, "any definition or category creates an inside/outside distinction and the logic of identity seeks to keep these borders firmly drawn".[12] I argue, however, that autopoiesis is not about the exclusive symmetry between system and environment but about the different ways in which difference appears within and outside the system. Retaining the difference between system and environment is not enough to avoid freezing the 'different' nature of environment into an ossified exclusion. Thus, Luhmann's autopoietic reminder that "the point from which all further investigations in systems theory must begin is not identity but difference",[13] must be seen as a licence for the multiplication of difference, and a quest for difference as identity. What I suggest here is that the epistemological simplification of one system/one environment has outrun its use and has begun posing as ontology. In its stead, a multiplication of different differences, variously inside and outside is to be posited, that produce identity (as difference) in an infinite series of repetition. Such repetition, however, and despite its name, cannot be contained by identity as sameness, but rather has to be seen as the difference of difference.[14]

A point of methodological clarification here: I do not think I am suggesting anything different to what Luhmann has already suggested. But I am certainly suggesting something different to what most current readings of the theory have produced.[15] Several factors are, I think, responsible for the misappropriation of the theory: an excessive emphasis on the system itself, which constructs it as a systematic form of organization, has led to an ossified understanding of the theory; a faith in either the empirically tested nature of Luhmann's theory or indeed its empirically untestable nature places the whole theory on some shaky pseudo-scientific ground of empirical confirmation, thus denuding the theory from its fundamental philosophical credentials (*pace* Luhmann, who emphatically considered himself a sociologist and not a philosopher); a fetishization of the concept of the boundary

12 I.M. Young, 'The Ideal of Community and the Politics of Difference', *in* L. Nicholson (Ed.), *Feminism/Postmodernism*, Routledge, New York 1990, p. 303.

13 N. Luhmann, *Social Systems*, J. Bednarz, Jr., Stanford (Trans.), Stanford University Press, Palo Alto (Ca.) 1995, p. 177; see also N. Luhmann, *Theories of Distinction: Redescribing the Descriptions of Modernity*, J. O'Neil *et al.* (Trans.), W. Rasch (Ed.), Stanford University Press, Palo Alto (Ca.) 2002, Ch. 5.

14 See Deleuze, 2004; also A. Philippopoulos-Mihalopoulos, 'Repetition or the Awnings of Justice', *in* O. Ben-Dor (Ed.), *Law and Art*, Routledge, London 2011.

15 Felicitous exceptions are not infrequent. See indicatively G. Teubner, 'Alienating Justice: On the Surplus Value of the Twelfth Camel', *in* J. Pribáň & D. Nelken, (Eds.), *Law's New Boundaries: The Consequences of Legal Autopoiesis*, Ashgate, Aldershot 2001; A. Schutz, 'The Twilight of Global Polis: On Losing Paradigms, Environing Systems and Observing World Society', *in* G. Teubner (Ed.), *Global Law without a State*, Ashgate, Aldershot 1996; U. Stäheli, *Sinnzusammenbruche: Eine dekonstruktive Lekture von Niklas Luhmanns Systemtheorie*, Velbrück, Weilerswist 2000; J. Clam, *Droit et Société chez Luhmann: La Contingence des Norms*, Presses Universitaires de France, Paris 1997; W. Rasch, *Niklas Luhmann's Modernity: The Paradoxes of Differentiation*, Stanford University Press, Palo Alto (Ca.) 2000, amongst others.

has led to a misunderstanding of the potential mobility of the concepts and the theory itself; and, finally, a sacrosanct dealing with Luhmann's writings that becomes blind both to the *substance* of the theory and its potentiality. Thus, closure, systems, sociology and indeed Luhmann's texts are still relevant, but their fetishization is not. What I suggest is simply a critical reading of autopoiesis, indeed a *critical autopoiesis* which, however, does not succumb to critique but carries on by unfolding itself along the object of its attention, moves alongside its body and employs its folds in order to construct concepts and conceptual practices that aim at a different reality. This reality, however, is neither a better place somewhere else nor an ideality of a topos never to be found. On the contrary, the proposed reality is simultaneously not yet actualized and immanent to the current conditions.

To Begin

In order to deal with difference, therefore, one has to begin with the environment. But how to begin with it? The environment is unobservable. This may suggest that to begin with the environment is not to begin at all, but to be thrown in the middle of something that closes in around. The environment is neither the origin nor the *telos* of a system – both these things are assumed by the system itself. To begin with the system is to begin with an origin, however constructed and even arbitrary this origin may be. To begin with the environment, however, is to recognize the fact that no construction, no representation of origin is good enough. The environment of a system is a space in which one is thrown and expected to create a topology of light, right there, in the middle of nothing. This cannot be represented as an origin but merely a moving along, a flowing along an already rapid catenation of bodies. Environment is neither the beginning nor the end, and it cannot assume the agency of such construction. The environment is right in the middle of the various self-assured systems. Deleuze and Guattari bring up precisely the space of the *middle* as the point of beginning. In so doing, they revolt against the habitual conceptualization of beginning that goes along the need for origin, but also concepts such as centre and boundary. Their book *A Thousand Plateaus* is precisely this kind of beginning: [16] throwing oneself in the middle of the text and moving along, without 'proper' beginning. To use a concept they are employing, just as the grass has no one root, central part or limits to its expansion, [17] in the same way to begin in the middle is to find oneself folded between the multiplicity of the world without a discernible origin, a specific centre and

16 G. Deleuze & F. Guattari, *A Thousand Plateaus: Capitalism and Schizophrenia*, B. Massumi (Trans.), Continuum, London 2004.

17 Grass is opposed to the tree with its defined root, trunk and volume. As Deleuze and Guattari write, "arborescent systems are hierarchical systems with centers of significance and subjectification". *Id.*, p. 16. For this reason, they urge to "make rhizomes, not roots, never plant! Don't sow, grow offshoots!". *Id.*, p. 24.

determined territorial limits. To be thrown into the mobile multiplicity of the grass is to follow the blades waving in the wind: one loses one's origin, one's preconceived ideas of location and destination, one's belief in the importance of the centre. One is lost in a horizontal plane of movement, and on this plane one begins by ebbing and flowing between strength and exposure. The environment of the law is grassy.

When one begins from the perspective of the environment, then one is faced with a system that lacks consistency. Indeed, a system that grapples rather desperately around, torn in tatters by the velocity of environmental flux. It seems that this system blindly gathers pieces, little shiny mosaics that might eventually form a mirroring surface on which the system will attempt to reflect on itself and its randomly constructed identity. This is exactly what an autopoietic system is. Nothing systematic about them. The term 'system' in Luhmann's theory is a misnomer because it gives the impression of systematicity, of normative promise and unfailing consistency, of a method, itself systematic, that produces systematized units of perfectly formed totalizing boundaries. But this system is nothing of the sort. [18] If, faithful to its etymology, the term denotes a *syn* ('together') and *histanai* ('to set up', 'to stand'), a togetherness that has been set up (is this setting up arbitrary? And who has set it up? Itself? Without discernible origin?), a transitive infinitive that stands alone and alone it *con*sists itself; if a system denotes a togetherness without *con*tent, without *periechon*, a *compearance*, [19] an assemblage of sorts without promise of future form, consistent boundaries, identifiable characteristics or positive functions; if a system is a *machine* in the Deleuze-Guattari sense that is nothing but connections and operations in a constant process of what they call *deterritorialization*, namely the relentless becoming other than itself, always at another stage which engulfs and is engulfed by its otherness; [20] if a system is that, that is, if a system *is* not, then a Luhmannian system is indeed a system. [21]

A system is thrown into the environment without mission and without function except to gather its amoeba-like topology and start surviving. While it is in the interest of the system to slow things down, in the environment as middle "things pick up speed". [22] In the environment of the law, the law evolves, changes, innovates, grapples with new concepts, crashes, fails, is co-opted, is abused – in short, the law *becomes* (the law or other than the

18 See also D. Schwanitz, 'Systems Theory According to Niklas Luhmann: Its Environment and Conceptual Strategies', *Cultural Critique*, Vol. 30, No. 1, 1995, p. 137-170 for a comparison with Derrida.

19 As J.L. Nancy & T.B. Strong, '*La Comparution*/the Compearance: From the Existence Of "Communism" To the Community Of "Existence"', *Political Theory,* Volume 20, No. 3, 1992, p. 371-398, call the appearing together but without bonds of communion.

20 Deleuze & Guattari 2004

21 See L.M.A. Francot, *Normativity's Re-Entry. Niklas Luhmann's Social Systems Theory: Society and Law,* Wolf Publishers, Nijmegen 2008.

22 Deleuze & Guattari 2004, p. 28.

law). But while in the autopoietic environment there are other systems, such as politics, religion, economy, the media and so on, that somehow indirectly vie for law's attention, the law manages to accommodate their calls relatively well. This means that the law "couples" with other systems by producing a common flow, a shared historicity of acting in parallel, sometimes successfully and others unsuccessfully. Thus, a constitution is a great example of a largely successful coupling between law and politics. Or regulation of banks is a great example of unsuccessful coupling between law and economy. But even the lack of success is mitigated by the fact that these systems eventually speak the same language, one of self-preservation and need for continuity. What remains excluded from this linguistic communication is environmental *matter*. The law, just as most other systems, cannot deal with that part of the environment that is constituted by and constitutes matter. Very quickly, matter is expelled to the extreme end of forgetting, assigned to an area without communicational potential. It is a well known criticism towards Luhmann that his theory excludes humans from society.[23] In my view, however, this is an accepted and indeed rather banal anti-humanist gesture shared by many theories and as such it has nothing to do with a deprioritization of the human. In fact, in Luhmann the human is everywhere in form and through channels of communication.[24] The problem lies elsewhere. It is the materiality of the human, the natural and, what is more, the post-human that is being left out. No bodies, no space, no doubts about what is the human body, or about the distinction natural/artificial. Indeed, the legal system sucks the material out of the materiality of the environment, converts matter into semantics, reduces bodies into subjects, spaces into property, love into signature, orgasm into contract.

This criticism is not entirely fair. Luhmann 'discovered' exclusion and with it his own *tristes tropiques* when in the early 1990s he visited the favelas in Brazil. The story is almost mythical in its recurrence, not least because of the spectacular new vocabulary that followed the journey. Expressions such as "existences reduced to the bodily [...] attempting to get to the next day",[25] and "physical violence, sexuality, the elemental and impulsive satisfaction of necessities" and "the observation of bodies" in *Die Gesellschaft der Gesellschaft*,[26] have narrowly although indelibly opened the text to the observation of the hitherto unobservable. I am not referring to human beings but to the *acknowledgement* of an outside – what William Rasch calls "the Spasm of the Limits".[27] Inclusion/exclusion appears to be a

23 See M. King, 'The Construction and Demolition of the Luhmann Heresy', *Law and Critique*, Vol. 12, No. 1, 2001, p. 1-32.

24 J. Paterson, 'Who is Zenon Bankowski Talking To? The Person in the Sight of Autopoiesis', *in* D. Nelken (Ed.), *Law as Communication*, Dartmouth, Aldershot 1996.

25 N. Luhmann, 'Beyond Barbarism', H.G. Moeller (Trans.), *in* H.G. Moeller (Ed.), *Luhmann Explained*, Open Court, Chicago 2006, p. 174.

26 N. Luhmann, *Die Gesellschaft der Gesellschaft*, Suhrkamp, Frankfurt am Main 1997, p. 633.

27 Rasch 2000, p. 119.

spectre of promises past that is here to haunt Luhmann's texts and their reader, and allow a flow of previously unencountered apparitions of bodies and spaces to enter his texts. This is the visibilization of the invisible:

> There are still immense differences between rich and poor, and such differences still affect lifestyle and access to social opportunities. What is different is that this is no longer the *visible* order, the order without which no order would be possible at all.[28]

Functional differentiation, Luhmann's Weberian trophy that divided the world in functionally differentiated systems, promised an invisibilization of social inequalities; but now the invisible has become visible (although still not instrumental for society, at least not in the way functional differentiation is) and the excluded has become registered.

LINES

Law's autopoietic position as one system in the wider social system is not usually accorded its full potential impact. To place the law within society, which in its turn is populated by other systems, is already to accept law's *affect*, that is law's ability of co-appearing with others, affecting and being affected (however indirectly) by them.[29] A strict systems theory understanding might dwell in the inability of closed systems to communicate with each other and a subsequent reinforcement of functional differentiation (law is law, politics is politics, religion is religion, and so on, each one serving a different function that emerged at the onset of modernity). A critical autopoietic approach, however, aims at exploding this process in such a way that society is eventually replaced by an affective sociality. This is not to prioritize connections over self-observation or indeed openness over closure. On the contrary, it is a reinforcement of closure as immanence. This understanding returns to the inner folds of the law and enables the unfolding of law's environmental awareness from within. The consequence of the above is double: first, the law is an immanent system, namely a system whose function is determined entirely by and within itself; and, second, this determination originates, not in a positive need to contribute to society, but in a perception of a space of unobservability within the system that takes the shape of material appearance of other bodies. The two consequences no doubt appear contradictory: for how can it be that, on the one hand the law remains closed, and on the other the law is determined by other bodies?

---

28 Luhmann 1997, p. 772 (added emphasis).

29 For the Deleuzian treatment of the Spinozian concept of affect, see G. Deleuze & F. Guattari, *What is Philosophy?*, H. Tomlinson and G. Burchell (Trans.), Columbia University Press, New York 1994.

Before I attempt to reconcile the above two propositions, let me briefly revisit the concept of function in Luhmann. In an enlightening passage, Luhmann concludes:

> Orientation by function alone is not sufficient. This follows from the simple fact that the reference to a function is *always an invitation to look for functionally equivalent alternatives, that is, to cross systems boundaries.*[30]

Function is co-appearing with its functionally equivalent alternatives, which, however can only come from a boundary transgression. This means that the legal system's function has less to do with law and more to do with enabling other systems to carry on their autopoiesis. The law achieves this by including them all in the form of an immanent environment, an environment that is no longer outside the system but folded within. In other words, function operates as the void – the necessary void – through which the continuation of other systems' autopoiesis materializes. Function is the gap produced when one removes a handful of wet sand from that part of the beach constantly beaten by the waves. The gap quickly fills with water and sand, a gap not quite a gap, whose palimpsestic territory is thick with receding and expanding boundaries. And since each function is unique to each system, function is nothing but the absence of other systemic functions. Any impression of causality that seems to favour system over environment, in that the former is observable, can now be supplemented by its converse – the cathedral properly comes before the buttress. Systemic function is an invitation by an absent host towards an alterity that is to remain unobserved.

The above understanding of function facilitates the co-appearance of both closure and unobservability within. However conceived at any point, law's function is determined by the movement of a space within the law that pulsates with exteriority. The law becomes a *plane of immanence,*[31] namely the term that Deleuze and Guattari reserve for the all-embracing sum of folds and falls and connections, where all causality is immanently contained within its boundaries. The plane of immanence is infinite. Its boundaries are virtually everywhere and actually including everything – not unlike a system whose boundaries are the world as the system knows it, potentially expanding to ingest more and more environment. The crucial point is that the law as a plane of immanence contains all there is to be contained. Its exteriority is always internalized but always powerfully appearing as a movement that pushes the boundaries ever further. This immanent exteriority is what Deleuze and Guattari call a *line of flight*, namely a line that traverses the plane and pushes

30 Luhmann 2004, p. 93 (added emphasis).

31 Also referred to as the *plane of consistency*. See throughout Deleuze & Guattari 2004.

the limits from within to further edges of creativity.[32] In this sense, the function of the law is to be found vibrating on its very own lines of flight, in its constant attempt at reaching out towards a creative transgression that remains immanently folded within.

Critical autopoiesis attempts to flesh out this necessary paradox of the law as both immanent *and* given to a certain exteriority. The practical aspect of this paradox is that the law needs to carry on doing two things: both carry on becoming-other-than-the-law, namely to embrace a foundational interdisciplinarity that addresses both object and method and which in its turn pushes the law into dealing with its environment in a way that disrupts and indeed imperils the perceived stability and reliability of the law; and, second, to carry on being the law, namely the system that captures the future by operating through its past, on a deliberatively slow and indeed conservative temporality that, at least in theory, provides a certain social reliability.[33] The difference from a more orthodox systems theory approach is that, here, the arguably tokenistic openness of a system to its environment is replaced by a radical immanence, indeed one could say a deeper closure, that contains future becomings. This immanence, however, is not controlled by the system. The law does not decide. It is the space of unobservability that decides what the law is to become. This is what Luhmann means when he writes "autopoiesis is above all the production of internal indeterminacy".[34] What is more, this space is moving precipitously towards a material appearance within the law. The law is now brought face to face with a material environment that accepts no representation, no construction and no substitution with a legal interpretation of the material through the usual legal codes. The law has invited its environment within, and it now has to deal with its guest.

Spaces and Bodies

The problem is not to bring law in contact with the material. The problem is not even to show that law is material. Indeed, the problem is to demonstrate that law is so steeped in matter and moving so closely to it that it ends up being without limits and, most importantly without limitations. But let me take this from the beginning. As I have already mentioned, an autopoiesis of materiality is a short leap, not only from Luhmann's later writings, but significantly from the very nature of the theory that is based on a non-metaphorical understanding of systemic topology. There is little doubt, therefore, that autopoiesis is

32 *Id.*

33 This has been put by Deleuze & Guattari, 2004, in terms of the distinction between logos and nomos. See my contribution to the matter in A. Philippopoulos-Mihalopoulos, 'Law, Space, Bodies: The Emergence of Spatial Justice', *in* L. De Sutter & K. McGee (Eds.), *Deleuze and Law*, Edinburgh University Press, Edinburgh 2011.

34 Luhmann 1997, p. 67 (original emphasis).

spatial. As *topos*, a system embodies Doreen Massey's definition of space: a product of interrelations and embedded practices, a sphere of multiple possibilities, a ground of chance and undecidability, and as such always becoming, always open to the future.[35] A system is a space of environmental happenstance that remains relevant because of the embeddedness of its operations; it is characterized by a multiplicity of contingent possibilities; and it is always and necessarily open to the future in the form of its environmental becomings. At the same time, a system, just as space, is characterized by a lack of *Grundnorm*, origin, objective or final destination. The system moves in a directionless way (at least in the sense of centralized direction), dragging along its unstable topology, unpredictably opting for movement or stasis. A system, just like space, can be measured, mapped and circumnavigated, but not controlled, contained, or embraced in its totality. The legal system is waking up to its spatiality – and this does not refer merely to some legal branches, such as the obvious property or environmental law, but the law on the whole and in all its particular manifestations. By spatiality I mean an emplaced materiality that affects the form of the law. The legal system is defined by its *longitude* and *latitude*,[36] namely the material elements that comprise its corpus in its movement and rest, and its capacity to enter into affect. Law's materiality is not just courts and wigs but the way the law emplaces itself, its measures, commands and prohibitions between other bodies, or between objects and thoughts, and in the distance and propinquity between them. Law determines these spaces through its longitude but also defines which bodies are to be brought in affective contact with the law, and through the law with each other. At the same time, law is affected by these bodies and connections. Its latitude changes to such an extent that the law has to move, thereby affecting its longitudinal emplacement. Law moves and in the process, it deterritorializes, namely it releases environment. This goes hand in hand with legal stratification, namely the reterritorializing and overcoding of space both in terms of matter and in terms of semantics (law's reference to its environment). Law provides readily available avenues of thought and action, it binds expectations of how to move, and in that way binds thought and behaviour in narrow, blind corridors of striation. But at the same time, law makes its own walls collapse, betrays expectations, reveals environmental smoothness where only pillars used to be. Even in its quality to be disobeyed, the law opens up smooth spaces of new distances and proximities. This is an intensely spatial process – nothing metaphorical here – grounded on material, shifting space.

It is clear that law's spatiality cannot be understood in isolation from its corporeality. Likewise, autopoiesis can no longer be thought without its bodily functions. Rather tellingly Luhmann writes: "the difference between corporeality and noncorporeality has (at least

35 D. Massey, *For Space*, Sage, London 2005.
36 Deleuze & Guattari 2004, p. 287.

for our present societal system) no social relevance".[37] This fits rather well with a Deleuzian definition of a body: "a body can be anything: it can be an animal, a body of sounds, a mind or idea; it can be a linguistic corpus, a social body, a collectivity".[38] While Luhmann clearly meant the distinction between corporeality and noncorporeality as a difference that was delegated to the side of the environment, it is time to recognize that now the difference makes a difference. From feminist and queer theory to environmental and geopolitical legal manifestations, the body has entered forcefully the system. That the law is able to see bodies of course can only mean one thing: that the law itself has woken up to its own corporeality. The legal corpus follows the same lines of movement and stasis as any other body. The difference between corporeality and noncorporeality passes once again on the side of the environment – but the environment is already in. The law, just as all other social systems, are bodies, themselves determined by their affective conflicts and confluences with other bodies. This is what, following Braidotti,[39] I would call the joyful moment of encounter between law and other bodies – law on its own cannot deliver itself. It needs to drive itself to its edge and there to produce its becoming. However, joy should be understood as a vitalistic force,[40] that pushes law from within and into forceful encounters with other bodies. The encounter encompasses the possibility of violence, of mutual destruction, of cannibalistic ingestion but also of new becomings and different power configurations. Such encounters are not limited between the bodies of social systems. They can also take place between the law and a human body, an artificially enhanced human body, animal body, mythical body, immobile or disabled body, senseless body, any body. Every body is material, "a matter-movement",[41] that generates order and chaos, opportunities for smooth spaces of nomadic movements and striated spaces of controlling movement. Rather than having a definitive function, a body's movement is always contextualized to the space on which it moves.

With this, we encounter the multiplication of difference between system and environment. The environment within the law is not a single, unitary space. Within it, different bodies move in different ways across different spaces. Along them, the legal topology is formed, a reaction and an action that attempts to understand what is happening with itself. The law fragments, its self-description forcefully replaced with illusions of unity that do not hold. The primordial gesture of distinction, the autopoietic feudal right of "the first distinction",[42] that Luhmann uses in order to differentiate between system and environment

37 Luhmann 1995, p. 246.
38 G. Deleuze, *Spinoza: Practical Philosophy*, R. Hurley (Trans.), City Light Books, San Francisco 1988, p. 127.
39 R. Braidotti, *Transpositions: on Nomadic Ethics*, Polity Press, Cambridge 2006.
40 *Id.*
41 Deleuze & Guattari 2004, p. 512.
42 G. Spencer Brown, *Laws of Form*, George Allen and Unwin, London 1979, p. 3.

(and between observed and unobservable), is no longer a property of the observer but of the distinction itself. It is the distinction that now moves between bodies and determines. There is no subject to the distinction, no one to call it the first distinction even ex post facto and arbitrarily. The distinction performs itself from the space of the middle, from this unobservable yet somehow privileged space of the environment within. The observer,[43] another cudgel of autopoietic theory that aimed at bridging the gap between the subject and the object, is now without a job. In the plane of immanence, everything has been replaced by what Deleuze and Guattari call *assemblages*,[44] namely reciprocal constitutions of difference that move along other assemblages, consisting a form of headless agency that is radically emplaced and foundationally affective. The body of law encounters the human body in a space of disputed movement and this sums up an assemblage that moves along other bodies/laws/spaces. A universe of systems within a system, breaths of conflict and co-appearance that claim the totality of the system by flowing along the performance of the distinction. This is a posthuman law through and through. Not simply in the Luhmannian way of excluding humans from society, but more importantly in the sense of including the artificial, the natural, the imaginary into the body of the human. To quote Deleuze and Guattari: "we make no distinction between man and nature: the human essence of nature and the natural essence of man become one within nature in the form of production of industry".[45] The human is no longer the effigy of a coherent or even incoherent subject,[46] but a body liberated from identity constraints, an element that couples with other natures and artifices and in so doing keeps on challenging the law. Likewise, a posthuman law is one that couples with abandon with the natural, the artificial, the uncategorisable, and constructs new jurisprudential assemblages with all of them.

Environment, again

Spatial, corporeal, posthuman, the law is now left in tatters. Trammelled by unpredictable lines of flight, its skin bloating with the movement of novel assemblages underneath, its exteriority ingested as a horizontal immanence, the law is radically challenged. It would have been a break down, if it were not for law's ability to delude itself. This is the other side of the paradox, the one that keeps the law together in the knowledge that there is nothing keeping it together. This is not a construction of unity, certainly not a representa-

43 N. Luhmann, 'The Paradoxy of Observing', *Cultural Critique*, Vol. 31, 1995, p. 37-55.

44 Deleuze & Guattari 2004.

45 G. Deleuze & F. Guattari, *Anti-Oedipus: Capitalism and Schizophrenia*, R. Hurley et al. (Trans.), University of Minnesota Press, Minneapolis 1983, p. 4.

46 A. Grear, 'The vulnerable living order: human rights and the environment in a critical and philosophical perspective', *Journal of Human Rights and the Environment*, Vol. 2, No. 1, 2011, p. 23-44.

tion. Just as the environment is fully here, in material appearance, so is the unity of the system. Allow me to quote Luhmann at some length here:

> Every question concerning the unity of a distinction, or, put differently, each attempt to observe the schema of observation, leads to a paradox, that is, to an oscillation between two opposite positions (lawful/unlawful, internal/external, equal/unequal), which can neither establish memory, nor produce structural complexity, nor secure connectivity. In that way, in other words, the legal system is not able to operate. On the other hand, if the legal system seeks to guarantee its autonomy, then it must include its negation of this very autonomy and the negation of all the conventions that support it. It must not exclude them. Or to put it differently: the legal system must include what is excluded and, in doing so, subvert the requirements of logic, such as the axiom of the excluded third question, the prohibition of contradiction, or the presupposition of identities free of oscillation.[47]

There is certainly oscillation between the sides of the paradox that the law has to put aside for otherwise "it is not able to operate". This is the self-induced illusion of unity for the law – that it cannot be both lawful/unlawful and so on. But this is not the coup of the text. Rather, the text reveals how the law assembles itself on the basis of its inability to assemble itself: "if the legal system seeks to guarantee its autonomy, then it must include its negation of this very autonomy". In exactly the same way, if the system seeks to guarantee its materiality, then it must include the negation of its very materiality. Materiality is the new autopoietic cudgel: simply put, materiality is the flipside of autonomy. Autonomy is open closure, whereas materiality is closed openness: the law shares the world through matter, while at the same time cutting a chunk of materiality and jealously guarding it for its own topological excursions. To include the exclusion of its materiality means for *the law to be through and through material, yet to put this on the side in order to carry on operating.*

This is precisely what we are currently witnessing. The discovery of materiality is not at all new. The law has come across it much earlier, before legal theory begun criticizing the law on this basis. The law is everywhere, steeped in things, bodies, distances. The law is matter, made out of matter. There is no difference between the law and material reality. The law, however, puts this materiality to the side. In this way, the law is both able to operate *and* able to control without making its appearance felt. I have elsewhere described

47 Luhmann, 2004, p. 460 (translation modified).

the concept of the *lawscape* as the reciprocal invisibilization of law and the city.[48] The city is a great example of legal saturation: take a walk and observe the law enabling, channelling, impeding, accelerating your movement; see the illegality of hoodies in shopping malls, veiled women in Paris, unveiled women in Afghanistan, walking in the nude in Utrecht. And then try to touch these bodies – the law will stop you; sniff out how the law allows smells to percolate and prohibits others in a classic bourgeois capitalist move where bread smell circulated through the air shafts is lawful in a supermarket, whereas smells from a restaurant percolating at the two-bedroom flat upstairs is unlawful. And so on, without even talking about planning regulations, zoning and privatization of public spaces. The city is thick with law, but fascinatingly, its thickness is such that the law becomes invisible. So invisible that it is as if it *is not* matter, that indeed it *does not* matter. Law presents itself as abstract, distant, closed up. But we exude law, we breathe and eat and defecate law – and not just in the city. We *are* the law – and this means that we cannot escape the law. The law has played a majestic trick on us, making us believe that our discovery of its materiality is the key to challenging the law, whereas it is exactly the opposite. It is through matter that the law controls.

To put it from a different perspective, the unity of the law is guaranteed by the inclusion of its fragmentation. The law relies on the corporeal, spatial, material multiplicity of assemblages in order to maintain its unity. Law and matter flow together in a way that it is impossible to tell them apart, capturing all in between. So where is the space of resistance? The space of justice? Where can one find a sliver of escape from the rapturous nuptials of law and matter? There is only one way, and this includes once again a movement, a body and a space. This time, the movement is backwards, as it were, a removal from the space of the law, a movement of bodies away from the embrace. Deleuze refers to this movement as *withdrawal.*[49] Like a veritable assemblage, withdrawal is not an isolated movement, at least in the sense of a directed displacement. Rather, it is a shift that mobilizes the space, the bodies on this space and the legality that trammels their connection. Withdrawal is a tectonic shift that takes with it all the surfaces on which the law appears. A distinction that draws itself, or indeed an assemblage that moves itself blindly away from itself. Withdrawal takes withdrawing with it and leaves a space of perpetual *stasis*, namely a pause that pulsates with revolt, with turning. The shift is a forceful declaration of appearance, of being *here*, fully embodied: a law moved by the spaces and bodies of its appearance.[50]

---

48 A. Philippopoulos-Mihalopoulos & S. FitzGerald, 'From Space Immaterial: The Invisibility of the Lawscape', *Griffith Law Review*, Vol. 17, No. 2, 2008, p. 438-454.

49 G. Deleuze, *The Logic of Sense*, M. Lester with C. Stivale (Trans.), Continuum, London 2004, p. 342.

50 A. Philippopoulos-Mihalopoulos, 'Spatial Justice: Law and the Geography of Withdrawal', *International Journal of Law in Context*, Vol. 6, No. 3, p. 1-16.

A body withdrawing is law withdrawing. But this is precisely the movement of *justice*. We know from Derrida that the judge has to destroy the law every time, with every judgement, in an attempt to confront the ghost of the undecidable, and with the ultimate aim of materialising justice.[51] But to destroy the law is to withdraw from it. One moves one's body away from the law, withdraws one's corporeal attachment to it and sees the law in full materiality ("timber!"). This is, however, a *separate* materiality – it *must* be seen as separate, for otherwise, that is if the negation of its unity is not included, the operation of destruction cannot take place. The materiality of the law is one with the materiality of the judge; yet this continuum must be disrupted, this unity must be severed *if* the destruction of the law is to take place. The body of the judge (lawmaker, citizen, *homo sacer*) withdraws from the falling body of the law. The space of justice opens up just here, at the edge of destruction and the beginning of reconstruction – the liminality of de- and re-territorialising waves of legality.

To this, another paradox should be added. The destruction can only take place from inside the legal edifice, hammering right at its foundations and up to its turrets. In withdrawing from the law one does not move outside. There is no better place outside. There is no better law, better society, better justice. It is all part of this infinite plane of immanence on which withdrawal moves: a stratum that simply shifts rather than escaping to an imaginary exteriority. If justice is to be materialized, withdrawal must be kept immanent. The space of justice is located here: deeper into the law, in an immanent environment that breaks the law from within. This is not simply a manipulation of the law, a new interpretation or a legal stuttering. Nor does it mean that one has to work with the system. Rather, it is a denial of the law, a questioning of its relevance, its validity and even its lawfulness. Withdrawal rides the waving banner of the unutterable legal paradox: is the law lawful? Take the example of a revolt against the government. Revolts work from outside the law in that they assume the difference in materiality between 'us' and 'them'. The policeman is not us, the fellow citizen is not them. It is a necessary suspension, an inclusion of negation. Yet whatever change takes place with a revolt, it will have to be within the law. Materiality reunited. Which law is that? A brand new law? No doubt; but also a very old law. A piece of the system must be preserved in order for the law to assemble itself every time after every withdrawal. The withdrawal has to be registered by the law, for otherwise the law cannot be destroyed. Speak the law's language, enter the law's dreams, touch the law's extremities. Revolting is withdrawing, but withdrawing is immanent. One cannot achieve justice by revolting alone.

51 Derrida, 1992.

However successful a withdrawal might be, itself cannot escape matter. Just as the thing it revolts against, namely the law, withdrawal is materially embodied and emplaced. It is always here, in the space opened up by the law, within the law as plane of immanence. Yet it resists precisely this materiality of the law. This is paradoxically done through the only means available, namely the space and body of the law. So, from within law and within matter: I have elsewhere called this movement *spatial justice*,[52] namely an emplaced justice that emerges at the spaces that the law leaves behind, revolting in stasis against the incestuous coupling between law and matter. Spatial justice is disconnected from historicization and thrown in at the space of *here*, namely the space that vibrates with history through its material appearance. Not an abstract history but a history of the *here*. Not a history that legitimizes atrocities but a history that accepts the need for bodies to be here, exactly where other bodies might also want to be. Justice is a conflictual space, full of erupting laws and spreading normativities. For justice away from the law is not a lawless justice. It is certainly a risky, potentially dangerous space, emptied of pillared security and smooth lines. It is also a space of constant reconstruction, rapid concept formation, applied acrobatics of thought and action. A space of justice – and indeed spatial justice – is a space where the law is being erected at every moment as if for the first time. Like a group of nomads that must set up home every time they stop for the night, in the same way the law is re-erected through a repetition that might create difference. No doubt there is legal repetition that simply generates identity, a sameness of application indistinguishable from case to case. In parallel to this, however, there is legal repetition, itself far from the materiality of a revolt, yet steeped into the materiality of the law, that destroys the law as it stands and builds it from scratch, every time new.[53] This kind of repetition, the 'pure' repetition as Deleuze calls it, generates the difference of justice.[54]

But not always. There is no guarantee, no prescription for the emergence of justice. Luhmann calls justice a contingency formula,[55] since its emergence is always contingent on the conditions, therefore not predictable. Spatial justice remains contingent, relying on law's materiality. Yet, and perhaps unsurprizingly, this space of justice is nearer than it seems. It appears at various moments, from within law's operations. Justice is already here, a latent promise that materializes with every movement. This is the nature of the environment of the law, itself folded safely away, deep within law's repetition.

52 Philippopoulos-Mihalopoulos *in* De Sutter & McGee (Eds.) 2011.
53 Derrida 1992.
54 Deleuze, 2004; for an elaboration on this, see A. Philippopoulos-Mihalopoulos, *in* O. Ben-Dor (ed.), 2011.
55 Luhmann 2004.

Is Law Cosmopolitan?

Peter Fitzpatrick[*]

The dominating principle of the universe is blindness. It makes possible juxtapositions which would be impossible if the objects could see each other.
(Elias Canetti)[1]

Introduction

Venerable academic usage has it that if you are about to say something utterly reductionist and even elusive, you call it schematic. So, the schematic configuration of what I will be saying schematically now follows. First, I will outline variations on the standard and close-to-standard notions of cosmopolitanism and, by way of devastating objections to them, arrive at a radical alternative which carries with it a seemingly opposed idea of cosmopolitanism. Then by way of not so devastating objections to that alternative, I come to an impasse – an impasse that provisionally proves generative of cosmopolitan law, of law as itself cosmopolitan. Next, I look at two types of cosmopolitan law – types that match the two notions of cosmopolitanism just considered. The conclusion from all of which is that the constituent compatibility and incompatibility between these two types of law reveal law as the cosmopolitan bond.

Standard Issue

At the outset, allow me to touch on a few of the obligatory pit-stops in the race through standard issue cosmopolitanism, not that they will offer many or any surprises I expect, but they may serve to set an enduring irresolution, a constituent dissonance in notions of the cosmopolitan. The first is usually operated by the Stoics who, whilst emphasizing the commonality of our humanity, did aptly recognize the conflict between its cosmic determination by a law of right reason and our freedom. With St. Paul in the next stop, once

* An earlier version of this paper introduced a Colloquium on Cosmopolitan Law hosted in conjunction with the Critical Legal Conference of 2010 by The Department of Legal Theory and the Working Group on Reflexive Modernization and Law in the University of Utrecht. My acknowledgements echo themes of the paper. They go to Bald de Vries and the School of Law in the University of Utrecht for unparalleled hospitality, to Samantha Ashenden for her elegant Kantian riposte, and to Anastasia Tataryn for intellectual companionship.

1 E. Canetti, *Auto da Fé* (trans. C.V. Wedgwood), Pan Books, London 1978, p. 63.

Saul of Tarsus where there was a school of Stoic philosophy, the dissonance disappears in what becomes a persistent line of resolution. That resolution takes Paul's vaunted universality – exemplified in *Galatians* 3:28: "There is neither Jew nor Greek, there is neither bond nor free, there is neither male nor female: for ye are all one in Christ Jesus" – and renders it as terminally conditioned. For Paul all have fallen, we all share in the fall of Adam (and presumably Eve), but we are, or can all be, saved in Christ, in a new covenant. Here the universal takes on an etymological exactness in *universus*, turned into one.

Next comes a distinctly unusual source whose presence derives from Mignolo's allocating it an originary role in the formation of modern cosmopolitanism.[2] As well as being an occasionally acknowledged ancestor of international law, Francisco de Vitoria is most conspicuously noted for being a defender of the Indigenous peoples of the Americas against the more resolutely murderous of the Spanish colonists. By way of an extension of scholastic theology and a revived Roman law, Vitoria found that the Indigenous peoples were members of a common humanity.[3] But along with that universal benefice came another which was less propitious. After rejecting papal generosity in distributing the lands of others and such like 'unjust titles', Vitoria nonetheless found that the same obliging quasi-Roman law, a *ius gentium*, allowed of certain modes whereby the colonists could acquire 'just title': "the legitimate titles by which the barbarians could have been subjected to Christian rule".[4] Vitoria gives predominant emphasis to two of these. The first came from a right to trade, to travel and to dwell in the countries of the barbarians – a right extending beyond trade narrowly conceived so as to include intercourse and communication generally.[5] The second right founding a putative just title was the right to proselytize: "Christians have the right to preach and announce the Gospel in the lands of the barbarians" and that even against their will, conversion being "necessary for their own salvation", with the barbarians being "obliged to accept the faith" if it were adequately presented to them.[6] Such rights being part of a universal natural law, the inevitable resistance of the *barbari* to their assertion could provoke the equally inevitable deduction that, at least in significant degree, the *barbari* were unnatural. So, and in terms that even then were far from original, the barbarians were found to be, among other things, cannibalistic, sexually perverted, and culinarily outrageous, so much so that they were considered well nigh impervious to a reforming natural reason.[7] Furthermore, a resistant response to the rights embedded in

2 W.D. Mignolo, 'The Many Faces of Cosmo-polis: Border Thinking and Critical Cosmopolitanism', *Public Culture*, Vol. 12, No. 3, 2000, p. 728-731.

3 F. de Vitoria, 'On the American Indians', *in* F. de Vitoria, *Political Writings*, Cambridge University Press, Cambridge 1991, p. 239-250.

4 *Id.*, p. 252.

5 *Id.*, p. 278-284.

6 *Id.*, p. 271, 284-285.

7 *Id.*, p. 290-291; F. de Vitoria, 'On Dietary Laws, or Self-Restraint', *in* Vitoria 1991, p. 207-230.

natural law made it "lawful" for the Spaniards "to do everything necessary to the aim of war" to ensure a compliance which Vitoria found necessary, and that "everything" extended to territorial acquisition by conquest and consequent imperial rule. [8]

In formal terms, the claim to a 'natural' universal had for Vitoria a theological justification, but the deity concerned was proto-modern, a deity contained within the world. This was a God which Vitoria found, again with considerable scholastic warrant, tied constituently to, even bound by, its creation. [9] That chimed with the not uncommon attribution to Vitoria of Protestant leanings because such a tamed deity conformed aptly to the post-Reformation scene in which the rulers of European states and principalities claimed a distinct ultimacy of rule imbued with its own quasi-deific authority. Such a claim to rule as universal through the particular was fused with a universalized cohesion of European rule by way of the commonality of Christianity. Yet even within the sixteenth century, this Christian commonality was becoming attenuated. With the advent of modern imperial rule, states and principalities could singularly take on a universal range as European even when not directly colonizing. [10] As Schmitt maps it, if somewhat abruptly, *Respublica Christiana* gives way to the *Jus Publicum Europaeum.* [11] And such cohesive labels as 'civilized' come to replace Christianity.

In all, Vitoria leaves us with two generative and enduring perspectives on cosmopolitanism. With one, some focal and surpassing, some universal entity provides the template for the world entire. The variety of these deific substitutes is considerable and would include the nation state, the comity of civilized nations, and varieties of normative transcendence. Some of these will be visited shortly when resuming the more standard story of cosmopolitanism's conceptual sources, but first there is Vitoria's other generative perspective on cosmopolitanism, this one being a more oblique, even unintended offering. That perspective entails the resistance and counter-assertion by the diversity of those included yet excluded by the first perspective. That generative perspective on cosmopolitanism provides the leitmotiv of this chapter.

8 Vitoria 1991 ('On the American Indian'), p. 282-283, 285-286, 291-292.

9 F. de Vitoria, 'De Homicide', *in* F. de Vitoria, *Obras de Francisco de Vitoria: Relecciones teológicas,* (trans. from Latin to Spanish Teófilio Ordánoz), Editorial Católica, Biblioteca de Autores Christianos, Madrid 1960, p. 1099.

10 And indirect participation in colonization could be considerable: see e.g. H. Kamen, *Empire: How Spain Became a World Power 1492-1763*, HarperCollins, New York 2004, p. 13.

11 Carl Schmitt, *The* Nomos *of the Earth in the International Law of the* Jus Publicum Europaeum (trans. G.L. Ulmen), Telos Press, New York 2003.

The well-worn bridge bringing a universalist cosmopolitanism into an acceptable modernity is provided by Kant, most notably in his tract *To Perpetual Peace.*[12] Here, and elsewhere with Kant, the state is ultimately supreme. Although *PerpetualPeace* envisages a federation of states, there is nothing in and as that federation to make it any different to the international law, so-called, refined by Vattel a short time before in which the community of nations can somehow exist in the face of, and emanate from, states each entirely "independent of all the others".[13] Nor can matters cosmopolitan be advanced in any way that would diminish or even question that surpassing sufficiency. And so we find that the specious argument advanced in Appendix II of *Perpetual Peace,* that tyrannical rule cannot be resisted, has its equivalent in *The Metaphysics of Morals* where our "submission to the state's authority" cannot be questioned – thus putting aside not only Kant's enlightened injunction *sapere aude* but also his elevation of the subject's freedom.[14] Aptly, and evoking Paul, if there has been a modernist death of God it is a death and resurrection for, still with *The Metaphysics of Morals,* Kant sheets sovereign authority home to God.[15]

It has, then, to be something of a puzzle as to how Kant's cosmopolitanism takes on a secular repute. Perhaps this is, at least in part, because that universalist cosmopolitanism is buttressed by his notorious racism.[16] The transcendence necessary for such a universalism becomes primarily a negative one, the civilized states exemplifying what the savages are not. Whilst this negative positioning ostensibly locates the universal immanently, within a world, it has nonetheless to be transcendent. As Deleuze and Guattari counsel, "whenever immanence is interpreted as immanent *to* Something, we can be sure that this Something reintroduces the transcendent".[17] The taking of immanence into an entity which asserts an enduring determinacy ramps that entity up to a quasi-transcendence.[18] In my account here there may seem an egregious omission of Kant's cosmopolitan law giving rights to

---

12 I. Kant, *To Perpetual Peace: A Philosophical Sketch* (trans. T. Humphrey), Hackett Publishing, Indianapolis 2003.

13 E. de Vattel, *The Law of Nations or the Principles of Natural Law Applied to the Conduct and to the Affairs of Nations and Sovereigns,* Vol. 3 (trans. C. G. Fenwick), Carnegie Institute, Washington 1916, p. 9.

14 Kant 2003 p. 37 (381); I. Kant, *The Metaphysics of Morals* (trans. M. Gregor), Cambridge University Press, Cambridge 1996, p. 95-97 (6: 319-320); I. Kant, *An Answer to the Question: What is Enlightenment?* (trans. H. B. Nisbet), Penguin, London n.d. p.1.

15 Kant 1996, p. 95 (6: 319).

16 As to which, and for a qualification spurred perhaps by Kant's universalism, see P. Kleingeld, 'Kant's Second Thoughts on Race', *The Philosophical Quarterly,* Vol. 57, No. 229, 2007. Cf. Mignolo 2000, p. 732-733.

17 G. Deleuze & F. Guattari, *What is Philosophy?* (trans. G. Burchell & H. Tomlinson), Verso, London 1994, p. 45.

18 All of which could, perhaps should, be read as a criticism of the received view of Kant's cosmopolitanism. Other offerings from Kant could be brought to bear on, and refine, his cosmopolitanism, e.g. I. Kant, *Critique of Pure Reason* (trans. J. M. D. Meiklejohn), J.M. Dent, London 1993, p. 187-188 (Chapter II, Section III, 3C). And see S. Muthu, *Enlightenment Against Empire,* Princeton University Press, New Jersey 2003, p. 209.

human individuals as citizens of the world, but I will come to that in the next section and indicate its at best modest effect on an overwhelming state power.

Although there has been an abundance of neo-Kantian cosmopolitanisms which are essentially extraversions of the state, his positing of a substrate, such as citizenship of the world, has of late had the greater resonance. Prominent instances would extend to a proletarian pervasion and to varieties of normative comprehension such as a spreading 'human rights regime' and 'frameworks' for recognizing individuals as effective world citizens.[19] Although not all of these would be "driven by the will to control and homogenize" universally,[20] they do all share in the constituent commitment to a universalist determination.

Objection and Alternation

The objection to standard issue cosmopolitanism is, in a word, its "mononaturalism", a term taken from Latour's tellingly titled "Whose Cosmos, Which Cosmopolitics?".[21] What he objects to is the saddling of cosmopolitanism with a unified world view, or a supposedly rational naturalism, or a complete commonality of the human. Instead Latour would adopt "William James's synonym for cosmos [which] was pluriverse, a coinage that makes its awesome multiplicity clear".[22] In all, he finds that "what is at stake is precisely what is common in the common world to be built".[23] In broad, very broad, terms cognate instances abound. A sampling would include "solidaristic" cosmopolitanism, "abject cosmopolitanism", and "a critical cosmopolitanism" which "has to become border thinking, critical and dialogic, from the perspective of those local histories that had to deal all along with global designs".[24] All affirm a plurality of entities as constituting the cosmopolitan. And it is here that we would return to the company of those who provide the generative force of a cosmopolitanism in their resistance and counter-assertion to a universalist imperium of the type instanced by Vitoria.

19 M. Hardt & A. Negri, *Empire*, Harvard University Press, Cambridge Mass. 2000, p. 18, 156; S. Benhabib (with J. Waldron, B. Honig and W. Kymlicka), *Another Cosmopolitanism*, Oxford University Press, Oxford 2006, p. 17, 20; and the incisively depicted instances in S. Marks, *The Riddle of All Constitutions: International Law, Democracy, and the Critique of Ideology*, Oxford University Press, Oxford 2003, p. 106-109 and G. Leung, 'A Critical History of Cosmopolitanism', *Law, Culture and the Humanities*, Vol. 5, No. 3, 2009, p. 371-374.

20 Mignolo 2000, p. 723.

21 B. Latour, 'Whose Cosmos, Which Cosmopolitics?', *Common Knowledge*, Vol. 10, No. 3, 2004, p. 453.

22 *Id.*, p. 454.

23 *Id.*, p. 455.

24 B. de Sousa Santos & C.A. Rodriguez-Garavito, 'Law, Politics, and the Subaltern in Counter-Hegemonic Globalization', *in* B. de Sousa Santos & C.A. Rodriguez-Garavito (eds.), *Towards a Cosmopolitan Legality*, Cambridge University Press, Cambridge 2005, p. 12; P. Nyers, 'Abject Cosmopolitanism: The Politics of Protection in the Anti-Deportation Movement', *Third World Quarterly*, Vol. 24, No. 6, 2003, p. 1089; Mignolo 2000, p. 723, 744.

The obvious difficulty then becomes how, apart from a focal force of resistance, the plurality of entities can be rendered immanently as *a* cosmos. Attempts to link the entities in some cosmopolitan commonality have typically slanted the diversity, the rooted and the hybrid towards a domain of the quasi-universal.[25] At least a passing sympathy for that outcome may be provoked by a thought of Donald Davidson who has it that different entities all relating plurally would "make sense...only if there is a common coordinate system on which to plot them; yet the existence of a common system belies the claim to dramatic incomparability".[26] A pure plurality would entail no connections at all. And if, without more, the dramatically incomparable entities were to exist identifiably in common, then the only available commonality would be one where they were the same as each other and incomparability would be lost. So a condition of their singularity, of the singularity of each in being-together, is *some* identifiable, some determinate, commonality apart from them. Yet, and unless we resurrect the transcendent, that commonality cannot be apart in the sense that its constituent force is separately and ultimately beyond the entities relating plurally. To be *their* commonality it must relate responsively to them. With such a cosmopolitanism, then, there could be a "need," observed by Nancy, for "an acosmic cosmology", one that avoids determination apart and comes to its determinate commonality from within, which admittedly may not be a promising prospect since, as Nancy would have it, "[w]e do not yet have any cosmology adequate to this noncosmos".[27]

We seem to have arrived at an aporia, not just the aporia as classically confined – the aporia as no passage, an insuperable divide – but as well an aporia which in Derrida's perception would connect and be generative.[28] In his own engagement with cosmopolitanism in *Cosmopolitanism and Forgiveness*, where his compelling concern is with the asylum-seeker, Derrida engages with Kant's adoption of hospitality in *Perpetual Peace* as the ethic of cosmopolitanism.[29] The immediate point is that with Kant hospitality is inexorably conditioned. So it is by now a variation on old news to note with Derrida that:

> in defining hospitality in all its rigour as a law..., Kant assigns to it conditions which make it dependent on state sovereignty, especially when it is a question of the *right of residence*.[30]

25 See A. Phillips, *Multiculturalism without Culture*, Princeton University Press, Princeton 2007, p. 68-71.

26 D. Davidson, 'On the Very Idea of a Conceptual Scheme', *in* J. Rajcman & C. West (Eds.), *Post-Analytic Philosophy*, Columbia University Press, New York 1985, p. 130.

27 J.-L. Nancy, *The Sense of the World* (trans. J. S. Librett), University of Minnesota Press, Minneapolis 1997, p. 38.

28 J. Derrida, *Aporias* (trans. T. Dutoit), Stanford University Press, Stanford 1993, p.28.

29 J. Derrida, *On Cosmopolitanism and Forgiveness* (trans. M. Dooley and M. Hughes), Routledge, London 2001; Kant 2003, p.15-18 (358-360).

30 Derrida 2001, 22, (his emphasis).

The asylum-seeker pursuing this right of residence in Kant's cosmopolitan law would notionally be met with the "Third Definitive Article for a Perpetual Peace" and the stranger's straitened right to be treated without hostility, but would then find in the next sentence that the state "may send him away again, if this can be done without causing his death".[31] As against this preconditioned law of hospitality, Derrida would set an unconditional hospitality, a law of unconditional hospitality, an imperative of illimitable responsiveness to the other:

> Only an unconditional hospitality can give meaning and practical rationality to a concept of hospitality. Unconditional hospitality exceeds juridical, political, or economic calculation. But no thing and no one happens or arrives without it.[32]

Yet this conditional or conditioned hospitality is also imperative:

> *the* unconditional law of hospitality needs the [conditional/conditioned] laws, it *requires* them. This demand is constitutive. It wouldn't be effectively unconditional, the law, if it didn't *have to become* effective, concrete, determined...[33]

In sum, "[p]olitical, juridical, and ethical responsibilities have their place, if they take place, only in this transaction...between these two hospitalities, the unconditional and the conditional".[34] I will return to the quality of that transaction after considering what Derrida has revealed here as a mutually generative connection between law and hospitality, and after considering how that leads us to the connection between law and cosmopolitanism, and thence to the idea of cosmopolitan law.

---

31 The translation here comes from *id.* 22. For another and for the context see Kant 2003, p.15.

32 J. Derrida, *Rogues: Two Essays on Reason* (trans. P.A. Brault & M. Naas), Stanford University Press, Stanford 2005, p. 149. Perhaps something more of the force of the unconditional here could be sought in traditions where hospitality was and is close to the unconditionally imperative.

33 J. Derrida, *Of Hospitality* (trans. R. Bowlby), Stanford University Press, Stanford 2000, p. 79 (his emphasis).

34 J. Derrida, 'Autoimmunity: Real and Symbolic Suicide: A Dialogue with Jacques Derrida', *in* G. Borradori (ed.), *Philosophy in a Time of Terror: Dialogues with Jürgen Habermas and Jacques Derrida*, The University of Chicago Press, Chicago 2003, p. 130.

Cosmopolitan Law

Predominantly, engagements with cosmopolitan law would seem to espouse or at least assume some surpassing universalism.[35] Let me take initially and briefly a type of law often labelled cosmopolitan, that of human rights, with its well nigh standard setting in a common humanity. It is sufficient for Francis Fukuyama, for example, to ground human rights in "the species-typical characteristics shared by all human beings qua human beings".[36] But as Carl Schmitt decrees "whoever invokes humanity wants to cheat".[37] How can we, coming from within the uncontainable human, encompass and assuredly determine what it 'is'? Thence, even if not for that poignant reason, we have those abundant criticisms of human rights which would see them as serving and formed by 'dominant' values or powers usually labelled 'Western'.

Yet as uncontainable the human can be appropriated also by the many who are not 'dominant'. Let me concentrate matters by borrowing Upendra Baxi's terms of engagement. On one side of a divide, Baxi recognizes that human rights are taken to cohere as unitary and "universal", and as such this conception of human rights can assume a "dominant or hegemonic" position.[38] Yet on the other side of this divide, Baxi sees human rights as plurality, and he depicts a scene in which "human rights enunciations proliferate, becoming as specific as the networks from which they arise and, in turn, sustain", and such multitudinous human rights provide "sites of resistance and struggle", of subaltern assertion.[39]

Let me take a rather similar divide that will bring our concerns closer to an unadorned law. On one side of this divide is the association between the field of 'law and development' and cosmopolitanism. From the late 1980s, with what came to be called a return of or to law and development, the operative range of law and the resources devoted to its promotion both became enormous.[40] It is difficult to be at all exact about the resources because provision for promoting law, now usually put in terms of the rule of law, tends to be mixed in budgets of, for example, the World Bank, the IMF and the U.S. Agency for International Development, with accompanying imperatives evidently promoting democracy and human rights and pursuing 'the war of terror'. Although often put in international terms, the

35 This can be so even where the advocacy is a nuanced one coming to cosmopolitan law from within something like a pluriverse: see N. Feldman, 'Cosmopolitan Law', *Yale Law Journal*, Vol. 116, p. 1059.

36 F. Fukuyama, *Our Posthuman Future: Consequences of the Biotechnology Revolution*, Profile Books, London 2002, p. 101, 128.

37 C. Schmitt, *The Concept of the Political* (trans. G. Schwab), University of Chicago Press, Chicago 1996, p. 54.

38 U. Baxi, *The Future of Human Rights*, 2nd edition, Oxford University Press, New Delhi 2006, p. xv, 23.

39 *Id.*, p. xiv, 26, 47.

40 For the account which follows the unparalleled engagement is S. Humphreys, *Theatre of the Rule of Law: Transnational Legal Intervention in Theory and Practice*, Cambridge University Press, Cambridge 2010.

content of this law comes from relatively powerful nations either directly or through their dominance of the 'international' institutions issuing them. And although usually grouped under the rubric of the rule of law, this content extends to basic infrastructures of 'law and order', as well as to measures countering terrorism and ensuring 'security'. It is also the case that this is a rule of law of an Anglo-American variety, one that has a fairly distinct historical relation to the protection of property and the enshrining of liberties of a narrow range. All of this makes for a condign fit with inextricable imperatives also found in conditionalities and such – imperatives to do with a particular economic orthodoxy, that of neo-liberalism, and to do with its attendant deregulation, privatization, and liberalization of the 'environment' for investment and trade. Despite this descriptive sweep, the measures involved are often and operatively quite detailed, both as they appear in documents allocating resources to them and in their engaged implementation. Their overall import is far more tentacular than direct colonial rule. And the purposive cast remains instrumental, including centrally now an instrumental subordination of law. This is decidedly not law as the expression of the polity on which it is being brought to bear.

The alternative, a pointedly resistant alternative and one empathetic with Baxi's subaltern human rights, can be encapsulated in the title to a collection of case studies gathered by Boaventura de Sousa Santos and César Rodriguez-Garavito, *Law and Globalization from Below: Towards a Cosmopolitan Legality.*[41] The case studies, mainly from "the Global South", are diverse, but there is significant emphasis on "counter-hegemonic coalitions" which "aim to substitute [...] solidaristic, cosmopolitan legal frameworks for the existing corporate-friendly laws", all the while recognizing that "the plurality of efforts at counter-hegemonic globalization cannot be encompassed by an overarching theory".[42] Understandably and even aptly enough, the constituent demands noted earlier for a commonality in plurality or singularity remain in place and unfulfilled. Along with Nancy, we seem to be left with an "acosmic cosmos", or a "noncosmos cosmos" which comes not only with the absence of any pre-set or pre-determining universalism but also without the positioned prospect of any determinate commonality.[43] Might not that positioning be the law?

When we last left Derrida with the compressed account of law, hospitality and cosmopolitanism, we saw that two types of law in combination were necessary for there to be hospitality and cosmopolitanism. With one there was an unconditional law of utter responsiveness to the other, to alterity – including the diversity of the "pluriverse" as Latour has it.[44] This can only be a law incapable of containment by any surpassing determination. Without

41 Santos and Garavito 2005, p. 12.

42 *Id.*, p. 13

43 Nancy 1997, p. 38.

44 Latour 2004, p. 454.

more, such a law would be a pure plurality, a mere dissipation, a dissociated plurality. So as Derrida emphasized, that law depended on the other type of law, on the conditioned laws, to give it determinate effect. The determinate laws, in turn, depend on the unconditional law, the responsive law, for their own continuing existence.

This mutuality of dependence could be put in more homely terms by considering the rule of law, and by doing so in quite conventional terms. Of course the rule of law is usually typified in terms of an enduring determinacy, in terms of providing some assured stability of expectation, some definite normative hold on futurity. But to hold a determinacy invariant is impossible since that would entail a totalized comprehension of all that may ever come to and affect it. Yet for law to rule, it has also to be quite contrary to those standard attributes. It must be utterly responsive and ever capable of being other than what it determinately may be. If it failed to be so, it would cease to rule situations inexorably changing around it.

It is time for the promised return to the 'transaction' between unconditional and conditional hospitality – the transaction necessary for the operative existence of each.[45] That transaction we can now see replicated in the relation between an unconditionally responsive law and law as a conditioned determinacy – a transaction necessary for each to be, and for law as a putative whole to be. The transaction cannot be a trade-off or compromise for, even as each enters into and combines with and enables the other, each has still to sustain an ultimate autonomy.[46] And here there is a return of the aporia which set, as it were, the imperative of a determinate commonality for the being-together of singular entities and the imperative for that commonality to assume a self-vacating responsiveness to those entities. That left us in the seeming impasse of Nancy's unattained cosmos, a "noncosmos".[47] The singular entities relating in and as the cosmos had no determinate commonality, yet such commonality was imperative for there to be not only *a* cosmos but for there to be the very singularity of each.

Then the aporia paid an extensive visit to law. The law that emerged could match both "the law of hospitality" and the conventionally "juridical".[48] These two varieties of law became indistinguishable in providing the mediate matter making the aporia operative – making possible a being-together of singular entities in and as a cosmos. Yet the aporia

---

45 Derrida 2003, p. 130.

46 See J. Derrida and J.-L. Nancy, 'Responsabilité – du sens à venir', *in* F. Guibal & J.-C. Martin (eds.), *Sens en tous sens: Autor des travaux de Jean-Luc Nancy*, Galilée 2004, p. 179-180; and cf. J. Derrida, *Negotiations: Interventions and Interviews 1971-2001* (trans. E. Rottenberg), Stanford University Press, Stanford 2002, p. 12-14.

47 Nancy 1997, p. 38.

48 See Derrida 2000, p. 79 and Derrida 2003, p. 130.

retains its classic guise. As a "bond" the cosmos will always for Derrida "exceed" any determinate "community".[49] The bond could not be settled or resolved in some surpassing, much less universally set, community. And likewise the law of that bond, "the law of originary sociability", the "law of hospitality", always exceeds determinate law.[50] And as the rule of law, law has always to come from beyond any determinacy of rule. Yet with the drawing in of that beyond law must also be capable of self-separating from it, capable of assuming in and as itself a resolved determinacy:

> Let us grant [with Blanchot] that law is obsessed with exteriority, by that which beleaguers it and from which it separates via the very separation that institutes it as form, in the very movement by which it formulates this exteriority as law.[51]

That formative force coming from beyond signals the return to the outset of this chapter where Mignolo advanced the perspective of a "critical cosmopolitanism" generated by those included yet excluded by cosmopolitanism as a universalist arrogation.[52] Such a perspective provides a focal force for that impelling alterity ever beyond any determinate cosmos – beyond, but ever integral to the law of cosmopolitanism.

---

49 Derrida 2002, p. 241. This may not seem to accommodate Derrida's excluding "cosmopolitanism" when dealing with a similar bond at Derrida 2003, p. 130, but cf. C. Douzinas, *Human Rights and Empire: The Political Philosophy of Cosmopolitanism*, Routledge-Cavendish, Abingdon 2007, p. 293.

50 J. Derrida, *Politics of Friendship* (trans. G. Collins), Verso, London 1997, p. 231; Derrida 2000, p. 79; Derrida 2001, p.18.

51 M. Blanchot, *The Infinite Conversation*, trans. S. Hanson, University of Minnesota Press, Minneapolis, 1993 p. 434.

52 Mignolo 2000.

Great Expectations: Justice, Peace... or Profit?

The Universal Legal System of Vitoria and Grotius

Can Öztaş

Introducing Estella

> 'Tell me in my ear,' said Miss Havisham, bending down.
> 'I think she is very proud,' I replied, in a whisper.
> 'Anything else?'
> 'I think she is very pretty.'
> 'Anything else?'
> 'I think she is very insulting.'[1]

International law: an egalitarian and universal set of rules established during the enlightenment period aiming to bring peace, equality and justice to international relations. International law: a Eurocentric, colonial instrument used for legitimizing and normalizing the application of power to international relations. The first presumption presented is usually built on the arguments of humanist lawyers of the sixteenth and seventeenth centuries. The second is generally the critique based on the arguments of Eurocentric eighteenth and nineteenth century lawyers. However, recently scholars have demonstrated that universalist and righteous sixteenth and seventeenth century lawyers contributed to the founding of hegemonic imperialism, while others counter this by arguing that egalitarian lawyers were present in the eighteenth and nineteenth centuries.[2]

I aim to contribute to the demystification of the roots of international law. And I begin with Pip's description of Estella in the novel by Charles Dickens, *Great Expectations*. The

1 C. Dickens, *Great Expectations*, Penguin Books, 2002, p. 59-60.
2 There are indeed a vast number of books and articles that discuss this topic, some of which I quote throughout this contribution. An initial further reading could involve the related works of C. Schmitt, T. Todorov, S. Muthu, C. Covell, C. Douzinas, A. Anghie, E. Darian-Smith, P. Fitzpatrick, D. Kennedy, A. Pagden, R. Tuck, B. Kingsbury, K. Haakonssen, E. Keene, M. Koskenniemi, N. Berman, E. Jouannet.

analogy might take the discussion a step further. International law, similar to Estella, is pretty, proud and insulting. Or using less emotive words: potential, technical and ineffective. Similar to Estella, a daughter of a commoner who acts as if she belongs to a higher class, international law also pretends to bring higher values, but is after all a legal text no different from other instruments of government.

This contribution will shed light on the origins of international law and expose the role of historical events and their interpretations in forming the legal basis of our current international political and economic system.

I investigate the works of two scholars from the sixteenth and seventeenth centuries who are known as prominent theorists of *jus naturale* (law of nature), *jus gentium* (law of nations) and *bellum justum* (just war). I consider Francisco de Vitoria, for his contribution in setting the legal basis for Europe's relation with the West Indies (Americas), and Hugo Grotius for his influence and work on the East Indies (India and the Far East). Both Vitoria and Grotius were crucial figures in the formation of the universal legal system.[3]

Vitoria and Grotius relied on the fundamental principles of *jus naturale*; '*sui juris*' (free) and '*dominium*' (title and property) to establish the legal basis of a universal structure of political and economic relations, which if not obeyed could justly be punished by war. They argued that these principles, which comprised a wide range of rights like individual freedom, free trade and right to property, were also a part of *jus gentium*. *Jus gentium* implied having the consensus of 'all nations', and applied beyond political, religious and cultural boundaries. Violation of these underlying values of the universal system of political and economic relations of the period was considered 'injustice to humanity', punishable by 'just war'. However, the universality of the system existed only in appearance. In reality, the system required the exclusion of 'the other' in order to allow for their exploitation, which was needed in order to support the functioning of the system.

I argue in this contribution that the universal legal system, established four centuries ago by Vitoria and Grotius is an intriguing illustration of how legal theories legitimize a particular purpose or interest. Their system established an institutionalized simultaneous inclusion and exclusion of 'the other' in different forms and modalities, including the privileging of capital and economic growth over human suffering. Understanding their system, I believe, will shed a light to the interpretations of the legal basis of contemporary

3 The legal system Vitoria and Grotius constructed was more than international law as we understand today. It was a universal system of laws because not only it involved natural law and positive/human law principles but also they claimed that all human beings (rulers and subjects) were bound by it, even if they did not consent in advance.

international political and economic relations and to the implications of law in legitimizing self-serving aims.

FRANCISCO DE VITORIA: EXTINGUISHING THE SUN

> 'I begin to think', said Estella, in a musing way, after another moment of calm wonder, 'that I almost understand how this comes about. If you had brought up your adopted daughter wholly in the dark confinement of these rooms, and had never let her know that there was such a thing as the daylight by which she has never once seen your face – if you had done that, and then, for a purpose, had wanted her to understand the daylight and know all about it, you would have been disappointed and angry?' [4]

With the discovery of Americas, the Spaniards sought to legally justify the legitimacy of the Spanish invasion and invalidate the resistance of American Indians, who did not share the same legal or moral principles. Methods and reasoning had to be found to facilitate and regulate Atlantic trade to allow the easy flow of wealth to Iberia.

Francisco de Vitoria, a Spanish theologian tried to systematically respond to these challenging questions by applying Roman law and *jus naturale* principles of Thomas Aquinas. [5] He defined law as follows:

> Law is a function of reason because giving commands issues from reason and law is a kind of rule or measure for human activity, the word *lex* being derived from the verb *ligare* 'to bind, oblige'. It is clear that law belongs to our rational nature and can exist only in the senses or in the intellect. [6]

Vitoria rejected the injustices committed within the newly discovered territories towards the populations living there. He refused title by discovery and questioned the brutalities committed by the *conquistadores* and the system of *encomienda*, where Indians were treated as slaves. [7] Vitoria challenged Papal authority and divine law, arguing that the Pope lacked jurisdiction over the unbelievers. Vitoria claimed the Pope's authority was limited to the

4 Dickens 2002, p. 301.

5 R.A. Williams, *The American Indian in Western Legal Thought The Discourses of Conquest,* Oxford University Press, Oxford 1990, p. 96.

6 F. Vitoria, *Political Writings*, A. Pagden and J. Lawrence (Ed.), Cambridge University Press, Cambridge 1991, p. 155.

7 Williams 1990, p. 99.

spiritual dimension of the Christian world.[8] Vitoria argued that American Indians were not an inferior breed or natural slaves, but human beings with reason:

> They (the Indians) are not of unsound mind, but have, according to their kind, the use of reason. This is clear, because there is a certain method in their affairs, for they have polities which are orderly arranged and they have definite marriage and magistrates, overlords, laws and workshops, and a system of exchange, all of which call for the use of reason; they also have a kind of religion. Further, they make no error in matters, which are self-evident to others; this is witness to their use of reason.[9]

In the course of refuting the conventional basis for Spanish *dominium* in the West Indies, Vitoria created a new system of universal law, which reformulated the relationship between divine, natural and human law. This revised Roman law of *jus gentium* was a universal system based on a set of principles endorsed by all nations, regardless of temporal, regional legal, value and traditional differences. The system ensured that everyone, including the American Indians, were born free and had *dominium*. Because the rules were formed through a universal consensus of all societies, everybody, including those unaware of the existence of these rules, were bound by the system. Moreover, this principle of universality brought it closer to *jus naturale.*[10]

American Indians were recognized as human beings with reason and they were included in Vitoria's universal system ensuring that their *dominium* would not be seized without a just cause. However, having claimed to include them into a system that would ensure equality, Vitoria did not intend to emancipate them from the guardianship of Christian Europeans. Contrary to his criticisms, Vitoria believed in the 'justice' that was brought by the Spanish. For example, he did not question the Spanish rights to travel or proselytize in the Americas. As argued by a number of writers, such as Pagden, Williams and Anghie, Vitoria's principles while appearing to be based on human dignity, equality and universality, helped to legitimize the Spanish invasion and colonization of America.[11]

But how did he set the legal foundations for a global economic system based on increasing profit enforced through war? The answer lies with one of the pioneers of the Christian

---

8 A. Anghie, 'Francisco de Vitoria and the Colonial Origins of International Law' *in* E. Darian-Smith & P. Fitzpatrick (Ed.), *Laws of the Postcolonial,* University of Michigan Press, Michigan 1999, p. 93.

9 Vitoria quoted in A. Anghie, *Imperialism, Sovereignty and the Making of International Law,* Cambridge University Press, Cambridge, 2004, p. 19-20.

10 D. Kennedy, 'Primitive Legal Scholarship', *Harvard International Law Journal,* Volume 27, No. 1, Winter 1986, p. 16.

11 Williams 1990; Anghie 2004; Pagden 1991.

reformers of *jus naturale* and the one who inspired Vitoria, Thomas Aquinas. Aquinas established universal standards of justice and political morality based on human reason combining Roman *jus gentium* with Christian ethics. He treated *jus gentium* as a consistent part of *jus naturale* aimed to *advance the common good*. He taught that *jus gentium* comprised the general principles of *just conduct*, as with those regulating *commercial transactions*, which were observed in common among men as an essential basis for *social order.*[12]

Vitoria continued Aquinas's tradition within the context of the Spanish-Indian encounter. He replaced the divine law administered by the Pope with his universal legal system of *jus gentium,* which rules were administered by a secular sovereign that combined the principles of *jus naturale* and Christian morality. Claiming universality, this system did not distinguish between national, international, private or public spaces of law,[13] and was based on the principles of justice and morality that ensured legal obligation among the subjects of law without an external intervention.[14] In Vitoria's words:

> *Jus gentium* has not only the force of a pact and agreement among men but also the force of a law for the world as a whole being in a way one single state, has the power to create laws that are just and fitting for all persons.[15]

Jus gentium, purportedly, existed among all peoples, not merely among Christians. *Jus gentium* revealed a system of mutual rights and duties,[16] established by the authority of the whole world, precluding the ability for any one country to refuse to be bound by *jus gentium*. Vitoria argued that violation of these universal rules, whether in peace or in war, was a punishable, mortal sin.

THE ORIGINAL TRINITY OF THE UNIVERSAL LEGAL SYSTEM

Vitoria's universal legal system depended on three concepts: *dominium, jus gentium* and *bellum justum.*[17]

---

12 C. Covell, *The Law of Nations in Political Thought A Critical Survey from Vitoria to Hegel*, Palgrave MacMillan, London 2009, p. 6-8 (emphasis added).

13 Kennedy 1986, p. 15.

14 B. Hamilton, *Political Thought in Sixteenth Century Spain*, Clarendon Press, Oxford 1963, p. 160.

15 Vitoria quoted in Covell 2009, p. 28-29.

16 Williams 1990, p. 97.

17 M. Koskenniemi, 'Empire and International Law: The Real Spanish Contribution', *University Of Toronto Law Journal*, Vol. 61, 2011, p. 12.

The notion of *dominium* was a principle of *jus naturale*, according to which all human beings were free and property was held in common. Vitoria argued that the division of property was not made by natural law. He explained that property was divided with the establishment of different societies and states in the course of history in a natural and consensual way, [18] in order to preserve common good and peace. Even though it was not regulated by *jus naturale*, private property was not contrary to it. The fact that the appropriation of property in societies rested on the consensus of people, laid down in positive law, *jus gentium*, regulated the jurisdiction over issues related to property. Yet, there still existed land and facilities (e.g. forests, seas, rivers or ports) that were kept in common for the prosperity of society. Similar to the historical division of property, human beings gave their consent to delegate their *dominium* to princes who in turn ensured an orderly and just function of society and state. However, the prince was not entitled to intervene in the usage of personal *dominium* unless it was necessary for the public good or security. In other words, Vitoria's concept of *dominium* covered an extensive field of human interaction, from freedom to property, including trade and commerce. All humans with reason enjoyed the right of *dominium* in title and property as a part of their natural liberty.

Vitoria began his analysis of Spanish affairs in the West Indies, questioning whether the Indians had dominium before the arrival of the Spaniards. He concluded that they had and 'just like Christians… neither their princes nor private persons could be despoiled of their property without just cause'. [19]

The integration of the Indians into the universal system of law defined rights and duties that, in case of violation, could be punished. The integration of the Indian to Vitoria's system of *jus gentium* implied that the extension of the principle *jus peregrinandi* that gave the Spaniards the right of access to the Indies. [20] This *jus gentium* principle originated from natural law and was related to the rights of visitors to foreign lands and their humane treatment.

> The Spaniards have the right to travel and swell in those countries so long as they do no harm to the barbarians and cannot be prevented by them from doing so. The first reason come from the law of nations, which either is or derives from natural law… Second in the beginning of the world when all things were held in common everyone was allowed to visit and travel through any land he wished. Third all things which are not prohibited or otherwise to the

18 Vitoria 1991, p. 74.
19 Vitoria quoted in Williams 1990, p. 98.
20 Anghie 1999, p. 94.

> harm and detriment of other are lawful. It is reckoned among all nations inhumane to treat visitors and foreigners badly without some special cause, while, on the other hand, it is humane and correct to treat visitors well.[21]

Within the universal legal system according to Vitoria, the Spaniards possessed the right of travel, commerce and had access to common resources and free land through what Vitoria called the right of 'natural partnership and communication'. "Amity between men is part of natural law and it is against the nature to shun the company of harmless men."[22] This right gave the Spanish the possibility to conduct trade and commerce and to use seas, shores and harbours (with the resources that they provide) that are necessary to the survival of human beings and therefore, by the common accord of all men, were exempt from the original division of property.

> By natural law, running water and the open sea, rivers and ports are the common property of all and by law of nations ships from any country may lawfully put in anywhere. Moreover Barbarians themselves admit all sorts of other barbarians from elsewhere and would therefore do wrong if they did not admit the Spaniards. The Spaniards may lawfully trade among the barbarians so long as they do no harm to their homeland.[23]

And establish themselves on unoccupied land and the chance to exploit precious metals, such as gold and silver.

> In the law of nations a thing, which does not belong to anyone becomes the property of the first taker, therefore if gold in the ground or pearls in the sea or anything else in the rivers has not been appropriated, they will belong by the law of nations to the first taker [...].[24]

As long as the Spanish acted in peace, the Indians could not prevent them to use their rights:

> Since these travels of the Spaniards are neither harmful nor detrimental to the barbarians, they are lawful. It is unlawful to banish visitors who are innocent of crime. It is an act of war to bar those considered as enemies from entering a city or a country, or to expel them if they are already in... but since the bar-

21 Vitoria 1991, p. 278.
22 Vitoria 1991, p. 279.
23 *Id.*
24 *Id.*, p. 280.

> barians have no just war against the Spanish, assuming they are doing no harm, it is not lawful for them to bar them from their homeland.[25]

Moreover, the Spanish were to be respected by the Indians, because they had originally come to America as ambassadors representing the Christian nations.[26] And to emphasize the broader applicability of these rules, they were not unique to a special (colonial) relationship between the Spanish and the Indians, Vitoria added that these principles were the same as those regulating Christian commonwealths.

> It is certain that the barbarians can no more prohibit Spaniards from carrying on trade with them, than Christians can prohibit other Christians from doing the same. If there are any things among the barbarians which are held in common both by their own people and by strangers it is not lawful for the barbarians to prohibit the Spaniards from sharing and enjoying them.[27]

Vitoria regarded the right to engage in commerce and trade as a natural human right within the context of *dominium*. To refuse trade was seen as contrary to the mutual self-interests that all humankind shared. Such conduct was irrational, contrary to natural law and the universal system of law, and justly punished as an infringement of other states' natural rights. Justice could be achieved through *bellum justum*, the principle that secured the smooth functioning of the universal legal system.

The questions related to the Spanish-Indian relations were further complicated by the massive amount of wealth created by trade, commerce and mining of gold and silver. Making excessive profit was not approved by Christian dogma, but the trade with the Americas, producing enormous wealth for Europeans, transformed the nature of commerce in Europe.

In order to qualify the Spanish trade with the Americas as just, Vitoria again referred to the concept of *dominium* in combination with the principles of self-preservation and the common good, contributing to society and commonwealth. He argued that people had travelled and engaged in commerce since the time of Noah.[28] Profit-making, even in larger amounts, would therefore be acceptable as long as it could be understood as motivated by the concern for the good of the commonwealth. The good of commonwealth was an all-encompassing principle. By transporting scarce goods to the market, the merchant was

25 *Id.*, p. 278.
26 Williams 1990, p. 102.
27 Vitoria 1991, p. 280.
28 Anghie 2004, p. 20-21.

performing a socially useful service. In this respect, profit could be considered as a reward or motivation for the merchant. Banks and private finance providers thus facilitated trade by allowing merchants the financial resources and travel opportunities to engage in commerce.[29]

All of this reveals that the universal legal system Vitoria theorized was adapted to the international affairs of his era and justifying the Spanish political and economic enterprise in the Americas. The rights that emerged from Vitoria's concept of *dominium*, combined with the concepts of self-preservation and common good set the legal foundations for an economic system that could be identified by freedom of trade, liberty in profit making, finance provided by banks. The universal *jus gentium* provided that all these rights could be performed anywhere around the world, legally.

Vitoria's universal legal system depended on a third element to make sure the rights were not violated and the system functioned without any hindrance: *bellum justum*. Any resistance by Indians, by legal means or by taking up arms, could be interpreted as a violation of the rights of the Spanish, which in the end resulted in the termination of their *dominium* and allowed the Spanish to use whatever force deemed necessary to enforce 'justice'.

Although Vitoria denied religious, civilizing or personal gain as reasons for war and tried to impose a gradual escalation of hostilities,[30] the system he put forward excused war for the defence and preservation of commonwealth. He sanctioned the retaliation potential for the violation of universal system and injustices committed.

> If the barbarians attempt to deny the Spaniards in these matters, which belong to the law of nations, and they insist replying in violence, the Spaniards may defend themselves and do everything needful for their own safety. It is lawful to meet force with force. In other words, if the barbarians deny the Spaniards what is theirs by the law of nations, they commit an offence against them. Thence if war is necessary to obtain their rights, they may lawfully go to war.[31]

Once just war was instituted, the Spanish were permitted to exercise all public authority over the Indians.

---

29 Koskenniemi 2011, p. 17-23.

30 In the first place, the Spanish were permitted to wage war against the Indians for the purposes of self-defence. In the case of the Indians persisting in their hostility, the Spanish were entitled to subjugate the Indians and to seize their property, as through force of arms, and then to treat the Indians as enemies and hence liable to have enforced against them all the rights of war, such as their reduction to captivity and the overthrow of their rulers. Covell 2009, p. 30-31.

31 Vitoria 1991, p. 282.

> Once the Spaniards have demonstrated diligently both in word and deed that for their own part they have every intention of letting the barbarians carry on in peaceful and undisturbed enjoyment of their property, if the barbarians carry nevertheless persist in their wickedness and strive to destroy the Spaniards, they may then treat them no longer as innocent enemies but as treacherous foes against whom all rights of war can be exercised, including plunder, enslavement, deposition of their former masters and institution of new ones.[32]

Each encounter between the Spanish and the Indians therefore entitled the Spanish to 'defend' themselves against Indian aggression or to restore 'justice' and in so doing, allowed Spanish to expand their territory.[33] Thus, *bellum justum* opened the possibilities for the appropriation of non-free land.

Moreover, according to Vitoria's principle of *bellum justum* any violation of the universal legal system in any part of the world was a violation committed to all mankind, thus any prince could intervene in any injustice or any unjust society and restore justice.[34] However, there is a nuance in Vitoria's formulation of who could wage just wars. Vitoria argued that because non-Christians could not be granted rights in their hostile actions against the Christians, they could not wage just wars. It was the exclusive right of the Christian sovereigns to declare a just war and exercise the rights conferred through the laws of war.[35] Whereas non-Europeans who might try to defend their right of dominium were direct violators of law. Spanish war against the Indian consequently was inevitable and endless.

In Vitoria's system, while *dominium* donated equal rights for all mankind, it was *jus gentium* that regulated the distribution of rights, property and obligations and *bellum justum* served as the coercive force of justice. These principles although claiming to be universal, excluded the American Indians. However, the neutral language of the system naturalized and legitimized endless Spanish incursions into Indian territories, justified the economic system that was based on the exploitation of Indians and their lands, and brought wealth and profit exclusively to the Spanish.

It was Vitoria who developed the legal justifications of the Spanish system, which was mainly based on state enterprise in trade, direct control of the Indian land and military intervention by the state when needed. The universal legal system was forming, but it

32 *Id.*, p. 283.
33 Anghie 1999, p. 95.
34 Vitoria 1991, p. 288.
35 Anghie 1999, p. 98.

needed to be redrafted by Grotius in order to include private actors with sovereign powers into the system.

The Sun was an important political, cultural, religious and ancestral figure for many of the groups the colonizers encountered in the 'Americas'. This figure was extinguished and destroyed by the Spanish and the Portuguese in the Americas such that later generations, like in the analogy of Estella, did not know the inspirational daylight of their ancestors who lived before the arrival of 'justice'.

Hugo Grotius: Lighting the Cannons on Trade Ships

> 'Or', said Estella, 'which is a nearer case – if you had taught her, from the dawn of her intelligence, with your utmost energy and might, that there was such a thing as daylight, but that it was made to be her enemy and destroyer, and she must always turn against it, for it had blighted you and would else blight her – if you had done this, and then, for a purpose, had wanted her to take naturally to the daylight and she could not do it, you would have been disappointed and angry?' [36]

Hugo Grotius, a Dutch lawyer who served as a public official in various countries and positions, followed Vitoria's principles, especially in his work *Mare Liberum.* Schmitt defines his work as follows:

> That same freedom that Vitoria sanctioned for Spanish Catholics vis-à-vis heathen Indians, Grotius advanced for Dutch and English Protestants vis-à-vis Portuguese and Spanish Catholics. Thus a train of thought that a Spanish theologian had expounded as an altogether internal, Spanish-Catholic matter within the firm framework of the Dominican order and within the political unity of the Spanish-Catholic empire, was used only a few decades later against Spain by a polemical jurist of a hostile country as propaganda in European trade wars. [37]

During the seventeenth century, Europe was undergoing important transformations as new sectarian differences and nation states emerged. Such developments meant liberation from the Holy Empire, independence from higher Catholic laws and the grip of Vatican.

---

36 Dickens 2002, p. 301

37 C. Schmitt, *The* Nomos *of the Earth In the International Law of the* Jus Publicum Europaeum (trans. G.L. Ulmen), Telos Press Publishing, New York 2003, p. 116.

New states established new principles of conduct for their relations, not only amongst each other but also in respect to non-European territories. The non-European territories were no longer considered to be places for conquest and plunder, but for trade and profit, expansion and resource exploitation. The Dutch penetration in the East Indies through the Dutch East India Company (the Company) was part of the policy of liberation of the Netherlands from political and economic dependence on the Iberian Peninsula.[38] Its targets were Portuguese strongholds in the East Indies and its objectives were the diversion of the profitable East India trade from Lisbon to Amsterdam. In this war for independence pursued on military and economic fronts, in and outside of European territory, the Dutch violated some of the most respected and established principles of European legal relations.[39] With visionary perspective, Grotius seized the opportunity to legally theorize these developments. On the one hand he theorized on the expansion of private affairs, private wars, and on defending the rights of the private companies as equals to states at the international forums. On the other hand, he advocated in favour of non-European societies in such a way that it would, while undermining the monopoly of the Iberian powers, protect the rights of Holland. The fact that one of the principal actors in the turmoil of European power struggle and colonial competition was not a state but a private corporation was to be of enormous significance in the formation of Grotius's legal principles. This motivated him to write a major apology for the whole Dutch commercial expansion into the Indies.[40] Consequently, this further instituted the legal foundation of global economic and commercial relations, protected by weapons.

Practicality and utility of thought were important to Grotius. He adopted different doctrines in different periods of his life and did not try to offer a single comprehensive account of the world. Grotius adopted, what is usually referred to as an 'eclectic' methodology.[41]

---

38 Formed out of a union of various smaller companies in 1602, the Dutch East India Company received in its charters quasi-sovereign powers, which included the active and passive right of legation, the right to conclude treaties, to acquire territory and if necessary to wage war in order to overawe its rivals and offer help to dissident groups all over the Far East. When the Dutch challenged Portuguese monopoly of trade and navigation in the East Indies, it was Grotius that drafted the legal defence (*Mare Liberum* as part of *Jus Praedea*) against the Portuguese position, defending the right of the Dutch and collaterally the rights of East Indian communities. See C.H. Alexandrowicz, *An Introduction to the History of the Law of Nations in the East Indies (16th, 17th and 18th Centuries)*, Clarendon Press, Oxford 1967, p. 14-15.

39 For further reading for a brief history of the period see Alexandrowicz 1967; Schmitt 2003; and M. Vink, '"The World's Oldest Trade": Dutch Slavery and Slave Trade in the Indian Ocean in the Seventeenth Century', *Journal of World History*, Vol. 14, No. 2, 2003, p. 131-177.

40 R. Tuck, 'Introduction', *in* H. Grotius, *The Rights of War and Peace Book I-II-III*, R. Tuck (Ed.), Liberty Fund, Indianapolis (In.) 2005, p xii-xiii.

41 He is even praised for his approach by a great number of scholars, e.g. Covell, Maas, Keene, Haakonssen and Buckle. Remec defines the eclectic position of Grotius as follows: 'The writers who equate the law of nations with the law of nature are called naturalists. Those who seek rules of the law of nations primarily in the existing positive customs and conventions are called positivists. Those who combine both methods allegedly follow Grotius, who maintain that the positive law of nations supplements the fundamental regu-

Grotius, similar to Vitoria, argued that:

> God created man, "free and sui juris", so that the actions of each individual and the use of his possessions were made subject not to another's will but to his own. Moreover, this view is sanctioned by the common consent of all nations.[42]

Grotius built his entire theoretical legal structure on the rights of the individual. His system of *jus gentium* not only applied to states and their rulers in their mutual external relations, but also to private individuals in their relations within the international forums on an equal footing with states. Grotius's aim was to limit the unfettered dominance of the states in the international system.[43] Besides trying to give the individuals an equal footing with states, the legal order Grotius envisioned derived its rationale and moral strength from the parallel relationship between states rather than a vertical relationship between states and a higher order.[44] Thus his legal principles, claiming to be equal, aimed to address all three levels:

> All the differences of those who do not acknowledge one common civil right, whereby they may and ought to be decided; such as are a multitude of people that form no community, or those that are members of different nations, whether private persons, or kings, or other powers invested with an authority equal to that of kings, as the nobles of a state, or the body of the people, in republican governments.[45]

The two most fundamental and prominent rights of the free and rational individual were the right to self-defence and self-preservation.[46] According to the principle of self-defence, human beings were allowed to defend their own lives and avoid possible injuries. As for self-preservation, this principle gave human beings the right to take necessary measures to acquire essential items needed for life.

---

lations established among all men and nations by the law of nature'. For further reading see P.P. Remec, *The Position of the Individual in International Law according to Grotius and Vattel*, Martinus Nijhoff, The Hague 1960, p.52.

42 Tuck 2005, p. xviii.

43 W. Maas, 'Grotius on Citizenship and Political Community', *Grotiana*, Vol. 20/21, 1999/2000, p. 3.

44 C. Weeramantry, 'Opening Tribute to Grotius', *in* C. Weeramantry and N. Berman (Eds.), 'The Grotius Lecture Series', *14 American University International Law Review*, Vol. 14, 1998-1999, p. 1517.

45 Grotius 2005, p. 133.

46 These are referred as Law I and Law II in M.J. van Ittersum (Ed.), H. Grotius, *Commentary on the Law of Prize and Booty (De jure praedae)*, Liberty Fund, Indianapolis (In.) 2006, p.23.

Although men were free and sovereign, they nevertheless were not purely self-interested creatures, men had a natural tendency to form and live in societies (men's desire for sociability).

> Among the traits characteristic of man is an impelling desire for society, that is, for the social life – not of any and every sort, but peaceful, and organized according to the measure of his intelligence, with those who are of his own kind. [47]

Grotius argued that the free and rational individuals had *dominium* over themselves and voluntarily gave part of their *dominium* to build societies or states. This was due to the fact that the rational individual recognized that life in a society was in conformity with human nature, enabling a better achievement of man's natural aims. By forming a society, individuals aimed to protect their self and property in an orderly manner. [48] As a consequence human beings living in civil society, Grotius added two more principles to his system. [49] Individuals should not only refrain from injuring other citizens, but should protect them for the benefit of society. And citizens should refrain from seizing one another's possessions, whether these be held privately or in common and furthermore should contribute individually both to what is necessary to other individuals and to the whole. [50] It was *jus naturale* that set these principles of 'just conduct' that imposed normative constraints and limitations in man's social relations and furthered the development of Grotius' universal system, similar to Vitoria's usage of self-protection and common good principles. [51]

Grotius's arguments of humans being 'social', required them to live in societies with developed principles for life based on 'justice'. [52] When considered together, one finds out that Grotius's understanding of social peace and justice in a society, his concept of 'sociality', which is supposed to be the 'mother' of natural law, is nothing else than the

---

47 Grotius quoted in H. Bull, B. Kingsbury & A. Roberts (Ed.), *Hugo Grotius and International Relations*, Clarendon Press/Oxford Scholarship Online, Oxford 1992, p. 223.

48 Remec 1960, p. 61.

49 These are referred as Law III and Law IV in Grotius, 2006, p. 27.

50 R. Tuck, *The Rights of War and Peace Political Thought and the International Order from Grotius to Kant*, Oxford University Press, Oxford 1999, p. 87.

51 Covell 2009, p. 52.

52 Grotius divides justice into two, distributive justice and compensatory justice. Compensatory justice is peculiar to the individual and its function is two fold: The function of such justice is twofold, namely: in regard to good, the preservation thereof; in regard to evil, its correction. Hence these two laws arise: first, evil deeds must be corrected; secondly, good deeds must be recompensed. These are referred as Law V and Law VI in Grotius, 2006, p. 29.

duty to respect the rights of others.[53] Thus, the rules for justice in society were reduced to property rights, which implied:

> [A]bstaining from that which is another's and restoring possessions to their owner; reparation – making good a loss incurred through our own fault; and punishment – inflicting penalties according to faults, obligation to keep promises – *Pacta sunt servanda.*[54]

THE ORIGINAL TRINITY REVISED, QUATERNITY OR MORE?

Grotius gathered sources for his theories in an eclectic manner based alternatively on *jus naturale* and *jus gentium* and similar to Vitoria who placed justice as the fundamental norm. He defined natural law as:

> [T]he dictate of right reason, indicating that any act, from its agreement or disagreement with the rational nature as in it a moral turpitude or a moral necessity; and consequently that such act is forbidden or commanded by God, the author of nature.[55]

Jus gentium on the other hand meant a law valid between nations, not law of nations,[56] bringing forward a society of man rather than states. This distinction was important for Grotius in his quest to include private individuals on equal footing with states. The concepts of rights (of individuals), the division of *dominum* and *occupatio, dominium* and *imperium* (divisible sovereignty) were other key concepts in his universal legal system. Although it seemed similar to the one of Vitoria, Grotius' universal system was more committed to the individual. Private individuals and states were interchangeable with respect to *dominium,*[57] and he foresaw no limitations for private property by any obligation other than those entered into voluntarily through contract.[58] The responsibility of punishment, *bellum justum,* in case of violations of the principles of the universal system was ensured

53 K. Haakonssen, 'Hugo Grotius and the History of Political Thought', *in* K. Haakonssen (Ed.), *Grotius Pufendorf and Modern Natural Law*, Ashgate, Hants 1999, p. 38.

54 M. Wight, *Four Seminal Thinkers in International Theory, Machiavelli, Grotius, Kant and Mazzini*, Oxford Scholarship Online, Oxford 2004, p. 36.

55 Grotius quoted in D. W. Dickinson, *The Inequality of States in International Law*, Oxford University Press, London 1920, p. 40.

56 G.E. Sherman, 'Jus Gentium and International Law', *The American Journal of International Law*, Vol. 12, No. 1, 1918, p. 56.

57 R. Tuck, *Natural Rights Theories Their Origin and Development*, Cambridge University Press, Cambridge 1979, p. 63.

58 Haakonssen 1999 p. 39

to both states and private individuals. Thus Grotius acknowledged man's natural right to dominium, and natural right of punishment, eliminating the requirement of a higher authority or an external intervention to achieve justice.

Grotius argued: "every man is the governor and arbiter of affairs relative to his own property".[59] This is how Grotius related property to the key concept of his legal structure, *dominium*. Natural law and reason dictated that *dominium* could not be taken away from a person without injustice, thus *dominium* and the right to private property should be protected. This placed property as one of the first and most essential elements of justice, not only in a society as argued above but also related to *protection of self* as well.[60] Thus private property became an essential feature of self, protection of self, acquiring what is needed for self, human nature and peace and justice in a society. In other words, the theory of property was inextricably linked with conceptions of human nature and society, of psychology and history, of action and obligation, making the story of the development of private property the story of the creation of an individual right out of the 'right common to mankind'.[61]

Grotius argued that property was appropriated by volitional laws confirming man's occupation (possession) of it: "with respect to movables, occupancy implies physical seizure; with respect to immoveables, it implies some activity involving construction or the definition of boundaries".[62] Grotius, similar to Vitoria, based the institution of private property on human action and laws, and argued that the right to property was protected by *jus naturale*. Nevertheless he differed from Vitoria when he created the category of '*occupatio*' within dominium in his work *Mare Liberum*, which aimed to place the Netherlands on the map of colonization.

According to Grotius, the right to be 'free and sui juris' consisted of *dominium* and *imperium*. *Dominium* was usually equated with the right over things and *imperium* with the right over persons, although Grotius sometimes used them interchangeably. These two notions were derived from civil society by an agreement.[63] *Occupatio*, a component

59 Tuck 2005, p. xviii.

60 Thus property was also related to the Law I: "It shall be permissible to defend [one's own] life and to shun that which threatens to prove injurious", in Grotius 2006, p. 23.

61 S. Buckle, *Natural Law and the Theory of Property Grotius to Hume*, Clarendon Press, Oxford 1991, p. 3 and p. 29-35.

62 Grotius quoted in Tuck 1979, p. 61.

63 Y. Masaharu, 'Dominium and Imperium', *in* O. Yasuaki (Ed.), *A Normative Approach to War Peace, War and Justice in Hugo Grotius*, Clarendon Press, Oxford 1993, p. 149.

of *dominium* was a natural right pertaining to self-preservation, related only to the individual, independent of society.[64]

> The recognition of the existence of private property led to the establishment of a law on the matter, and this law was patterned after nature's plan. For just as the right to use the goods in question was originally acquired through a physical act of attachment, the very source of the institution of private property, so it was deemed desirable that each individual's private possessions should be acquired, as such, through similar acts of attachment. This is the process known as 'occupatio', a particularly appropriate term in connection with those goods which were formerly at the disposal of the community.[65]

Dominium over property arose either out of an explicit agreement by way of division or an implicit agreement by way of *occupatio*. The fact that *occupatio* did not require consent of civil society or the universal society of men initially allowed and legitimized the newly acquired Dutch land ownership in the East Indies. However it had a profound effect on acquisition and appropriation of non-European territory. With this distinction the European territorial system with its particular place in *jus gentium* based on agreements among states and private individuals was differentiated from the non-European territory. This division allowed the invasion and seizure of most of the non-European territory with the claim that the territories were *terra nullius*[66] since they did not satisfy the criteria of land appropriation and ownership.[67]

Grotius argued that vacant lands, wastelands, or areas that were not used by the local communities could be occupied by societies in need of that space since *occupatio* was related to the principle of self-preservation.[68] Grotius also treated the land used by hunter-gatherer people as vacant because it was uncultivated and remained common, and thus available for appropriation. Grotius maintained, "waste or barren land must be given to strangers at their request, or it may be lawfully possessed by them because whatever remains uncultivated, is not to be esteemed property [...]".[69]

---

64 E. Keene, *Beyond the Anarchical Society Grotius, Colonialism and Order in World Politics*, Cambridge University Press, Cambridge 2004, p. 53

65 Grotius quoted in Buckle 1991, p. 13.

66 *Terra nullius* in natural law is the term related to land that the pre-social entitlement, or natural right, to property could be invoked.

67 D. Boucher, *The Limits of Ethics in International Relations Natural Law, Natural Rights, and Human Rights in Transition*, Oxford University Press, Oxford 2009, p. 9.

68 Grotius 2005, p. 573.

69 Grotius 2005, p. 448.

The concept of need was flexible for Grotius. Need could be anything from the transfer of excessive population, or farmers needing lands to cultivate. Or it could be framed in terms of continuing an activity, like trade, which is related to the principle of self-preservation.

As for the territories where there were fewer 'vacant' lands available, like India, Grotius came up with the principle of duality of *dominum* and *imperium* (division of sovereignty).

> Jurisdiction is commonly exercised on two Subjects, the one primary, viz. Persons, and that alone is sometimes sufficient, as in an Army of Men, Women, and Children, that are going in quest of some new Plantations; the other secondary, viz. the Place, which is called Territory. But although Jurisdiction and Property are usually acquired by one and the same Act yet are they in themselves really distinct; and therefore Property may be transferred, not only to those of the same State, but even to Foreigners too, the Jurisdiction remaining as it was before.[70]

Imperium is acquired by a ruler extending power over occupied land and inhabitants on that land and it could not be transferred. In contrast *dominum* acquired by a ruler could be transferred to subjects or foreigners. This transfer would not necessarily affect the status or the *imperium* (sovereign) rights of the ruler.[71] This division allowed the Dutch to be more flexible, practical and cost efficient in the quest of colonization, contrary to the Spanish. It allowed the Dutch to have *dominium* rights of a port or a piece of territory in a strategic location, without affecting the *imperium* rights of the local ruler. This division eventually led to the concept of 'indirect rule', an important principle used mainly by the Dutch and later the British colonial administrations.[72] Thus the Company could make profit by inserting itself into already existing systems of trade and taxation without having to deal with costs of administration of local population.

An interesting instance that highlights the fact that Grotius's universal system was made on the premise of increasing profit is revealed in the way Grotius changed his legal positions according to the Dutch interests. Grotius argued for free trade and free usage of sea in East

70 Grotius 2005. p. 457-459.
71 Masaharu 1993, p. 151.
72 The most important principle of indirect rule was that the independence of indigenous 'semi-sovereign' rulers was constrained by imperial and moral considerations. Their sovereignty was acknowledged, but they were not only obliged to obey the European power in matters related to strategic and security concern, but because they were considered less civilized, they were also under the strict control in matters related to misgovernment. The European powers did not hesitate to interfere in the affairs of local rulers time and again when they believed it was necessary to do so. Keene, 2004, p. 93-94.

Indies in *Mare Liberium* against the Portuguese monopoly, but changed his position when the British challenged the Dutch monopoly in the same region.[73]

In *Mare Liberum*, Grotius insisted that everybody had the right to free trade and the sea was common to all and could not be owned for navigation or fisheries.[74] He based his argument with respect to the free use of the seas on *jus naturale* and his arguments on free trade were based on *jus gentium*.

Intending to undermine Portuguese trade, he emphasized the sovereign status of the East Indian communities: "These islands we speak of have, and always had their kings, their common-wealth, their laws and their liberties".[75] The Portuguese could not have a monopoly on the trade by papal donation or custom or possession or any other unilateral act carried out in disregard of the sovereign authorities governing the countries of the East Indies.[76] Grotius defended the rights of the Dutch, with the principles of *liberum commercium* and *libera mercatura*, strongly influenced by Vitoria.

However when the English challenged the Dutch position in the East Indies a few years later, Grotius changed his position. By this time the Dutch were settled in the East Indies and held a monopoly, which was threatened by the English penetration. The Dutch emphasized that they had entered into treaties with local rulers for exclusive trade in particular areas and that these treaties were binding all nations according to *jus gentium*. The English stated that these treaties had established unjust monopolies, which could not find support in jus naturale and *Mare Liberum*; they quoted chapter eight of Grotius' treatise. Grotius who argued previously against the Portuguese on the basis of *jus naturale* principles regarding the free sea and *jus gentium* principles ruling out the titles and rights originating from positive law against the Portuguese, this time referred to the superiority of positive laws over the natural law principles against the British. He claimed that although the English relied on the principle of liberty based on *jus naturale*, the Dutch based their claims on validly concluded treaties and thus the right to contract justified by *jus gentium* took precedence over the *jus naturale* principles. Thus Grotius limited one of his most important principles, the principle of right to free trade, to contracts and the sovereignty of the local communities were ignored. Although Grotius did not drastically change his position on the free usage of open seas, this event made him revise his position and put limits on the use of certain parts of the seas and other commonly held places; his revised position was

73 In both instances Grotius served as the primary legal council to the Dutch.

74 H. Grotius, *The Free Sea*, translated by Richard Hakluyt, Liberty Fund, Indianapolis (In.) 2004, p. 10 and p. 49.

75 Grotius 2004, p. 13.

76 Grotius 2004, p. 51-53.

reflected in his arguments in the chapters two and three of the second book of his trilogy on *The Laws of War and Peace.*[77]

While working to open trade with the East Indies, Grotius argued freedom of trade based on natural law. Once the Dutch secured their privileges, in defence of Dutch position, he relied on the positive law that overruled natural law. Thus, his concern was neither to establish a legal system based on concrete principles, nor the sovereignty of East Indian princes or the regulation of relations between the European and non-European powers. Grotius did not mention the reasons of the conflict, which were the colonial rivalry of European powers over the non-European territory in which the non-Europeans played a figurative role. His main concern was to create a legal basis to regulate a peaceful and profitable trade in favour of the Netherlands.

The universal legal system of Grotius also depended on *bellum justum* as its coercive force. According to Grotius, refusing the rights given by the system (either by European or local communities) could be punished by *bellum justum* either by states or by private individuals.

> Is not the power to punish essentially a power that pertains to the state? Not at all! On the contrary, just as every right of the magistrate comes to him from the state, so has the same right come to the state from private individuals; and similarly, the power of the state is the result of collective agreement... Therefore, since no one is able to transfer a thing that he never possessed, it is evident that the right of chastisement was held by private persons before it was held by the state.[78]

Grotius argued that reason prohibited all use of force that took away what rightly belonged to others.[79] He tried to limit the absolute right to engage in war. By reformulating *bellum justum*, along the natural law principle of 'redress of wrongs'. He gave a concise definition of war in his work *Commentary on the Law of Prize and Booty*:

> Armed execution against an armed adversary is designated by the term 'war'. A war is said to be 'just' if it consists in the execution of a right, and 'unjust' if it consists in the execution of an injury. It is called 'public' when waged by the will of the state, and in this latter concept the will of magistrates (e.g. princes) is included. Moreover, public war may be either 'civil' (when waged against a

77 Grotius 2005, p. 420-479.
78 Grotius quoted in Tuck 2005, p. xx.
79 Tuck 2005, p. 101.

> part of the same state) or 'foreign' (when waged against other states). What is known, as a 'war of allies' is a form of foreign war. Those, which are waged otherwise [than by the public will], are 'private' wars, although some authorities have preferred to describe such conflicts as 'quarrels' rather than as 'wars'. These conflicts, too, may be either civil or foreign.[80]

Grotius aimed to distinguish righteous wars from unrighteous ones, imposing limits to the frequency of wars and the violence of belligerents.[81] Yet each state and private individual sought to protect what they believed to be their rights and to impose punishment on those in opposition. With his classification of *bellum justum* Grotius created a legal principle that excused war in the name of justice. Grotius presented war as natural and even neutral in the sense that it could be tool to protect one's rights and property.

Moreover, Grotius argued that a violation, which might constitute a just cause for war, could also be used to determine the legal interests that should be protected not only by a war of restitution but also by punitive war. Grotius admitted that wars of restitution based on wrongful acts could have a dual just cause 'recovering damages' and 'exacting punishment'.[82] Grotius believed that the right to defend oneself extended beyond merely responding to an immediate attack but included possible threats as well. As a result *bellum justum* extended to the exercise of violence against a third party by whom one is not directly threatened. However Grotius did not develop the legal justification for this proposition and left it rather vague.

> [T]he state inflicts punishment for wrongs against itself, not only upon its own subjects but also upon foreigners; yet it derives no power over the latter from civil law, which is binding upon citizens only because they have given their consent; and therefore, the law of nature, or law of nations, is the source from which the state receives the power in question.[83]

An important implication by giving the right to private individuals (like the Dutch East India Company) who are engaged in complicated power and profit struggles around the world is that the European traders found themselves in the position of making judgments about morality and justice, with a prerogative to punish those believed to be guilty.[84] This

80 Grotius 2006, p. 50.
81 Cornelius F. Murphy, Jr., 'The Grotian Vision of World Order', *The American Journal of International Law*, Vol. 76, No. 3, 1982, p.4 80.
82 Furukawa Terumi, 'Punishment', *in* Yasuaki, 1993, p. 231.
83 Tuck 2005, p. xx.
84 Tuck 2005, p. xxvii-xxviii.

suggested a more conceptualized and extensive violator of the system that Vitoria had foreseen: the pirate.[85] The notion of the pirate is interesting, since Grotius exclusively classified the pirate as *hostis generis humani* (the enemy of humanity). Grotius maintained that since pirates were associations banded together for illegal behaviour, they did not qualify as societies or states. Therefore Grotius did not accord them either sovereignty or *dominium*, prohibiting their inherent right to freedom. They could not make contracts or agreements; agreements made with such entities were not valid. The classification of pirates was left to the responsibility of states or private individuals. Once named as pirate, the enemy of humanity, the person or group of persons would lose all their rights as human beings, totally excluded from the legal system. Since the right to free trade and property were two important concepts for Grotius, the obstructers of these freedoms, regardless of their intention, (e.g. the indigenous people defending their territory or their trade rights) were sporadically classified as pirates.

The right to free trade, which allowed the exchange of goods for all over all material resources that one wanted and needed, was based on Grotius's Law II.[86] The other reference for this right was in *The Law of War and Peace*:

> Even amongst Divines it is a received Opinion, that whoever shall take from another what is absolutely necessary for the Preservation of his own Life, is not from thence to be accounted guilty of Theft: That Sentiment is not founded on what some allege, that the Proprietor is obliged by the Rules of Charity to give of his Substance to those that want it; but on this, that the Property of Goods is supposed to have been established with this favourable Exception, that in such Cases one might enter again upon the Rights of the primitive Community.[87]

The right to trade justified by acquiring all, which are useful for life led to the creation of 'a useful ideology for competition over material resources in the world'.[88] However, this did not only stay as a competition, the universal legal system paved the way to a system of such liberty in economic relations that involved rights to property, trade and taking possessions anywhere in the world against any authority and all these rights could be enforced by just wars.

---

85 "[W]ar may be justly undertaken against those who are inhuman to their parents... against those who eat human flesh ...and against those who practice piracy." Grotius 2005, p. 1022-1024.

86 Law II, it shall be permissible to acquire for oneself, and to retain, those things, which are useful for life. Grotius 2006, p. 23 also see, *supra* footnote 46.

87 Grotius 2005, p. 433-436.

88 Tuck 1979, p. 62.

Historically trade and commerce were the main occasions of interaction among different peoples. These activities created the environment of exchange and learning. They were meant to be peaceful interactions, yet once the cannons of trade ships lit, their function changed, bringing destruction rather than trade goods. Just like the analogy of Estella, the light of the ships became something to be feared similar to a ruthless enemy.

RETHINKING ESTELLA WHILE CONCLUDING

> 'So', said Estella, 'I must be taken as I have been made. The success is not mine, the failure is not mine, but the two together make me.'[89]

Vitoria established the principles of his *jus naturale* based universal legal system on three concepts: *dominium*, *jus gentium* and *bellum justum*. These concepts not only helped the Spanish conquest, settlement and administration of the West Indies, but they permitted free trade and excessive profit making that boosted the Iberian, and consequently European, economies. However the colonial and commercial system was costly and in the end resulted in the decline of the Spanish Empire. Grotius developed Vitoria's concepts further and while basing the principles of his system eclectically on *jus naturale* or *jus gentium*, he used *occupatio*, *dominium* and *imperium* as fundamental concepts of his system. He elevated the status of private companies as equals to states and allowed private and punitive wars extending the definition of *bellum justum*. His concepts helped the Dutch to join the colonization race and prosper through a cost effective trading empire.

Contrary to the differences explored above, the basics of both systems remained the same. Both Vitoria and Grotius reacted to the growth of trade, commerce and the expansion of European rule around the world by producing a legal and political vocabulary that emphasized expansion as natural and articulated the social world as a universal system of inter-state-individual relations.[90] They both defended individuals and their rights as *jus cogens*, related the right to private property closely to it and claimed to have built a universal system, irrespective of cultural or religious distinctions. The systems did not function by the direct discrimination of 'the other' not being granted rights. Vitoria acknowledged the *dominium* of the American Indians and Grotius recognized alternatively the *dominium* and *imperium* of local rulers of East Indies. The conquest, colonization and exploitation did not take place due to the lack of rights; it was done through the notion of rights. Because they were included in the universal system, the American Indians had to respect the rights of the Spanish and the peoples of East Indies had to recognize the rights of the Dutch.

89 Dickens 2002, p. 302.
90 Koskenniemi 2011, p. 35-36.

Otherwise they could be punished by *bellum justum*. The rights of the non-Europeans were limited when they were claimed against Europeans (e.g. in Vitoria's case, the non-Christians could not wage just wars, in Grotius's case their rights were valid as long as it profited the Dutch). The non-Europeans were included in the system to increase profit and excluded in terms of rights in order to be exploited. And this was made in the name of individual rights, social peace and justice, or in other words: for the prosperity of humanity. Thus the persistent significance of Vitoria's and Grotius's work lies in their construction of a system of law that is in appearance egalitarian, but built on the exclusion of the non-European other. The legal system was instrumental in maximizing the political and economic interests of their respective countries.

The legal structures envisaged by Vitoria and Grotius remain as foundations of modern law. Contemporary international law is also enshrined with the protection of individual rights and the common good for humanity through the concept of justice. The right to private property exists as a fundamental human right protected by international conventions and courts (e.g. European Court of Human Rights) and punished when violated. The contemporary international law with its different legal practices (e.g. international human rights law, humanitarian law) still has a tendency to declare universal rights, whilst recognizing the necessity of their adaptation to each type of culture, without compromising its universal character. However, the basic 'non-resolved exclusion' of Vitoria and Grotius still remains the same. The 'other' continues to be included while being excluded with the assertion that individuals had, or should have rights. This allows for continued legally sanctioned creation of wealth and influence, exploitation and the distribution of material and spiritual resources through the exercise of private power disguised within a system that claims universal rights and equality.

International law is what we make of it and how we construct it, it is not an idolized system of higher universal values. International law and the legitimacy it creates could be used instrumentally for a particular purpose or interest, disguising itself in the discourse of human rights or universal justice. The present economic crisis, as well as violence and resistance to the hegemonic universal system through continuous demands for change around the globe, suggest, like Estella rethinking her life after she returned from her unsuccessful quest to live in high society, that it is time to rethink the idolized property rights with its legal basis and its implications in international law.

Reconciling Rwandan Reconciliations

International Criminal Law versus National Politics in the Mirror of Humanity

Eugene Mc Namee[*]

> The UN Security Council [...] Convinced that in the particular circumstances of Rwanda, the prosecution of persons responsible for serious violations of international humanitarian law would [...] contribute to the process of national reconciliation and to the restoration and maintenance of peace [...]
>
> [...] Decides hereby, having received the request of the Government of Rwanda (S/1994/1115), to establish an international tribunal for the sole purpose of prosecuting persons responsible for genocide and other serious violations of international humanitarian law committed in the territory of Rwanda and Rwandan citizens responsible for genocide and other such violations committed in the territory of neighbouring States, between 1 January 1994 and 31 December 1994 and to this end to adopt the Statute of the International Criminal Tribunal for Rwanda annexed hereto [...]
>
> UN Security Council Resolution 955, S/RES/955 (1994) 8 November 1994

Introduction

By now there is a huge literature surrounding the events of the Rwandan genocide, its genesis and its aftermath, to the extent that a historiography of the genocide has been written which has identified various strands of approach to the topic – often at radical variance from each other.[1] The literature can be divided into various sub-genre categories; those that detail the events of the genocide, those that seek to place the genocide in historical context and those that try to account for the genocide in more thorough sociological,

* I am grateful to Nesam Mc Millan and Sara Ramshaw for their insightful comments on earlier drafts.

1 S. Strauss, 'The Historiography of the Rwandan Genocide', *in* D. Stone (Ed.), *The Historiography of Genocide*, Palgrave Macmillan, Basingstoke 2008.

political or anthropological terms. A unifying feature of the field of literature at this point is that the genocide itself is accepted as having been multi-factorial in its causality over both the long and short durée of history, and that this history was heavily conditioned by complex networks of relations between Rwandan and other regional and global state and non-state actors. The simple story of an outbreak of inexplicable atavistic ethnic murder has been thoroughly debilitated through multiple contextualizations. For most political or historical commentators on the genocide, its historical genesis and its aftermath, the International Criminal Tribunal for Rwanda (henceforth ICTR) process merits little more than passing comment, and often such comment has the derogatory flavour of 'too little too late'.[2]

Yet there is also by now an extensive literature surrounding the processes of the ICTR, chiefly regarding the novelty of certain of the convictions, for example the first conviction on an actual charge of genocide, the first international criminal conviction of a serving head of government, the first conviction for rape as a crime of genocide, the likely effect of the ICTR as a forerunner to the permanent International Criminal Court.[3] The fact that the 'Statute' (constitutional document) of the ICTR limits its remit to 'the prosecution of persons responsible for genocide and other serious violations of international humanitarian law committed in the territory of Rwanda and Rwandan citizens responsible for genocide and other such violations committed in the territory of neighbouring States, between 1 January 1994 and 31 December 1994' is certainly pertinent here, in that the time limitation imposed is one which cuts out the consideration of contextual factors which form the bulk of any more comprehensive historical or political analysis. Although such factors might be regarded as providing a broad context, it is understandable that the ICTR, in an effort to achieve timely provision of justice, would proceed on the basis that the broad context had only remote relevance to the much narrower category of what would be considered in court because of its specific evidential relationship to a precisely defined crime. This reductive legalism, while perhaps operationally necessary, and while opening up the legal process to standard legal critical attention in terms of the quality of justice produced, in processes such as the ICTR creates a deep paradox. This paradox at times surfaces even within the processes of the Tribunal itself, for example when in *Prosecutor v. Kayishema*

---

2 See, for example, G. Prunier, *The Rwandan Crisis: History of a Genocide*, Hurst, London 1997.

3 C. Bassiouni, *Crimes Against Humanity in International Criminal Law*, Kluwer, The Hague/ London 1999; S. Zappala, *Human Rights in International Criminal Proceedings*, Oxford University Press, Oxford 2003; S. Darcy, *Collective Responsibility and Accountability Under International Law*, Transnational Publishers, Arsdley (NY) 2007; C. de Than and E. Shorts, *International Criminal Law and Human Rights*, Sweet and Maxwell, London 2003; L.J. van den Herik, *The Contribution of the Rwanda Tribunal to the Development of International Criminal Law*, Martinus Nijhoff, Leiden 2005.

and Ruzindana,[4] the court recognizes a need to contextualize the conflict, but also recognizes the extra-legality of doing so, leading to an uncomfortable compromise position:

> The Trial Chamber [...] is of the opinion that an attempt to explain the causal links between the history of Rwanda and the suffering endured by this nation in 1994 is not appropriate in this forum and may be futile. It is impossible to simplify all the ingredients that serve as a basis for killings on such a scale. Therefore, the account presented below is a brief explanation of issues relating to the division of ethnic groups in Rwanda, a brief history of Rwanda's post-independence era, including a look at the 1991 constitution, the Arusha Accords, and the creation of militias.[5]

The nature of the crimes and what the international community want to achieve by trying them would seem to rule out the insulation of the legal process from the historical and socio-political issues within which the trial is implicated, yet the paradox is that such insulation is maintained in order for the trial process to function. There is no such operational reason for academic commentary to maintain such a stance, yet what is lacking is a body of literature considering together the broad context of the genocide and the issue of the ICTR and its processes. A notable exception is Mullins and Rothe's *Blood Power and Bedlam: Violations of International Criminal Law in Post-Colonial Africa*,[6] which, in an attempt to develop a criminology of state crimes, goes some way to a consideration of the ICTR through the same (post-colonial) analytic categories as the genocide itself. A second exception is the account by Kingsley Moghalu in *Rwanda's Genocide: The Politics of Global Justice*,[7] which offers a fascinatingly detailed account of intertwined legal and political issues in the setting up, ongoing operation and effects of the ICTR, without, however, adopting an overall theoretical explanatory framework. Both of these works are heavily (and understandably) biased towards a retrospective analytic approach.

This essay attempts to complement such work through suggesting that the differing ways in which the future is tied to the key concept of 'reconciliation', which grounds both the ICTR process and the Rwandan governmental efforts at post-conflict social repair, and of course a vision of the future implies a version of the past, opens up a fruitful territory for investigating certain aspects of the politics of global justice. The idea of 'reconciliation'

4 *Prosecutor v. Kayishema and Ruzindana*, ICTR-95-1-T, p. 21. See generally p. 21-29, 'Historical Context of the 1994 Events in Rwanda'.

5 *Id.*, p. 21. See generally p. 21-29, 'Historical Context of the 1994 Events in Rwanda'.

6 C.W. Mullins and D. Rothe, *Blood, Power and Bedlam: Violations of International Criminal Law in Post-Colonial Africa*, Peter Lang, New York 2008.

7 K. Moghalu, *Rwanda's Genocide: The Politics of Global Justice*, Macmillan, London 2005.

that lies at the heart of the justification for the legal process is specifically political, indeed might be regarded as having become in recent times 'a regulative ideal in political discourse', in its unassailability constituting the 'telos and closure' of politics.[8] It is certainly striking that the ideal of reconciliation is so strongly promoted in the context of a trial for genocide, where the notion of reconciliation might seem not only alien but potentially unjustifiable; if genocide is evil then could it ever be just to be reconciled with the perpetrators?[9] It is also striking that national reconciliation is also the acknowledged aim and goal of post-conflict legal and social processes in Rwanda itself, once again raising the issue of 'telos' and 'closure'. It is here, in the contrast between 'reconciliations' that this essay finds its point of focus, bearing in mind this question of whether 'reconciliation' has come to constitute an arch-politics. Having first laid out a brief context to the setting up of the ICTR, this essay tries to identify the idea structure behind the idea of 'reconciliation' as it operates as a feature of the ICTR process, and to contrast this with the idea structure of how ostensibly the same concept of 'reconciliation' is brought into play in paradigmatic legal and public policy processes in Rwanda itself. What emerges is that not only are these 'reconciliations' different, but they are conflicting. Reconciliation becomes recognizable as a politically mobilized concept with attendant power struggles over its meaning and significance, and which in the context of the ICTR provides a function of insulating 'the International community' from more developed forms of practical responsibility under the guise of a gesture of generosity and justice.

Context to the Establishment of the ICTR

> The most authoritative rendering of the truth is possible only through the crucible of a trial that accords full due process. Such trials can generate a comprehensive record of the nature and extent of the violations, how they were planned and executed, the fate of individual victims, who gave the orders and who carried them out… When the world community fails to prevent genocide from occurring, it should as least seek to ensure the prosecution of the allegedly responsible individuals in an institution that is fair and is seen as fair. In this regard, the Rwanda Tribunal serves as the conscience of the international

8 E. Christodoulidis and S. Veitch, 'Introduction', *in* S. Veitch (Ed.), *Law and the Politics of Reconciliation*, Ashgate, Aldershot 2007.

9 In her report on the Eichmann Trial, Hanna Arendt notes in passing that Eichmann mentioned at times that he would 'like to make peace with his former enemies', a sentiment that he shared with many ordinary Germans and a sentiment that was behind proposals to create a 'conciliation committee' to bring together Nazi murderers and Jewish survivors. She regarded such ideas as completely fantastic and utterly devoid of reality, serving only to give 'an extraordinary sense of elation' to the speaker, as they embarked on this gross adventure in self-deception. H. Arendt, *Eichmann in Jerusalem: A Report on the Banality of Evil*, Penguin Classics, London 2006.

> community. It is the manifestation of the moral outrage of humanity over the transgressions of civilizational norms and ethics.
>
> Statement of Malaysia, U.N. GAOR 51st Sess., at 18, U.N. Doc. A/51/PV.78 (1996)

Most reasonably informed people above a certain age have a general idea of what happened in Rwanda in 1994. In that year the hitherto obscure (to a Western audience) African country exploded into the global news with graphic and terrible reports of the mass murder of men, women and children of one ethnicity by the men, women and children of another. The reports were often so horrific as to be practically unbelievable; detailing the torture and slaughter of thousands upon thousands by neighbours armed with crude machetes and farming instruments. Many people will remember that the UN forces present at the time were largely pulled out rather than engaged to try to stop the carnage.[10] As time went on and more diverse reports of the situation emerged, it became more difficult to grasp a simple version of what was going on, and this became even more the case as the genocide gave way to a massive humanitarian refugee crisis as displaced Rwandans flooded into disease ridden camps along the border with Congo and Tanzania and reports emerged of thousands of deaths from preventable diseases such as typhoid and cholera. The displaced people were Rwandan Hutus, while the genocidal campaign had been conducted against Tutsis. The attention paid to the refugee crisis arguably deflected attention from the aftermath of the genocide, in particular the plight of the survivors. The international community, it seemed, was much more ready to intervene to provide humanitarian aid relief than to intervene militarily at an earlier stage when the genocide itself might have been averted and this non-political politics has been the subject of much debate.[11] As is the way of things, new global calamities came to grab the headlines and to divert attention from Rwanda and the aftermath to the genocide, and public media reports were replaced gradually by a mass of more considered literature trying to make sense of that period.[12]

The attention of the UN was not so easily diverted. It had been the object of heavy criticism not only from the media but also from many of its own members for its response to the

---

10 R. Dallaire, *Shake Hands with the Devil*, Arrow, London 2004.

11 See, for example, S. Žižek, 'Against Human Rights', *New Left Review*, Vol. 34, 2005; M. Mamdani, 'The Politics of Naming', *London Review of Books*, Vol. 29, No. 5, 2007.

12 G. Prunier, *The Rwandan Crisis: History of a Genocide*, Hurst, London 1997; A. Des Forges, *Leave None to Tell the Story: Genocide in Rwanda*, Human Rights Watch 1999; P. Gourevitch, *We Wish To Inform You That Tomorrow We Will Be Killed With Our Families*, Picador, London 2000; M. Mamdani, *When Victims Become Killers; Colonialism, Nativism and the Genocide in Rwanda*, Princeton University Press, Princeton 2001; L. Melvern, *Conspiracy to Murder: The Rwandan Genocide*, Verso, London 2004; L. Melvern, *A People Betrayed; The Role of the West in Rwanda's Genocide*, Zed Books, London 2000.

crisis in Rwanda. For example, Kofi Annan, in response to a deeply critical independent report on the conduct of the UN in relation to the genocide – which he himself as Secretary General commissioned – expressed publicly his deep remorse at the UN's failure to prevent or stop the genocides.[13] Annan, at the time of the genocide, had been the UN High Official in charge of the Rwandan mission. In the autumn of 1994, just a few months after the mass killings had stopped, authorized under UN Resolution 935, the UN sent in a team of investigators to make an initial report on what had happened. The investigators found that there was widespread evidence of a genocidal campaign against the ethnic Tutsis of Rwanda, and evidence of the mass-killing of ethnic Hutus on the basis of their real or supposed opposition to the exterminations, or because they were mistaken for Tutsis. The report found that Tutsis had been targeted as a group, the Hutus as individuals. On the basis of this report the UN concluded that genocide had occurred, and an International Criminal Tribunal for Rwanda was set up, through a similar *ad-hoc* process and along similar lines to the recently established International Criminal Tribunal for Former-Yugoslavia, to try those most responsible for the outrage. The ICTR was set up under the mandate of UN Resolution 955 of 8 November 1994, in the preamble to which was stated: 'Expressing once again its grave concern at the reports indicating that genocide and other systematic, widespread, and flagrant violations of international humanitarian law have been committed in Rwanda [...]'.

The juridical response to trying those responsible for the genocide in Rwanda has come in two forms; the domestic Rwandan response, based on the Rwanda legal system, and the international response, based on International Law. Rwanda has adopted a twin-track process for trying those accused of genocide. Those accused of the most serious crimes, for example organizing and fomenting the original scheme are tried through a formal court process and may be awarded prison sentences (up until the abolition of capital punishment in 2007, the death penalty was also available and applied).[14] Those accused of more minor crimes, for example crimes against property, are tried through the *gacaca* process,[15] where local justices adjudicate through more informal processes and award compensation or require imprisonment. The ICTR tries those that it regards as being most seriously implicated in the genocide, and awards prison sentences up to a maximum of life imprisonment. To some degree the functioning of both these structures of justice complements each other. For example, the participation of the international community

13 See UN Security Council, *Report of the Independent Inquiry into the Actions of the United Nations during the 1994 Genocide in Rwanda*, 15 December 1999.

14 The abolition of the death penalty was undertaken in order to facilitate the eventual transfer of accused from the ICTR, as part of the completion strategy, which the ICTR would not countenance while the death penalty stood.

15 To be discussed in further detail below.

under the auspices of the UN in the body of the ICTR carries sufficient weight to have persuaded many countries throughout the world to extradite accused persons – amongst whom were some of the chief architects of the genocide – who had fled into exile on their territory after the genocide, something which the government of Rwanda was unable to do. For example ex-prime minister Jean-Paul Kambanda was extradited to the ICTR from Kenya in 1997 to face trial in Arusha and in 1998 became the first ever head of government to be convicted of genocide. However, the ICTR could only ever be an instrument to administer justice in relation to a very limited number of accused due to the complex and expensive nature of its processes (some trials have now been running for more than five years) so that the administration of justice in relation to the mass of those involved was necessary as a feature of domestic Rwandan legality. Despite the seeming complementarity of the processes, however, the initial support of the Rwandan government for an international tribunal quickly gave way to an attitude of reservation as to the proposed form and location of such a tribunal, and the relationship between the actual ICTR since its inception and the Rwandan government has often deteriorated to something approaching mutual hostility.[16] There have been diverse reasons for this breakdown in relations, most notably the Rwandan government's ongoing annoyance that the massive expenditure disbursed to fund the ICTR was not allocated to reconstruction and reconciliation efforts on its own soil, either as direct grant or by virtue of the Tribunal having its seat there. Beyond matters of resources there have been three chief objections by the Rwandan government to the actual legal processes of the ICTR; the first is the notion that the formal criminal legal structure as instituted places too much emphasis on the perpetrators rather than the victims, the second that the maximum penalty for those found guilty did not extend to the death penalty, and the third that at certain points the idea of trying members of the Rwandan Patriotic Front (the invading 'Tutsi army' which militarily defeated the then Rwandan government to end the genocide) for involvement in crimes against humanity was mooted.[17]

The two different patterns of juridico-political response to the genocide exist, of course, within two different worlds of possibility. The international response is a product of the entire gamut of international structures that both compose and influence the conduct of the UN, while the Rwandan response is entirely local and with regard for wider geopolitical or global developmental ideas only insofar as these are perceived to serve the national interest at present – that national interest having to bend itself to the pressing concerns of national reconciliation and reconstruction. And it is on this ground of 'reconciliation' that the conceptual programmes of both the ICTR and the Rwandan justice system

16 K. Moghalu, *Rwanda's Genocide: The Politics of Global Justice*, Macmillan, London 2005.
17 *Id.*, p. 125-153.

ostensibly find their common ground. This term has gained particularly prominence within international humanitarian thinking as a result of what seems the more or less successful transition of South Africa away from the Apartheid regime to a multi-cultural democratic polity, aided by the novel justice mechanism of a 'truth and reconciliation commission'. This is not the only arena in which 'reconciliation' has been mobilized as a basic idea within which justice processes should be organized, in obvious contrast to more classical (Kantian) ideas of justice mechanisms serving a higher form of ideal abstraction of itself; the purity of judgement and punishment in relation to the existential and deontological matter of the crime. The reasons for the ascendancy of reconciliation are based in the marriage of political uncertainty of both conceptual and practical hue. [18] The conceptual uncertainty that has taken hold of international systems of justice is everywhere evident, as to the value of an over-riding Western notion of justice provision and justice mechanisms that gain global prominence because of the historical and actual pre-eminence of Western nations within international governmental and non-governmental agencies, but which are increasingly conceded to be inappropriate for local circumstances in particular areas of the world. In terms of practical politics the requirement for reconciliation in the wake of situations of conflict is generally dictated by the fact that the foundational structure, the nation-state, on which international relations is based cannot be regarded as a flexible entity, so that there is generally no option but that the citizens of a territory that has gone through conflict must somehow be reconciled to each other at least to the extent that they can inhabit the same national territory. Whatever the efficaciousness of either the ICTR or the Rwandan justice system in relation to the genocide, there is no doubt that they both aim to facilitate reconciliation. The question opens up of what particular reconciliation is being constituted in each site. [19]

The ICTR and Reconciliation

> Political and social stabilization in Rwanda depends on whether all citizens, regardless of their ethnic origin, can be reconciled. Such national reconciliation would imply the due administration of justice, first of all to ensure that the guilty parties no longer feel they can act with impunity, which would act as a deterrent. Secondly, it would enable victims and their families to feel that justice was being done and that the real perpetrators were being punished, which would dampen any feelings of revenge. If justice is not done, there may be no end to hatred, and atrocities could go on and on, with the executioners believing

18 A. Schaap, *Political Reconciliation*, Routledge, London 2005.

19 For an introduction to the multiplicity and generality of debates on reconciliation see Schaap 2005 and S. Veitch 2007.

> they were immune to prosecution and the victims' thirst for revenge fuelled by a sense of injustice and the idea that an entire ethnic group was responsible for the atrocities committed against them. In this regard it is of paramount importance that justice be done, because this will help replace the idea of collective political responsibility with the idea of individual criminal responsibility.
>
> First ICTR President (Judge) Laity Kama, addressing U.N. GAOR, 51st Session: 5, U.N. Doc. A/51/PV.78 (1996)

It is a gauge of just how successful has the idea of reconciliation become in recent times that in the quote given above from the (then) leading judge at the International Criminal Tribunal for Rwanda, a court trying 'an ideal type case of violations of international criminal law',[20] justice, rather than simply proposed as good, correct and necessary in its own right, is cast as a support player in relation to the leading role given to national reconciliation. Criminal prosecutions are presented in quite classical legal terms as necessary to guard against impunity and so to have a deterrent effect, but also are presented, in much less classical terms, as necessary to serve the role of replacing 'collective political responsibility with individual criminal responsibility'. The role of the criminal law, in other words, is explicitly cast as being less about punishing the guilty few because they are guilty, but because by punishing the guilty few the implication is to recognize the innocence of the many. Law is proposed as a vital vector instrument to provide an escape from a corrosive politics and to ground a new future. Through this gesture the many who might have seemed to bear some political responsibility because of some perhaps minimal involvement which may have been thrust upon them – they, after all, escaped the violent maelstrom and also failed to stop it – thus come to constitute a decontaminated political community, and we might further say, translating a vocabulary of political responsibility into a more personal language but without violence to ideas at play, is that an aspect of this decontamination is to take away their shame.

Such emotional language does enter into the judge's statement, but from another direction and to another end. There are repeated references to the idea of 'feelings', in particular to the feelings of the victims. The judge seems to be willing to ascribe to the court the responsibility of ensuring not alone that justice be done, but also that the victims should *feel* that justice has been done. This feeling of justice having been done is linked on one side to the attribution of guilt to the responsible criminals, and on the other side to the prospect of national reconciliation: the victims will feel that justice has been done if they

20 D. Rothe & C.W. Mullins, *Symbolic Gestures and the Generation of Global Social Control: The International Criminal Court*, Lexington Books, Lanham 2006, p. 5.

can come to understand that the responsibility lies not with an entire ethnic group but with a small group of individuals, and when they come to this realization then they will be in a position to reconcile with the innocent majority as opposed to the 'real perpetrators'. This realization will be enough to diffuse the 'thirst for revenge' harboured by victims and replace it with a sense of justice having been done. Once again law here is portrayed as the purifier of politics, except this purification process is directed to the victims (rather than those who might be thought politically responsible) and is directed forward in time, the purging of feelings of revenge that they might carry forward, rather than the purging of, for those potentially to be held politically responsible, the notion of previous culpability. The law is a double filter of social process and social affect; it transforms perverse politics into law, leaving the ground ready for a new politics, and it transforms grand negative social emotions into positive emotions, leaving the ground ready for a new community. The double sense of its operation is captured by the term 'reconciliation', a concept from which the judge does not shy in the slightest.

A third element that undergirds those two already mentioned, and which has entered obliquely into the discussions above, is that of time, or more precisely the relationship between reconciliation and time. The law deals with the past and opens the way to the future. In classical legal terms this two-directional quality is heavily biased towards an attention on the past; the law deals with the past and there is an implicit assumption that the future will take care of itself as a matter of society and politics. The statement from the judge is a statement of recognition that the weight of attention has shifted much more towards the future, to the idea of the importance of reconciliation in the grand scheme of things and the relative putting in perspective of the past, that is, the crimes which have been committed in the past. To the extent that the past has a value there is an inference that it has a value in order to ground a positive future; the idea is re-conciliation, the projection backwards in time of a notion of concilarity, of being in council, in order to ground the supernormative 'reconciliation'. Politics in the sense of social practice is purified, politics in the sense of affect is purified, politics in the sense of previous structures of social meaning is purified (through an imaginary projection of a natural order of 'conciliation' backwards and forwards in time). The law as simple process of adjudication, how could it not in the face of such power, prostrates itself before reconciliation.

Such an attitude is not, of course, without its critics. Take, for example, the following:

> Reconciliation has too often come to signify in the political discourse of our times the call not just to put the trauma's of the past behind us but also, in a sense, to put behind us the very politics of the past. Against this our main concern has been to emphasise that 'reparation of historical injustices' requires

> that we face up to these injustices. That is what it means to do justice to them and reconciliation can only, properly, be the contingent response, not the unconditional outcome, of how societies face up to precisely that task.[21]

This marks out distinctly a latent theoretical danger of the kind of instrumentalization of (criminal) justice in relation to a projected future that lies at the heart of the discussion in the text above: namely that past injustices of a political nature by their conversion into tamer legal problems are swept under a carpet rather than resolved. What if, in other words and to respond directly to the quotation from Judge Laity Kama (page 106-107 above), the more true pattern of the past has been precisely 'collective political responsibility' for massive crimes against humanity, and the transference of criminal responsibility to the few in the service of reconciliation is an instance of over-determining an outcome which flies in the face of justice in a broader sense than that narrowly encompassed by criminal notions of intent and guilt? In this reading the new 'decontaminated' political community envisaged by the judge takes the paradoxical form of a legally constituted non-political political community, in the sense of a political community which must forget the conditions of its own coming into being in accepting the status of *tabula rasa*. Furthermore, the deep imbrications of law within politics, even if the particular events seem to warrant a generous and helpful intervention, has perhaps the effect of destroying the most valuable qualities of law as standing above a fray and adjudicating from a point of objectivity. The idea that the law must find people criminally responsible in order to create a political effect takes on a pattern of circularity; if the legal process has been set up on the basis that genocide occurred and the criminal law of genocide presumes an intent to commit genocide, and the future good of the political community requires reconciliation, and reconciliation requires the translation of ideas of political responsibility to those of individual criminal responsibility, and the court recognizes its own function as providing reconciliation, then the legal process will find that genocide has occurred and it will find individuals who will fulfil the conditions to be convicted of it.

But perhaps it is unwise to treat this matter too categorically, in the sense of assuming that perceived paradoxes of logic and circularities of argument are enough to ground fundamental objections. The judge's statement under examination is an extract from a speech by a lawyer (the chief lawyer) from the ICTR and certainly made various claims about the legal process, but it was made to the General Assembly of the United Nations, and thus perhaps it was not only fitting that the speech should have blurred the boundaries between politics and law, but also that a certain amount of rhetorical excess might have been expected. Furthermore, as is well known and frequently acknowledged, the nature of

21 Christodoulidis and Veitch 2007, p. 1.

international law in its current course of development is still such that its nature as law (with expected 'rule of law' characteristics of clarity and consistency of operation) is frequently called into question, and its close links to politics are frequently and unavoidably apparent.[22]

Finally, one might well claim that the focus on reconciliation as prior to (in importance) and post (in time) legal process creates a field of considerations (conceptual, practical, temporal) that is appropriate to the subject matter and in its complexities and paradoxes appropriately recalls profound theorization around questions of justice, rather than presumes justice as a simple function of law.[23] In this light one might say that the ICTR, and legal processes like it which self-consciously span the boundary of law and politics, are in a sense rescuing law (or attempting to do so) from a frequently perceived – and perhaps characteristically Modern – sterility,[24] to return to paying attention to considerations of justice (including affect[25]) that are, after all, the *raison d'être* of law.

Adopting a slightly different vocabulary we might say that on certain liminal occasions law and politics approach each other to constitute 'transitional justice' which as a term is perhaps rescued from accusations of being either self-contradictory (logically paradoxical) or axiomatic (logically circular) by its usual modest employment as a rough and ready generic term to cover transition to liberal democracy, the deeper theorization of which (along with more profound questions of justice) is usually bracketed out.[26] Such a transitional justice optic through such a bracketing out or assumption of the basic ameliorative qualities of rule of law/democracy, open an opportunity for more detailed attention to the 'constructivist' qualities of legal process.[27] That is to say, what forward directed social effect is produced by the operation of diverse ostensibly legal processes, even if these processes recognizably do not contain all the elements that they would within a settled sphere of the operation of normal democratic politics. In this light statements and attitudes such

22 See Rothe & Mullins 2006; and, in particular, Mullins & Rothe 2008, for discussion and bibliography. See also K. Moghalu, *Global Justice: The Politics of War Crimes Trials*, Prager, New York 2006. For further discussion, see P. Zumbansen, 'Transnational Law and Societal Memory', *in* Veitch 2007. For comparison, see R. Kerr, *The International Criminal Tribunal for the Former Yugoslavia: An Exercise in Law, Politics and Diplomacy*, Oxford University Press, Oxford 2004.

23 See, paradigmatically, J. Derrida, 'Force of Law: The "Mystical Foundation of Authority"', *in* Gil Anidjar (Ed.), *Acts of Religion*, Routledge, New York/London 2002.

24 C. Douzinas, *The End of Human Rights*, Hart, Oxford, 2000; S. Motha, 'Reconciliation as Domination', *in* Veitch 2007.

25 P. Goodrich, *Languages of Law*, Weidenfeld Paperbacks, London 1990.

26 R. Teitel, *Transitional Justice*, Oxford University Press, Oxford 2000; C. Bell, *On the Law of Peace: Peace Agreements and the Lex Pacificatoria*, Oxford University Press, Oxford 2008; C. Bell, 'Transitional Justice, Interdisciplinarity, and the State of the "Field" or "Non-Field"', *International Journal of Transitional Justice*, Vol. 3, 2009, p. 5-27.

27 Teitel 2000.

as those quoted from Judge Laity Kama and Kofi Annan, which highlight the role of the ICTR in furthering reconciliation, could well be regarded as legitimate in that they are not descriptive but performative; connecting reconciliation to criminal justice as a means to promote this as an idea not to make verifiable claims as to its truth. To push this idea a little further one might recognize the parameters of the acknowledged force of law as connected not just to physical force, but to its symbolic power, this power in itself having some qualities of the mystical, in other words to remark that the repetition of 'reconciliation' is more than performative in a secular sense, but also performative in a more basic sacred sense, it is incantatory to an idea of reconciliation in the sense of reaching out for shared humanity. The reconciliation in question, in other words, is also that between the global community and the Rwandan victims, an acknowledgement of a deep sense that the court process constitutes a species of atonement for (a general political) shameful abandonment.[28] The legal process is a formal prayer to justice, not its accomplishment.

Reconciliation and Rwanda

> Reconciliation is not just one of the many other options for us Rwandese, it is rather a non-negotiable obligation. An obligation to give ourselves hope for our old age; an obligation to leave to our children a better Rwanda to grow old and live in.
>
> Statement from Antoine Rutayisire, Vice-President of the Rwandan National Unity and Reconciliation Commission, on the NURC website

On 1 October 2010 the UN released the official version of its 'Report of the Mapping Exercise documenting the most serious violations of human rights and international humanitarian law committed within the territory of the Democratic Republic of the Congo between March 1993 and June 2003'. The Report, widely leaked in advance of its official release, accused the Rwandan Patriotic Army (the victorious invading 'Tutsi' force which had routed the forces of the previous government to end the genocide), of having committed numerous crimes against humanity in the course of its pursuit of ethnic Hutus who had refused repatriation into Rwanda during the RPA incursions into DRC in 1996-7, ostensibly carried out with a view to closing refugee camps which had become bases for hostile attacks on Rwanda. Such crimes against humanity were alleged to have included activities that could, if fully investigated and confirmed under more stringent evidential requirements, constitute acts of genocide. The impact of the report, and perhaps even more so of the

28 N. McMillan, '"Our" Shame: International Responsibility for the Rwandan Genocide', *The Australian Feminist Law Journal*, Vol. 28, 2008, p. 3-29.

numerous leaks of the draft report, was profound. President Paul Kagame made a speech to the General Assembly of the UN in which he condemned the draft report, protesting that:

> 'it has become clear that the UN has evolved into a two-tier organization, reflecting a world that seems to be divided into two major categories: one with inherent laudable values, rights and liberties, and another that needs to be taught and coached on these values.'[29]

Foreign Minister Louise Mushikiwabo rubbished the report as 'flawed and dangerous from start to finish', 'a moral and intellectual failure as well as an insult to history', and 'a threat to regional stability'[30] and threatened to withdraw Rwandan troops from their roles in UN international peace-keeping missions, including in the Sudan where the majority of the UN force and the force commander were Rwandese. Further developments in the shape of an International Tribunal to investigate further the issues raised, or recommendations for criminal prosecutions through the ICC or some *ad-hoc* process are to be expected (although note there that Rwanda is not a signatory to governing protocols of the ICC and thus not subject to its jurisdiction).

While any state might be expected to react angrily to allegations that its forces had been involved in crimes against humanity up to and including genocide, the allegations (and the reason why the foreign minister could refer to the report as an 'insult to history') were particularly galling and worrying to the Rwandan government in that its own version of history is that it managed to stop a genocide when the international community stood idly by, and that, furthermore, it was forced into its excursions into the DRC because of the inactivity of the UN to protect Rwanda from further aggression from genocidal forces even in the wake of all that happened in 1994. The international prestige of the Rwandan government, and the internal legitimacy of its governance has relied heavily on this version of events, in the face of periodic but persistent claims (and the power interests here are clear) that the situation in Rwanda in 1994 was not as black and white as it has been presented, and that, in fact, could more accurately be portrayed as a situation of mass civil strife with random atrocities on all sides and, to the extent that there was planning of genocide, that what occurred was a 'double genocide' of fanatical extremist Hutus against Tutsi, but also of RPA Tutsi military against Hutu civilians. The allegation of potential acts of genocide in the Congo therefore has a much deeper resonance with internal issues of legitimacy in Rwanda itself.

29 Speech to the General Assembly, 24 September 2010.

30 Quoted in C. McGreal, 'Delayed UN Report Links Rwanda to Congo Genocide', *Guardian*, 1 October 2010.

These issues of legitimate governance are particularly sensitive for the Rwandan government because of the policies that it has put in place to reconstruct the country in the aftermath of the genocide. The policy of 'National Unity and Reconciliation' put in place in 1999 and confirmed by the Rwandan constitution in 2003 in effect delegitimizes (and this has been instituted into various legal measures against 'divisionism') the idea of ethnic identity in favour of the strong promotion of national identity, predicated on the promotion of an accordant national historical narrative of relatively benign pre-colonial conditions that were corrupted and racialized by colonial intervention to the extent that the conditions for genocide were sown years in advance and subsequently aggravated by various extreme material conditions on the ground; unemployment, poverty, mis-governance, malign foreign interventions.[31] The issue of the framing of the historical narrative of the most recent UN report is then also an issue, in that it fails to acknowledge what the Rwandan government has promoted as its core story of responsibility; that of the colonial powers, chief amongst which form the core membership of the UN Security Council. In adopting such a strong historical narrative the Rwandan government has drawn the implication that the narrative of the future must be equally strictly controlled, hence the authoritarian attitudes towards what are regarded as 'revisionist' tendencies, chiefly either a questioning of the core story of the genocide, which, while attaching immediate responsibility to Hutu genocidaires, does contain the mitigating elements for the Rwandan population as a whole of attaching overall historical responsibility to colonial powers (both in terms of immiseration of Rwanda and of the inculcation of destructive oppositional identity patterns along a 'divide and rule' axis, both sides of which were subjugated to dominant white colonial power). The categories of Hutu and Tutsi are, in current legislation, abolished, not just as a matter of formal identification through state bodies, but also as a matter of public discourse and political representation, to the extent that any such public or political discourse might be legally judged to have 'divisionist' effect and to result in criminal prosecution and stiff penalties.[32] In practical terms, it is often alleged, what this means is that an ostensibly democratic government is in fact an elite clientelist Tutsi authoritarian plutocracy, centred around the charismatic President Paul Kagame, leader of the invading Tutsi forces into Rwanda at the time of the genocide and since then two-term President, on the most recent occasion ostensibly elected with over 90% of the popular vote – a noted and active proponent of this anti-government theory is Paul Rusesabagina, hero of the popular fact-based film 'Hotel Rwanda'.[33] The shield that the Rwandan government uses against such

31 S. Buckley-Zistel, 'Nation, Narration, Unification? The Politics of History Teaching After the Rwandan Genocide', *Journal of Genocide Research*, Vol. 11, No. 1, 2009, p. 31-53.

32 E. Zorbas, 'What Does Reconciliation After Genocide Mean? Public Transcripts and Hidden Transcripts in Post-Genocide Rwanda', *Journal of Genocide Research*, Vol. 11, No. 1, 2009, p. 127-147.

33 I am grateful to Nesam McMillan for pointing out the irony that both Kagame and Rusesabagina are feted as heroes in the West, with little or no acknowledgement of their incompatible historical and political analyses and visions of the future.

attacks is the moral authority it has garnered through its having stopped the 1994 genocide, and the idea that such measures which may seem to have an authoritarian tang of suppressing freedom of thought and expression, are in fact entirely necessary as an accelerated programme of re-education that is up against the clock of potential re-lapse back into an available, deep-rooted through colonial imposition, pattern of ethnic division, mutual hatred and violence. The idea that they were themselves responsible for genocide calls all this structure of legitimation into question, melts it down into a relativist 'two sides to every story' quagmire. That is no basis on which to build a future.

The institutional structures which have been set up in Rwanda to counter the potential of a relapse into what it would regard as negative and incorrect understanding of the genocide both in its immediate operation and in its historical (determining) context and which are most generalized in the country, are the *gacaca* legal process and the *ingando* re-education process. Each of these processes is promoted as having an antecedent in the pre-colonial history of Rwanda. The former is a community legal process adjudicated by trained local personnel who take the role of the 'elders' in more traditional practice and who pass judgement on the less serious cases in relation to genocide, passing sentence that may run to incarceration but which may also be limited to or include reparation or community or victim oriented work.[34] The focus is not alone on the passing of judgement, but on the opening up of a public forum for the expression of public accounts of what happened, and of instituting a space where there is a sense of community involvement in the provision of justice and therefore of opening a space for a shared reconciliation. The degree to which this functions efficiently is highly contested, and there are obvious plausible difficulties even from a theoretical point of view in that many victims are dead and so there may be few available witnesses to particular events, the witnesses may feel intimidated from speaking, opportunists might take the chance to accuse innocent people with a view to gaining some unwarranted revenge or personal advantage and so forth.[35] Nevertheless, the attempt is to create this process as a site for reconciliation through general expression and coming to terms with truth as personal testimony as well as with the truth of the eventual result. *Ingando* is a mass re-education process, originally conceived as a tool specifically for former combatants and released prisoners (of whom at one stage there were well over 100,000 imprisoned in relation to genocide crimes) but which has been broadened into a much more comprehensive civics programme for genocide survivors, community leaders, university students, women's groups and youth groups. Topics are covered under

34 P. Clark, *The Gacaca Courts, Post-Genocide Justice and Reconciliation in Rwanda*, Cambridge University Press, Cambridge 2010; D. Temple-Raston, *Justice on the Grass*, Free Press, New York 2005.

35 Clark 2010; Temple-Raston 2005; Buckley-Zistel 2009; Zorbas 2009.

five central themes: analysis of Rwanda's problems; history of Rwanda; political and socioeconomic issues in Rwanda; Africa, rights, obligations and duties; leadership.

What is evident in the two institutions described briefly above is that there is a coherent promulgation of the core narrative of the fundamental danger of ethnic divisionism, the roots of such divisionism in the colonial period, and the remedy for such divisionism in the recovery of a more pure pre-colonial period of community relative harmony which can be brought up to date and used to invigorate a sense of common Rwandan identity. The contrast with the implicit and sometimes explicit understandings which ground the ICTR process is very distinct. For the ICTR the route to reconciliation is to transform collective political responsibility into individual criminal responsibility. For the Rwandan government there is no question but that there was collective political responsibility and mass participation. However, the roots of this political responsibility are located in a perverse Rwandan sociality that itself was the result of the colonial period. The prosecution and conviction of those considered most responsible in the sense of having positions of leadership and responsibility or having participated actively in murder is a matter of justice and not particularly related to reconciliation. The contemporarily innovative but historically based community restorative and mass education programmes of *gacaca* and *ingando* are designed to construct and promote a strong national narrative, a shared sense of history, a plausible responsible 'Other' that displaces the potential re-emergence of Tutsi-Hutu rivalry and conflict and a sense of shared future on the basis of common understanding of the past.

This programme of reconciliation is itself situated within a wider social project of economic development along the pattern of standard indices of development; health, education, infrastructural development, sanitation, transport, good governance. In 2000 the Rwandan government released its 'Vision 2020' document, including a foreword by President Kagame in which he stated:

> The Vision 2020 is a reflection of our aspiration and determination as Rwandans, to construct a united, democratic and inclusive Rwandan identity, after so many years of authoritarian and exclusivist dispensation. We aim, through this Vision, to transform our country into a middle- income nation in which Rwandans are healthier, educated and generally more prosperous. The Rwanda we seek is one that is united and competitive both regionally and globally.
> To achieve this, the Vision 2020 identifies six interwoven pillars, including good governance and efficient State, skilled human capital, vibrant private sector, world-class physical infrastructure and modern agriculture and livestock, all geared towards national, regional and global markets.

This document has been followed up by series of detailed policy documents and programmes which pursue the market based development principles laid out in Vision 2020, the latest of which is the 'Economic Development and Poverty Reduction Strategy 2008-2012' document of 2007 which charts the progress up to that point and lays out the pathway for projected future development. This is not the time and place for an assessment of the plausibility of the projections in this and similar documents, but simply an occasion to remark that the Rwandan government explicitly models Rwandan development on 'Asian Tiger' economic development and seeks the transformation of the Rwandan economy from a subsistence agrarian economy to a 'knowledge-based' 'middle-income' economy by the year 2020. It recognizes the absolute necessity of such development given that the population is projected to double from eight to sixteen million people by then, and given that the lack of resources has been acknowledged as a co-factor in the development of the genocide. In other words, the Rwandan government seems clear-eyed about the very serious social trouble that lies ahead if there is not sufficient economic development. The very clear sub-text to many documents such as the two mentioned is that reconciliatory practices have to be read in the context of this most basic of objectives, hence the extremely hard line on what might be regarded as 'divisionist' in the sense of creating obstacles to a unified population working to progress economically with a shared understanding of past and potential (brighter) future.

CONCLUSION

> The International Criminal Tribunal for Rwanda delivered the first ever judgment on the crime of genocide by an international court. This judgment is a testament to our collective determination to confront the heinous crime of genocide in a way that we never have before. I am sure that I speak for the entire international community when I express the hope that this judgment will contribute to the long term process of national reconciliation in Rwanda. For there can be no healing without peace; there can be no peace without justice; and there can be no justice without respect for human rights and the rule of law.
>
> Kofi Annan, preamble message to ICTR document, *Challenging Impunity*

The ICTR, which began operating in 1997, is still on-going, although subsequent events elsewhere guarantee that it has a low profile in global news coverage. To date forty nine people have been tried to completion at first instance, with forty one of those having been found guilty of crimes of genocide and/or crimes against humanity, of whom nine are currently pursuing appeals. Eight people have been acquitted. Twenty cases are currently in progress and two people are detained awaiting trial. Ten named accused are still at large.[36] A 'completion strategy' for the Tribunal has been finalized, which envisages the possible end of trials in Arusha by the end of 2011, and the subsequent timely completion of any appeals processes (heard in The Hague). This is undoubtedly a rather slender tally of results in relation to an event of genocide wherein the estimates as to those killed generally vary between half a million to one million people. The legitimation of such a paucity of trials, as discussed above, is that only those considered *prima facie* most responsible and who have escaped the jurisdiction of Rwanda are indicted at the ICTR, and that the ICTR must be understood as complementary to the domestic Rwandan justice system in producing an adequate overall justice process. This essay has focused on the somewhat confusing further attempts to go beyond the legitimation of the ICTR on the grounds of justice considerations in relation to heinous crimes and further legitimation on the grounds of a contribution to an undoubtedly desirable outcome, some form of 'reconciliation' for Rwanda itself, with all due caution to the flexibility of such a concept. The claims as to this further contribution to Rwandan reconciliation rest, as discussed above, on a notion of the symbolic power of the law in a transitional context to create reconciliation by virtue of the repeated annunciation of the same, a form of exemplary justice, and a recognition that the legal process is part of a larger social imperative. However, as this essay has gone on to detail, the symbolic power of law in this context is reliant on its ability to convert mass political responsibility into individual criminal responsibility. This is a conversion process which is directly counter to the reconciliation paradigm which operates inside Rwanda itself, where the story is of mass political responsibility where ultimately such responsibility comes to rest with the structuring force of colonial relations. The incapacity of the legal forum to attend to wider notions than individual criminal intent serves as an insulation from consideration as pernicious the very features on which the Rwandan government focuses its attention as the root of the genocide.

Putting this argument bluntly, it is that the legal institution itself, whatever the outcome of the trials, displays, reproduces and rests on a structure of ideas, a political form, that is closely related to the structure of the long term colonial relations between Rwanda and the colonizing Western powers and which persists in the post-genocide period. In this reading the attitude displayed by Judge Laity Kama in the quotation on page 106-107 above is approved to the extent that the court is recognized as not principally a legal institution, but rather an exhibition of a deep political structure which happens to take the form of a court, although the political quality of the court is read in much more negative fashion than the interpretation offered by the judge. The political structure is that which seems to

36 Accurate as of 1 June 2011. For up-to-date information see <www.unictr.org/Cases>.

be given as a gift or paid as a debt due, actually operates as a gift to self. Specifically in relation to the ICTR, the gift of the international community to the Rwanda people in recognition of their loss and its own inability to act sooner, is the gift of a kind of mirror within which the West finds its own returned humanity. The ICTR acts as 'the conscience of the international community'.[37] It did not act in time to stop the genocide but has the ability to destroy the impunity of the responsible and so to contribute to reconciliation. Except that the structures of meaning within which it wants to frame the genocide in order to make this gift, have the effect of directly countering the basic narrative of responsibility on which the Rwandan government has based its entire programme of reconciliation. Reconciliation for Rwanda is nominally a principal goal of the ICTR, but is structurally secondary to the West's reconciliation with its own sense of itself as benign, a sense of self which allows to emerge intact an idea of genocide, of the Rwandan genocide, as having its roots in the evil conduct of a limited cohort of Rwandan citizens. Whatever the questions which hang over the good faith and good conduct of the Rwandan government in regards the issue of reconciliation, it is important that the structural inadequacies of the UN justice response through the ICTR should not be allowed to be hidden by the idea that domestic criminal processes can be translated onto a transnational sphere and somehow become in politics but not of it. This clumsy translation can only function to let the International Community see what it wants to see, itself staring back in pious self-satisfaction.

37 Page 102 above.

Torture and Systems Theory[1]

Costas Douzinas

A Ticking Bomb?

One can only admire Niklas Luhmann's prescience. Many years before 9/11, an eon before Abu Ghraib, Guantanamo Bay and 'extraordinary renditions' became household names, to open an essay on 'indispensable values' with a discussion of the 'ticking bomb' hypothesis is quite prophetic.[2] Would one torture a terrorist suspect who may have knowledge about the whereabouts of a bomb about to go off and kill '10, 100, 1000' innocents? Would the answer change if the immediate family of the hesitating torturer was involved or if the "terrorists have an atom bomb?"[3] Luhmann bravely and prophetically anticipates some of the proposals we have been hearing recently. Torture can be allowed if regulated and supervised by "internationally supervised courts, closed-circuit observation of the scene in Geneva or Luxemburg, long-distance control through telecommunications, displacement of the just/unjust distinction to the victim's option of being either hero or traitor".[4] Luhmann adds without much explanation that these solutions are not satisfactory (morally, one assumes) but they become inevitable if one realizes that "doing nothing" would sacrifice "innocent-bystanders to the fanaticism of terrorists".

This is as strong an opening in an essay on norms and values you are likely to come across. The choice of example to illustrate the malleability of 'indispensable norms' is brave but troubling. Indeed, torture in one of the few acts that the post-WWII Western consensus found totally abhorrent. Torture was seen as part of a past that the West had left behind for good. A number of international treaties explicitly banned torture and a whole convention was dedicated to the abolition of the practice. In Europe at least torture seemed a relic fit for the history seminar. Article 3 of the European Convention on Human Rights not only bans "torture, inhuman and degrading treatment" but also makes the prohibition

---

1 This article is reprinted with permission of the publisher. The article was published in: Willam Rasch (ed.), '"Tragic Choices". Luhmann on Law and States of Exception', *Soziale Systeme* 14 (2008), p. 110-125, Stuttgart: Lucius & Lucius.

2 N. Luhmann, 'Are There Still Indispensable Norms in Our Society', *Soziale Systeme*, Vol. 14, No. 1, 2008a, p. 18-37.

3 *Id.*, p. 3, 4.

4 *Id.*, p. 26.

absolute, disallowing its suspension even in times of war or emergency "threatening the life of the nation" (Art. 15).

It was understood, of course, that in extreme cases, certain exceptions might be necessary. The Israeli Supreme Court for example had allowed, in *Hamdan*,[5] the internal security forces to apply "moderate physical pressure" during the interrogation of suspects. This blanket authorization, which was condemned by the UN Committee on Torture, was repealed in 1999 when widespread abuses against Palestinians were uncovered by human rights organizations.[6] Indeed, this juridical reversal demonstrates the slipperiness of the legal slope. Mild torture in extreme cases of a 'ticking time bomb' (in *Hamdan*, the torture victim, according to the court "possesse[d] extremely vital information, the immediate procurement of which would prevent an awful disaster, would save human lives, and would prevent very serious terrorist attacks") can easily mutate into extreme torture techniques widely applied. No information leading to the avoidance of disaster was discovered by the torture of Hamdan.

Luhman's article was written in 1993.[7] Yet it comes straight out of current debates. In the last few years, the hypothesis has been a mainstay of newspaper commentators, moral philosophy seminars and conferences on applied ethics, one of the main ways through which professional moralists have come to discuss the morality and legality of torture in the 'war on terror' and not only. Lawyers, such as Alan Dershowitz and liberal commentators, including Michael Ignatieff and Bruce Ackerman, are prepared to enter into debate about the morality and legitimacy of torture and to develop detailed ways of legalizing it through 'torture warrants', 'sunset clauses' and judicial supervisory regimes.[8] These procedures introduce an element of judicial or other external supervision and therefore make the exercise of torture 'limited' and 'lawful'.

We can understand the 'ticking bomb' scenario as a game played in University seminar rooms. As every law professor knows, a good 'problem question' on an exam paper should be able to compel the 'right' answer. We have no evidence that information about ticking bombs was ever acquired by torture, including in Israel. The trick is that we have to say yes or no to an unreal situation that never happens. The answer appears to be the outcome of moral deliberation, reasoned argumentation and choice as befits the seminar room; but

5 *Hamdan et al*, HCJ 8049/96.

6 *Public Committee against Torture in Israel et al*, HCJ 5100/94 et al.

7 N. Luhmann, *Gibt es in unserer Gesellschaft noch unverzichtbare Normen?*, C.F. Müller, Heidelberg 1993.

8 A. Dershowitz, *Why Terrorism Works*, Yale University Press, New Haven 2002; M. Ignatieff, *The Lesser Evil*, Edinburgh University Press, Edinburgh 2004; Bruce Ackerman, *Before the Next Attack*, Yale University Press, New Haven 2006.

it would take a moral absolutist of heroic proportions to argue anything other than 'yes'. The appearance of freedom is as false as that which accompanies, according to Luhmann, the "supply-society leaving the individual with meaningless decisions".[9] The choice is forced; the scenario is constructed in such a way as to make torture pre-emptively justified. But this undergraduate game has dire consequences. It lowers the threshold of acceptability of torture and makes it a topic apt for civilized conversation and moralistic disputation. One of the few moral certainties of our civilization is on the retreat.

Why should Luhmann choose such a problematic example to illustrate his argument about 'indispensable norms' aka human rights? One obvious answer is that the ban on torture is precisely the most 'indispensable' of norms and therefore the best test case for his critique of the idea. But it also serves the wider purpose of bringing together a number of strands in the history of ideas, legal history and jurisprudence, which help illustrate his own systems theory. Let us briefly follow some of these steps.

INDISPENSABLE NORMS OR FUNDAMENTAL RIGHTS?

Luhmann's concern, typical of a German educated in law, is with 'indispensable norms' (constitutional rules for example), the values lying behind them (human dignity, freedom or equality) and the permissible and necessary balancing ('tragic choices') when these norms/values clash amongst themselves or with other public policies. Luhmann's warnings against the triumphalist excesses of the values, 'indispensable norms' and rights brigade is extremely timely. His indictment is long and compelling.

Values are essential for political manifestoes and constitutional court decisions because they are presented as self-evident and self-evidently good. One is for peace, freedom and humanity and not for war, slavery and the inhuman. While values have no need for justification, they can justify any number of policies. Their political usefulness is therefore great but their philosophical value limited. Their incontrovertible 'goodness' serves to stop reflection about their nature or import. The great and proliferating number of values, their abstraction and vagueness mean that while they are endemically in conflict, they offer no intrinsic advice about its resolution. Values allegedly help make decisions indisputable; in reality, they are of no use in deciding specific issues. As a result, value conflicts are treated at the level of the individual case which, under-determined by grand principle, operates in a situational and casuistic context in conditions of 'self-generated uncertainty'. Values, supposedly necessary for decisions, "bring this necessity into the form of contingency".[10]

9 N. Luhmann, 'Beyond Barbarism', *Soziale Systeme*, Vol. 14, No. 1, 2008b, p. 38-46.
10 Luhmann 2008a, p. 20.

One possible response to the problem of undecidability would be, according to Luhmann, to take the legal route: concentrate on the individual case, follow the elaborate procedures and protocols the law has developed for resolving conflicts and remember that a decision must be made. Luhmann mentions certain legal techniques for resolving normative clashes which resemble our own 'presumptions in interpretation'.[11] Instead of constructing ever more complete and hierarchical lists of values, with their foundational, basic or ground norms (an exercise that will inevitably fail), a more appropriate strategy would move "in the direction of precedents, typical of the common law, coupled with a correspondingly complex demand for proficiency in decision-making and less conceptual argumentation".[12] The civil law of fundamental values and basic norms should try to approximate the common law model.

The relationship between civil and common law, this 'peculiarity of the English' according to Max Weber, is too complex and evolving to be discussed here in any detail. To test the advice in our area of immediate interest let us turn briefly to the case-law that comes closest to the 'conflict of values': human rights. By combining high value and legal technique, rights-based adjudication may be the answer to the problems under-determined values and indispensable norms create but cannot resolve.

If we turn to the Anglo-American discourse of rights, the German rhetorical excess of values is repeated and even exceeded. For the rights fanatics, rights trump policies, give right and certain answers to hard cases, they unbelievably enjoy 'objectivity' and promote the values of dignity, autonomy and equality. We live in the age of rights, we are told. The North and the South, left and right, state and church, globalizing imperialists and anti-globalization protesters, first world liberals and third world revolutionaries, they all use the language of rights. In our age of 'posts', where the 'end of history' alongside modernity, class, ideology and something called 'the human' has been proclaimed (rather hastily; Fukuyama, its celebrated proposer, has recently admitted that reports of the death of history have been premature) rights is the last universal vocation, the only institution that allegedly enjoys catholic approval. Rights are the ideology after the death of ideologies, the only

11 Such presumptions assisting judicial interpretation when more than one meanings can be attributed to a statutory provision include the following: when two statutes are in conflict Parliament must be presumed to have repealed the earlier Act (the so-called 'repeal by implication'); Parliament must be presumed not to wish to violate international legal obligations; or, the use in an Act of Parliament of the masculine pronoun 'he' must be presumed to include the feminine 'she', unless clearly indicated to the contrary. There are many such presumptions, some of which contradict each other. As is obvious by the examples given, their assistance in deciding cases involving conflict of values is strictly limited.

12 Luhmann 2008a, p. 21

ideology or 'idolatry' in town, according to Michael Ignatieff, its apologist in chief.[13] But can rights give 'right answers' to the hard choices of our day and replace the difficulties of values and norms?

The jurisprudence of human rights shares the problems Luhmann identifies in the field of fundamental norms and values. Human rights provisions more than all other law are profoundly ambiguous and must be interpreted in complex political and legal situations. Human rights are the one area in which the realist and critical legal claims have been almost universally confirmed.[14] In brief summary, the critics argue that human rights provisions are indeterminate; that they are always subjected to wide and similarly indeterminate restrictions;[15] that rights are inescapably involved in conflicts with other rights (freedom against security, free speech and press against privacy) or with the same rights of others; that their open-ended language means that they acquire meaning and effects in acts of interpretation and application, in which all kinds of non-principled considerations are involved; finally, that the context of application is much more important than the text of the provisions.

The claim, for example, in Article 2 of the European Convention on Human Rights that "everyone has a right to life" gives no answer whatsoever to questions about the legitimacy of abortion, euthanasia or the use of lethal force by the military against civilians and the security services against presumed terrorist threats.[16] Human rights provisions do not wear their meaning on the sleeve of the relevant treaty clause. Whether, for example, events

13 I use the term ideology here in its strict Althusserian definition, as the 'imaginary way in which people relate to their real conditions of existence'. L. Althusser, 'Ideology and the State', *in* L. Althusser, *Lenin and Philosophy and Other Essays* (trans. B. Brewster), Monthly Review Press, London/New York 1971, p. 127-181.

14 Duncan Kennedy, *A Critique of Adjudication,* Harvard University Press, Cambridge (Mass.) 1977), p. 304-309; M. Koskenniemi, 'The Effects of Rights on Political Culture', *in* Philip Alston, *et al* (eds.), *The European Union and Human Rights,* Oxford University Press, Oxford 1999, p. 99-116; David Kennedy, 'The International Human Rights Movement. Part of the Problem?', *European Human Rights Law Review,* Vol. 3, 2001, p. 245-267.

15 The right to freedom of expression in Article 10 ECHR is subjected to such "formalities, conditions, restrictions or penalties as are prescribed by law and are necessary in a democratic society in the interests of national security, territorial integrity or public safety, for the prevention of disorder or crime, for the protection of health or morals, for the protection of the reputation of the rights of others, for preventing the disclosure of information received in confidence, or for maintaining the impartiality of the judiciary". A cynical soul might observe that every possible restriction on speech can be justified under this litany of exceptions.

16 In a number of cases the European Court has stated that states retain a 'margin of appreciation' (in other words discretion) in deciding their obligations under the Convention (*Handyside v. UK*, Series A, ECHR, No 24, Judgment of 7 December 1976); that "even if one assumes that Article 2 protects the unborn life, the rights and interests involved have been weighed against each other in a reasonable way" (*Open Door Counselling Ltd v. Ireland,* ECHR, Series A, No 246, Judgment of 29 October 1992); that "the value of life to be protected can and must be weighed against other rights of the person in question" (*McCann and others v. UK*, ECHR, Series A, No 324, Judgment of 27 September 1995).

in Rwanda amounted to genocide (according to the Security Council they did not) or, whether the persecution of Albanians in Kosovo to a 'humanitarian catastrophe' (no according to the Security Council, yes according to NATO) is not answered by treaties and conventions but by the politicians, diplomats or judges interpreting them in the context of state interests. As an international lawyer put it "any substantive issue could be labelled as a human rights violation".[17] If one combines this recognition with law's intrinsic indeterminacy, which means that "the legal argument inexorably and quite predictably, allows the defence of whatever position",[18] it becomes clear that the trust put on lawyers' ability to resolve conflict through the tool of human rights is seriously misplaced.

Replacing values with rights and entrusting decision-making in hard cases to lawyers does not solve the problems Luhmann rightly identifies. Indeed, if that was the case, if technical solutions at the individual level could respond to the ills of domination and exploitation, violence, war and the end of history would be nigh. Does the ubiquity and inflation of rights discourse mean that we have transcended conflicts of interests and the clash of ideas? A cursory perusal of the daily news indicates not. Luhmann agrees; his diagnosis of the world order is even more accurate today than at the time of the writing. Economic development takes place through the exclusion of masses of people; democracy is imposed through despotism and invasion; rights are guaranteed through dissent and resistance.[19] He is right to dismiss the cosmopolitan solutions of Kant (universal rights guaranteed by world federation) and Habermas (rights legislated through deliberative democratic procedures) for being naive and ignorant of the law.[20] Reason, uncoerced communication, basic values or fundamental rights cannot pacify conflict or remedy massive injustice. Legal technique cannot cure deep and widening domestic and international rifts. Freedom is far too general a concept with many antagonistic conceptions (consider the irreconcilable interpretations held by the American government and the insurgents in Iraq) and equality (before the law) far too formal to guarantee anything more than the most generic recognition of personhood. Luhmann is absolutely right in his critique of values although he should not expect much better from the jurisprudence of rights. As he emphasizes, the right not to be tortured does not mean just that – people are tortured all the time. The boasting, rationalization and bad conscience of the values enthusiasts have been often repeated by the human rights brigade.

17 K. Tomasevski, *Responding to Human Rights Violations: 1946-1999*, Martinus Nijhoff, The Hague 2000, p. 405.

18 M. Koskenniemi, 'Letter to the Editors of the Symposium', 93/2 *American Journal of International Law*, Vol. 92-3, No. 2, 1999, p. 351, 354.

19 Luhmann 2008a, p. 24.

20 C. Douzinas, *Human Rights and Empire: The Political Philosophy of Cosmopolitanism*, Routledge-Cavendish, London 2007, Chapter 7.

Rights and Systems Theory

What is the import and function of rights according to systems theory? For Luhmann, rights offer a programme for the 'unfolding of paradoxes'. In this they resemble values: the persistent contingency of what is presented as necessary ironically makes "the indispensability of norms – the autopoiesis of the system".[21] Rights give objective validity to subjective rights, they recognize individuality socially and make "the individual's unsociability the basis for regulating the legal system of society".[22] This is a rather modest account with one major advantage: it does not confuse what the Europeans call 'subjective rights' with 'fundamental' or human rights. Subjective rights were created by the early modern legal system. The rise of the legal form of rights is a clear indication of the emergence of capitalism and its close companion, individualism. Marx famously said that commodities cannot go to the market and sell themselves, the indispensable action of capitalism. They must be taken there by people (legal subjects) exercising rights. Rights and legal persons claiming them are the logical prerequisites and outcomes of a market economy and a positive legal system which, to meet capitalist needs, regulates social life by means of general precepts. Rights follow rules, but there is nothing glorious or exalted about them. They are the indispensable building blocks of a socio-economic system based on the market and of a legal system that facilitates it. In Luhmann's felicitous phrase, rights turn 'the individual's unsociability' into the basis of the social bond.

Human rights are different. As a positive legal institution, they are a sub-category of rights, protecting certain important claims, commonly against state powers. Luhmann emphasizes the paradoxical nature of rights and distinguishes them from human rights.[23] His followers who have written more extensively about rights tend to be more lyrical (and less realistic. I am not qualified to judge whether they remain faithful to the canon).[24] According to Gert Verschraegen, human rights enable and legitimize free choice, strengthen the dominant characteristics of free inclusion and social mobility and constitute the unnoticed and elementary condition for participation in modern society. While the pre-modern individual was subjected to total social inclusion, the functionally differentiated modernity makes social inclusion heterogeneous. Rights are a compensation for the loss of total inclusion and fixed social position. People have now access to various systems such as education, the economy, law, politics etc. which allow them to follow their personal preferences and

21 Luhmann, 2008a, p. 22.

22 *Id.*, p. 22.

23 *Id.*, p. 22.

24 G. Verschraegen, 'Systems Theory and the Paradox of Human Rights', *in* M. King & Ch. Thornhill (Eds.), *Luhmann on Law and Politics,* Hart, Oxford 2006, p. 101-127. G. Teubner, 'Human Rights Violations and Private Actors', *Modern Law Review*, Vol. 69, 2006, p. 327-346.

free them from moral precepts. In this sense, human rights protect both individual spheres of influence and the differentiation between different systems by imposing a self-limitation on the political system.[25]

The slide from rights to human rights is evident. The theory of the disciples becomes an example of the ills the master identifies in the rhetoric of indispensable norms. How can we resist this over-inflation of rights discourse? If human rights are given to people on account of their humanity and not of membership of narrower groups such as citizenship, ethnicity or class, we may conclude that human rights do not exist: those who have only humanity to protect them, the 'unlawful combatants' of Guatanamo Bay, the migrants who drown in the Mediterranean or get blown up in the minefields of the Greco-Turkish border trying to get to the 'promised land' of Europe, the 'one use humans' of the refugee camps, all these *homines sacri* of the new world order have no 'human' rights and therefore no humanity. Or, it may make us realize that rights do not belong to humans or "protect the freedom and interest of individuals" as Verschraegen claims;[26] rather rights construct our 'humanity' as a receding horizon, as a humanity that is always still to come.

Either way, the claim that the purpose of rights is to protect the differentiation of functional systems is not convincing. Natural and human rights have been won through struggles and campaigns for their recognition or expansion. I have not come across yet any protest banners demanding that 'system differentiation' be protected. This is not a facetious point. The attempt to turn rights into institutions policing the borders of systems necessarily falls into the most ahistorical type of naturalism. "Constitutional and human rights are not a creation of the law", argues Verschraegen, "but are pre-legal as a social institution, as a self-protecting device of society".[27] This is eighteenth century naturalism of the most naïve kind craving for pre-legal and pre-social institutions but without the attendant social contracts. One should be reminded however that without the struggles of dissidents, rebels and revolutionaries none of these institutions would have arisen.

Luhmann takes a different tack in his article. He believes that the use of human rights should be restricted to the worst cases of injury to dignity and atrocity and that the tendency to turn them into a rule-book for global social work should be resisted. The juxtaposition of human dignity with social work is troubling. It harks back to the old debate about negative and positive freedom and the Cold War argument that social and economic rights are not proper rights because, unlike civil and political rights, they are not justiciable

25 Verschraegen 2006, p. 105, 106, 110, 113-115.
26 *Id.*, p. 107.
27 *Id.*, p. 103.

(legally enforceable) and potentially violate individual freedom. Warming to this theme, Luhmann disparagingly and distastefully adds that human rights are the "foundation for poorer countries' demands on richer countries".[28] To avoid this expansionist use of human rights by the poor to seek redress for past injustices, Luhmann proposes that the language of rights should be replaced by that of human duties. This is clearly a Sisyphean task for a legal system based on the principle of the rights of the 'unsociable individual'. Indeed a right-based legal system cannot support independent duties and responsibilities; the only duties it understands are those imposed on third parties as a result of the operation of rights. And this is why Luhmann bizarrely argues that the most important 'human' duty is that of states to provide order, if need be by torturing its enemies.

At this point, the critical legal position has to abandon the fellow-travelling with systems theory. We have covered quite a lot of common ground at the level of description or observation. But when Luhmann moves to the normative position (as all trained lawyers are likely to do even when they protest their prescriptive agnosticism), the conservative nature of systems theory emerges clearly.[29] If antagonistic values, conflicting norms and contradictory concepts clash and cannot be synthesized or made to cohere at the level of the individual decision, Luhmann's advice is to return to legal technique. This is because the law has historically exhibited the ability to co-opt and integrate counter-principles and antinomian practices and has promoted its autonomy and closure in this manner. The example offered is the recognition, since Rome, that the law can be violated for 'reasons of state', a state of exception or emergency can be declared and an 'eminent domain' created in order to serve supreme public ends (*salus populi*). Luhmann proposes the extensive adoption of this technique as an antidote to the exaggerated rhetoric of values and human rights. The unlawful can be legalized, the outside domesticated, if it is imported into the law and regulated. Torture, by definition illegal and abhorrent, can become lawful, if it is supervized or certain procedures are followed. This approach brings the exception or negation of law into the legal system and allows its bipolar coding of lawful/unlawful to reveal fully its paradoxical nature.

28 Luhmann 2008a, p. 27.

29 Chris Thornhill after a careful reading of Luhmann's political theory finds its implications problematic. These include an "attachment to nineteenth century models of administrative positivism and limited state-legalism" and the "obvious appeal of some of his ideas to quite standard versions of reactionary theory (especially neo-liberalism)", Thornhill, 'Luhman's Political Theory', *in* M. King and C. Thornhill (Eds.), *Luhman on Law and Politics*, Hart, Oxford 2006, p. 99.

According to Giorgio Agamben and much contemporary critical theory, the legalization of the unlawful and the wholesale normalization of the exception have happened already.[30] As Walter Benjamin put it starkly, *a propos* of the Third Reich, the state of exception has become permanent.[31] Luhmann does not refer to Carl Schmitt and his famous definition of the Sovereign as he who can suspend the law in order to save it.[32] Giorgio Agamben's extensive programme of research around the figure of the Sovereign and the state of exception has shown that this suspension of the law is a permanent characteristic of Western polities: it grounds politics on the programmatic exclusion of certain people (the *homines sacri*) from the domain of legal protection. Order is based on exclusion; meaningful life on meaningless existence. It is not so much that the law adopts the exception in order to achieve functional differentiation; rather the law is based on this originary exception.

We can now understand the importance of the 'ticking bomb' scenario. Its narrative construction leads inexorably to the justification of torture. Its inevitable conclusion meets the realism of the observational technique and deconstructs the idealistic rhetoric of the 'indispensable norms' brigade. But it does much more. It introduces the paradoxical nature of decision-making (system theory's mainstay) and places the theoretical premium not on the bodily integrity of people (who, in systems theory, are the 'environment' of the functional systems) but on the integrity of the systems themselves for which the maintenance of order is supreme necessity ("the state organization [...] first and foremost [is] the international address for questions about the provision of order").[33] Human rights are turned into the state's duty to protect the *ordre publique* in a *dance macabre* of paradoxicality. But there is a different kind of paradox that permeates the operation of human rights to which we now turn.

The 'Shell' of Natural Law

Luhmann's attack on the rhetoric of indispensable norms is important and timely. It is prefaced by a brief and rather clichéd review of the history of natural law from Plato to Nato. Natural law, in its various transfigurations, is presented as the main source of fundamental values. The brief history concludes with the ringing declaration that natural law is

30 G. Agamben, *Homo Sacer. Sovereing Power and Bare Life*, Stanford University Press, Stanford 1998; G. Agamben, *State of Exception*, Chicago University Press, Chicago 2005; M. Hardt & A. Negri, *Empire*, Harvard University Press, Cambridge (Mass.), 2000.

31 W. Benjamin, 'Theses on the Philosophy of History', *in* W. Benjamin, *Illuminations* (trans. H. Zohn 1968 ed.), Pimlico, London 1999, p. 238.

32 C. Schmitt, *Political Theology: Four Chapters on the Concept of Sovereignty*, MIT Press, Cambridge (Mass.) 1985, p. 46. For an excellent discussion of Schmitt's theory of sovereignty see W. Rasch, *Sovereignty and its Discontents*, Birkbeck Law Press, London 2005.

33 Luhmann 2008a, p. 28.

> an empty shell of a word, applicable in flowery phrases ... nothing results from the historically deducible meaning of natural law that could answer our question as to the validity of indispensable norms.[34]

Indeed, natural law may be an empty shell or a 'floating signifier'. It is true that the author of natural law and the content of its rules have changed considerably throughout history. Successive versions have been discredited, fallen into disrepute or disuse. Luhmann is right that none of the earlier versions could survive the change in social conditions which gave it substance and legitimacy. The purposeful cosmos of the Greeks, ordered by *dike* and implanted in the *physis* of all things animate and inanimate; the philosophical cosmopolitanism of the Cynics and the spiritual *logos spermatikos* of the Stoics could not survive the Roman positivization of *dike* into *jus* and the turning of cosmopolitanism into imperialism. Christian natural law could not survive the disenchantment of the world and the cold critical eye which invented theodicy and completed God's trial with the 'death of God'. Similarly, the ideal natural rights proclaimed in the great revolutions of the eighteenth century could not survive the final triumph of capitalism in the nineteenth and the rise of mass democracy in the twentieth. Natural rights mutated from grand statements of revolutionary fervour into the legal canons, protocols and procedures of human rights inscribed in laws, constitutions and international treaties. The positivization of natural rights repeated earlier examples: the age of rapid industrialization and colonial expansion which followed the revolutions needed strong governments, social engineered and productive populations, controlled and pliable bodies in the place of rebellious and romantic dissidents.

It is true that in all these mutations, established powers displayed a great ability to assimilate natural law to their cause. We no longer believe in a purposeful cosmos, an overarching reason, divine legislation, natural entitlements, or asocial needs and desires. It could not be otherwise. Most striking however is that despite the successive deaths of its authors, despite the repeated and inevitable rejections of every specific content, the 'empty shell' keeps coming back. The eternal return of natural law is more interesting than the passing away of every single one of its versions. In the latest mutation, international law has replaced God as the author of superior law (human rights); this source will also fade away in time. But the wide acceptance of human rights, the latest great bonanza of naturalism, tells a different story from Luhmann's dismissal of the tradition. What survives the various historical incarnations of natural law and their rejection or transcendence by later generations is precisely the 'shell' of natural law, a form, an attitude that unites its differing versions despite their widely differing content. To understand this we need to take a different approach to the history of the idea.

34 *Id.*, p. 11.

For Greek philosophy, nature (*physis*) and its law are born together in an act of resistance against traditional authority. In pre-classical Greece, law and convention, right and custom were identical; the root of all authority was the ancestral. The philosophical 'discovery' of the idea of nature brings this claim to an end. Nature is a critical concept; it must be discovered because it is occluded by a combination of convention, law and ancestral authority. By discovering nature, Plato and Aristotle departed radically from that tradition. For the classical philosophers, nature is not just the physical world, but a term of distinction, a norm or standard used to separate the work of philosophical and political thought from what obstructs or hides it, namely the combination of customary law and conventional opinion. 'Philosophy now appeals from the ancestral to the good, to that which is good intrinsically, to that which is good by nature.'[35]

Nature is philosophy's tool, its ' discovery' and elevation into an evaluative standard and weapon against convention emancipates reason from the tutelage of power and gives rise to natural right. Nature presents itself as what was hidden by culture because philosophy cannot come into existence or survive, if it submits to ancestral or conventional authority. Philosophy and nature are born against the law. To this day when knowledge and reason are subjected to authority they are called 'theology' or 'legal learning' but they cannot be the philosophy practiced by the Greeks.[36] In this sense, turning nature into norm, into the standard of right was the greatest early step of rational civilization but also a cunning trick against priests and rulers. The Sophists used nature against custom and law. In setting *physis* against *nomos* and individual opinion against tradition, they gave *physis* a normative meaning, in which "to reason" meant to "criticize".[37] Socrates and Plato, in turn, deployed nature to combat the moral relativism of the Sophists and to restore the authority of reason. Their response to the Sophist challenge was to re-establish the normative character of nature by showing that, far from contradicting law, it sets the fundamental norm of each being. This is how nature, this most cultured of concepts entered the world: as a critical idea that expresses resistance to the sclerosis of established powers and the intolerance of received opinion.

We can observe a similar process in modernity. Natural rights in the eighteenth century and human rights after Word War II were invented to protect people and arm them in their struggle against unjust power. They may have been co-opted to imperial and disciplinary projects; their positivization may have turned them into legitimation tools for socio-political arrangements and ideological weapons against those who disagree with the

35 Leo Strauss, *Natural Law and History*, Chicago University Press, Chicago 1965, p. 91.
36 *Id.*, p. 92.
37 *Id.*, p. 7-9.

West. It is true, as Luhmann insists, that natural rights have been repeatedly 'politically assimilated'. They began as a means of expressing moral and political dissent and rebellion against existing authorities "only to be appropriate [*sic*] by these very authorities as instruments for consolidating and justifying their power to promote their own partial interests".[38] But as the current expressions of the naturalist legacy they retain a distance – even if minimal – from the reality of social relations, legal rights and imperial aspirations. Natural right and its descendents enter the historical agenda directly and indirectly, disguised as religious duty, legal right or political ideology, every time people struggle "to overthrow all relations in which man is a degraded, enslaved, abandoned or despised being".[39] This was the case in the great revolutions of the eighteenth century, in the post-WWII 'never again' declarations, in popular uprisings against fascist and communist rule in the late twentieth century and every time the oppressed, exploited and dispossessed invoke them in their struggles. Human rights, whether positivized or not, belong to a long and honourable tradition of dissent, resistance and rebellion against the domination of power, the oppression of wealth and the injustice of law. They are parts of the legacy of the left.

This is what I mean by the 'shell' of natural law. In its various permutations, it has marked a distance between the naturally and socially given and the eternal aspiration for its transcendence. Natural law is one main expression of the often reasoned and always felt 'sense of injustice'. What is important about natural law is not so much its changing authors or content (today the different types of human rights) but its persisting form: the desire to resist, criticize and change the existing world for a better place. This is what Luhmann rejects by turning natural law not into a 'shell' but into a meaningless, amorphous skin.

JUSTICE AND LAW BETWEEN SYSTEMS AND DECONSTRUCTION

Human rights are full of paradoxes. Rights give objective existence to subjective entitlements. The duty-bearer who must deliver individual entitlements is the state; but it is law, the language of the state, that enforces these rights. The greatest paradox is that after their positivization, a statement of right refers both to a legal entitlement and to what a higher source (nature, morality, international law, etc.) demands. When a Chinese political dissident claims that he has the right to free speech, he is both wrong (he evidently does not under extant law) and right. His assertion is against the current state of law but this is not just a moral claim; it is a call to arms for the reform or transformation of the political and legal system. In this usage, the naturalist or moral element of human rights is an integral

38 Luhmann, 2008a, p. 10.
39 Block, op. cit. p. xxvii-xxix.

part of the whole and is in permanent tension and occasional conflict with their putative legal status.

This confounding of the real and the ideal is characteristic of human rights discourse. The very nature of rights is paradoxically both of the law and of something beyond it, call it justice if you will. Against the moral poverty of legal positivism (law and morality are totally separate) and the moral imperialism of rights fanatics (all law is moral and rational), the critical legal position makes the relationship between law, justice and force, the key of political philosophy and jurisprudence.[40] For the positivists, justice is identified fully with the law. Legality, the rule of law, the impartiality of the judiciary, the following of formal procedures, this is the essence of justice. Any contamination of law by value will compromise its ability to turn social and political conflict into manageable technical disputes about the meaning and applicability of pre-existing public rules. Morality as much as politics must be kept at a distance; indeed the main requirement of the rule of law is that all 'subjective' and relative value should be excluded from the operation of the legal system. This insulation of law from ethico-political considerations allegedly makes the exercise of power impersonal and guarantees the equal subjection of citizens and state officials to the dispassionate requirements of the rule of rules as opposed to the rule of men.

In the positivist worldview, law is technical reason, a poor remnant of the *orthos logos* and *recta ratio* of the classics. Justice on the other hand is associated with emotions and passions. To assert that a legal system is unjust, says Alf Ross, is an "emotional expression [...]. To invoke justice is the same thing as banging on the table: an emotional expression that turns one's demand into an absolute postulate".[41] Non-formal conceptions of justice are "illusions which excite the emotions by stimulating the suprarenal glands".[42] When "someone says 'that thing is unjust' what he means is that the thing is offensive to his sentiments".[43]

The similarities between this crude positivism and systems theory are remarkable. The bipolar code guaranteeing the closure of the legal system is that of lawful/unlawful. Justice, on the other hand, is one of the values Luhmann strongly dislikes and suspects. The emphasis on legal technique, judicial competence, rules of interpretation and legal procedures repeats the main preoccupations of positivist jurisprudence. The function of rights as promoters of the differentiation and closure of functional systems moves in the same direction. For Luhmann, the just/unjust bipolarity was highly problematic,[44] and has been

40 C. Douzinas & A Gearey, *Critical Jurisprudence*, Hart, Oxford 2005, Chapters 1 and 4.

41 A. Ross, *On Law and Justice*, Stevens & Sons, London 1958, p. 274.

42 *Id.*, p. 275.

43 F. von Hayek, *Law, Legislation and Liberty*, Routledge and Kegan Paul, London 1972, p. 168, note 30.

44 Luhmann, 2008a, p. 4.

abandoned in favour of the legal (lawful/unlawful) coding. While systems theory attacks the excesses of the neo-Kantians, it fully adopts a strict and simplistic law/morality divide evident in early legal positivism.

This approach to law is both cognitively wrong (deciding what is lawful is impossible without an evaluation about the moral, just or desirable outcome) and morally impoverished (it reduces morality either to private 'subjective' choices and/or to a predication of legality). It became the legitimation and rationalization of the great atrocities of the twentieth century. The eternal return of (new versions of) naturalism despite its repeatedly proclaimed 'fallacy' indicates that law and morality are not opposed. They are linked in inner paradoxical ways. For the Greeks and Romans, justice was the prime, albeit missing, virtue of the polity and the spirit and reason of law. A just constitution was a legitimate constitution and a just legal system has a valid claim to the obedience of its citizens. We find similar ideas in the writings of the common lawyers. Justice is cumulatively the foundation, the spirit and the end of the law. As law's immemorial and unwritten foundation, justice links the common law with divine will and its expressions in nature and reason. After the Reformation, justice as equity is explicitly associated with the divine order and becomes law's spirit. When law and justice, in the form of equity, are in conflict, the law must give way to higher reason. In all these formulations, justice is seen as the "primitive reason" of law, [45] its virtue and ethical substance, an ideal or principle that gives rules their aim and limit and remedies their defects. But justice is also something outside or before the law, a transcendent principle that gives it overall direction, a higher tribunal or reason to which the law and its judgments are called to account. In this sense, a law without justice is a law without spirit, a dead letter, it can neither rule nor inspire.

Modernity repressed the inner link between law and justice to its detriment. We could describe postmodern jurisprudence as the latest return of the repressed. In our disenchanted world, the transcendent must be found in the immanent, the principle of justice in history. When law violates its established procedures and harms someone; when it does not recognize or uphold rights which have been given already or are reasonably expected; when it breaches basic principles of equality and dignity – in all these cases the law acts unjustly according to its own internal criteria of justice. We can call this first type of justice, legal justice, because it is internal to the law and operates when the law matches its own standards and principles.

But legal justice is only one facet of justice. A different conception has inspired the jurisprudence of deconstruction from Jacques Derrida to Jean-Luc Nancy and critical legal

45 Sir H. Finch, *Law, or, A Discourse Thereof in Four Books*, Society of Stationers *at fol.*, London 1627, p. 57.

theory. It starts from the statement of Emmanuel Levinas that justice operates in the relationship to the other person. The other is a singular, unique finite being with certain personality traits, character attributes and physical characteristics. But to me, this finite person puts me in touch with infinite otherness. According to phenomenology, I cannot know the other as other, I can never comprehend fully her intentions or actions, I can never have an appropriate adequation or presentation, because no immediate access or perception of otherness exists. We need criteria in order to be just to the other but they are not readily available. Indeed any attempt to turn justice into a theory (as some Marxists did) or a series of normative statement and commands (as Kantians do) is necessarily a violation of justice. Theories and laws need to be applied; but every application would turn the uniqueness of the other into an instance of the concept or a case of the norm and would immediately violate their singularity. The principle of justice is to respect the singularity of the other – a very different axiom from Luhmann's access to many functional systems.

The infinite dwells in the finite, justice dwells in the law but also challenges the law since the law forgets the infinity of the other. The law has to deal with many others and it must compare and contrast them. To do that it puts them on the same scale and compares them by using rights, duties and other common denominators that allow the different to become similar and the other same. Justice is immanent to the law but this immanence means that law is unequal to itself, it contains within itself what opens to a new law, a new politics, a new place or non-place (utopia). Justice lies within the law as a gap, a chasm, which judges both specific instances of injustice and violence but also the overall direction of the law. Both inside and outside, justice is the horizon against which the law is judged both for its daily routine failings and for its forgetting of justice. Whether we see the law as a historical institution or as a system of rules and decisions, the deconstruction of its operations discovers either the violence of origins in its daily operations or unravels the ordered bipolarities (fact-value, public-private, objective-subjective, lawful-unlawful) and shows that they cannot stabilize the legal system.

According to Michael King, law has:

> only two ways of responding to perturbations from its environment – one is not to recognise the issue as relevant to law; the other is transform it into an issue which can ultimately be resolved through law's coding of lawful/unlawful.[46]

If this is the case, systems theory is unable to 'observe' the internal split of human rights, their double reality partly positive law and partly a distancing from and judging of positivity as part of its nature. No bipolar code can account for their integral 'moral' component which doubles the legal condition: it can neither be accepted as relevant to law nor can it be resolved through the lawful/unlawful coding the very operation of which it is meant to challenge perpetually.

The 'ticking bomb' hypothetical and the domestication of torture indicate the limits of liberal theory. The value/rights idealists (the neo-Kantians Habermas, Dworkin, etc.) identify rights with right and improbably believe that reason and principle have all the answers. They are proven daily wrong but this only makes their claims louder and shriller. The systems realist, on the other hand, anxious to prove the probity of his theory, leaves us cynically exposed to the dictates of power, if its exercise seems to confirm the autopoietic prescriptions. As Luhmann keeps insisting, the question "what is to be done" must be preceded by "how can one observe and describe accurately" as if, at the beginning of the twenty-first century our lack of knowledge is the main impediment to action.[47] As King honestly admits, "Luhmann's *usefulness* might well lie in the *uselessness* of his theory as a blueprint for improvement of social systems".[48]

For the neo-Kantians, norms and rights have all the answers. For the systemics, reason is no panacea for our ills and every line of resistance becomes a further twist in the paradoxical operation of systems. In both cases, we are left with no much hope; Luhmann is at least honest about it. We need more however if we are to resist the brutality of our times. Hegel famously said that the owl of Minerva flies at dusk. It may be that at this late stage the modernist priority of knowledge over action or of *techne* over praxis is in the process of being reversed against the advice of systems theory – and this is the unacknowledged wisdom of our age.

---

46 M. King, 'What's the Use of Luhmann's Theory?', *in* M. King & Ch. Thornhill (Eds.), *Luhmann on Law and Politics*, Hart, Oxford 2006, p. 47.

47 Luhmann 2008a, p. 29.

48 King 2006, p. 52.

Walter Benjamin's Other Law

Marc de Wilde[*]

Introduction

In this paper, I intend to show how Benjamin, in his essay *Critique of Violence*, develops an alternative approach to law based on a notion of responsibility, a responsibility *before* the law. As I will explain, Benjamin's essay contains not only a critique of violence, but also a critique of law. On Benjamin's view, there is an intrinsic relation between violence and law, because violence can only be criticized and evaluated as part of a moral sphere that is defined by concepts of law and justice.[1] Therefore, Benjamin's critique of violence is essentially a critique of *legal* violence, a critique of the kind of violence which the state yields through coercively binding its subjects to law. In emphasizing law's structural dependence on violence, Benjamin's essay is a deeply troubling text. It asks us to radically question those aspects of law which we may find most valuable, including those we may consider essential to liberal legal systems and the rule of law.

In the text, Benjamin defends the idea of a general, revolutionary opposition to the coercive character of law. He thus expresses his admiration for the proletarian revolution, which, on his understanding, categorically refuses the force and authority of law. He even relates the revolutionaries' refusal of law to the theological vision of a divine law-destroying violence – a violence that promises to bring all human law and its structural dependence on violence to an end. Benjamin's endorsement of a law-destroying violence has led some commentators to conclude that, for him, law and justice are incompatible. In this sense, Jacques Derrida, in *Force of Law*, argues that Benjamin attempted to develop "a sort of justice without law, a justice beyond law [*une sorte de justice sans droit, une justice au-delà du droit*]".[2] On this reading, as law is intrinsically tied to violent coercion, justice can be

* I would like to thank Bald de Vries and Lyana Francot for organizing the Critical Legal Conference 2010, which inspired me to write this paper. I presented an earlier version of the paper during a workshop on Benjamin's Law at the Centre for Law and the Humanities of the Birkbeck School of Law. I am immensely grateful to Peter Fitzpatrick and Chris Lloyd for organizing this workshop and to Esther Leslie, Patricia Tuitt, James Martell, and an exceptionally engaged audience for their thoughtful questions and comments.

1 W. Benjamin, *Critique of Violence*, *in* M. Bullock and M.W. Jennings (Eds.), *Walter Benjamin: Selected Writings, Volume 1, 1913-1926*, Harvard University Press, Cambridge (Ma.)/London 1999, p. 236. All parenthetic citations are from this edition and refer to the page number of the text.

2 J. Derrida, *Force of Law*, *in* G. Anidjar (Ed.), *Acts of Religion*, Routledge, New York/London 2002, p. 286.

attained only outside of law; it would become possible only if we are prepared to go beyond law, to refuse law, to refuse the generality of its rules and its claims to authority.

However, towards the end of his essay, Benjamin himself suggests that it is possible to imagine another kind of law, a law that is no longer fatally dependent on violence. This would mean that Benjamin's critique is perhaps not directed against law as such, but only against certain conceptions of law. It would also imply that, contrary to Derrida's interpretation, Benjamin does not exclude the possibility that justice may be attained within a sphere that is governed by law. Indeed, as I will argue, for Benjamin, justice is possible only in relation to law; it becomes possible through, what I call, a responsibility *before* the law – a responsive engagement with the law's imperative, which always also includes the possibility of its refusal. Interestingly, Benjamin's alternative approach to law turns out to be related to certain religious motifs; it is, more specifically, developed in the context of a discussion of the biblical commandment 'thou shalt not kill'. As I will explain, Benjamin regards the commandment as the model for another kind of law; for him, it contains the promise of a law that is no longer dependent on violent coercion, but that originates, instead, from the responsibility of those bound to it.

In this paper, I have three aims. First, I want to describe briefly Benjamin's critique of law and violence, and to discuss his main objections against the manner in which modern legal systems have become involved in practices of state oppression. I will show how this critique is directed not against law as such, but against certain conceptions and practices of law. Second, I will sketch the contours of Benjamin's alternative approach to law based on a different Jewish tradition of understanding the biblical commandment 'thou shalt not kill'. On this understanding, the law is believed to be radically open: it is believed to be open to future possibilities of interpretation, future conditions that may change the law's meaning, including the possibility that it may have to be abandoned in view of exceptional circumstances. Finally, I intend to show how Benjamin's alternative approach to law remains relevant for critical legal thinking today. I will thus analyze a landmark decision of the European Court of Human Rights from the perspective of Benjamin's conception of law, thereby articulating some of its main implications for today's legal theory and practice.

Benjamin's Critique of Legal Violence

Benjamin begins his critique of legal violence by discussing the two mainstream conceptions of law of his time, i.e., natural law and legal positivism. He argues that these theories are not capable of effectively criticizing law's dependence on violence, because they understand violence instrumentally, as a means to certain ends. Thus, natural law justifies the use of violence if it serves to promote just ends, while legal positivism accepts violence if it is recognized by the law as a legal and legitimate means. Natural law and positive law thereby seek the criterion for the justification of violence outside of violence itself, in a consideration of ends and means. They focus on the legality or legitimacy of violence, instead of evaluating violence itself as "a principle". On Benjamin's view, they therefore fail to answer the question under which circumstances violence itself might be justified (p. 236-237).

According to Benjamin, there are several examples of a violence that cannot be understood instrumentally. For instance, the legal order's interest in a monopoly of violence vis-à-vis individuals shows that violence does not always serve as a means to certain ends. When in the hands of individuals, violence threatens the legal order not because of the ends it serves, but because of its mere existence outside of the law. Therefore, the law seeks to monopolize violence not as a means, but as a principle, its mere existence outside of the law being a threat to the authority and force of law (p. 239). Similarly, Benjamin argues that the figure of the "great criminal" through his violence arouses the "secret admiration of the people", even if they reject the ends he pursues. The people tend to regard the great criminal's violence not primarily as an illegal means to certain illegal ends, but as a principle that violently disrupts the normal functioning of the legal order. In both cases, then, violence cannot be understood as a means. It is not a means, but a "manifestation" (p. 248).

In the first part of the text, Benjamin examines the implications of his notion of violence as a manifestation for the critique of state violence. He argues that the legal order is dependent on an immediate violence, which does not relate to any ends and cannot be understood by reference to its normative meaning or function. He calls this immediate violence a "lawmaking violence [*rechtssetzende Gewalt*]", and distinguishes it from a "law-preserving violence [*rechtserhaltende Gewalt*]" (p. 241). On Benjamin's view, the lawmaking violence is revealed in the positing of law, the act by which law is established or reaffirmed. Benjamin regards the positing of law itself as an act of violence, for it turns persons into legal subjects who become potentially guilty and legally accountable. As Benjamin argues, the act of positing shows that a law-making violence is at work in the legal order. It resides in the "force of law [*Gesetzeskraft*]", that is, law's claim to authority. Thus, each time a law is posited, authority is claimed and legal subjects are coercively bound.

However, as Benjamin also explains, lawmaking and law-preserving violence relate to each other in a way that prevents them from being pure and delineated forms of violence that can be criticized and evaluated independently of each other. Thus, lawmaking violence anticipates the law-preserving violence upon which the laws will depend for their application. And, conversely, law-preserving violence, in the act of applying the laws, reaffirms and re-establishes these laws. Thereby all law-preserving violence, in its duration, indirectly weakens the lawmaking violence it represents; in the end, it threatens to become a lawmaking violence itself, recreating the laws it was supposed to preserve.[3] As Benjamin suggests, this leads to a "dialectical rising and falling in the lawmaking and law-preserving forms of violence", which causes legal institutions to fall into decay (p. 251). Thus, the law-preserving violence undermines the authority of law by suspending the laws in exceptional cases. This lasts until the law-preserving violence replaces the hitherto lawmaking violence, becoming a lawmaking violence itself and founding a law of its own, which is destined in turn to decay.

For Benjamin, the *police* provide a particularly troubling example of this dialectic. The police represent quite literally the force of law. Their task is to preserve the laws. However, as Benjamin points out, the police do not actually limit themselves to their law-preserving task. While preserving the laws, they tend to restrict or extend the laws' application in exceptional cases instead. On Benjamin's view, they therefore embody a "spectral mixture [*gespenstische Vermischung*]" of law-preserving and lawmaking violence: the police are capable of re-positing and re-creating the laws they were supposed to preserve. Because of this confusion of lawmaking and law-preserving violence, both forms of violence tend to lose their mutual limitations. Lawmaking violence can penetrate all spheres of the legal order, also those of mere administration and preservation. This means that the laws are constantly threatened by their possible suspension in "exceptional cases". Benjamin, therefore, calls police's authority "ignominious [*schmachvoll*]": "its power is formless, like its nowhere-tangible, all-pervasive, ghostly presence in the life of civilized states" (p. 243). For Benjamin, the police even bear witness to the "greatest conceivable degeneration of violence", because, in combining a lawmaking and law-preserving violence, they dispose of a violence that is practically unlimited and that cannot be legally constrained.

This raises the question whether it is possible to bring the catastrophic dialectic between lawmaking and law-preserving violence to an end. Benjamin thinks it is, and he explains his position by exploring the possibility of so-called "pure means [*reine Mittel*]". Pure means are said to be non-violent "means of agreement" through which conflicts can be resolved in a peaceful manner. They do not depend on either lawmaking or law-preserving violence, but, instead, interrupt the working of these forms of violence. Their profoundest example is human conversation in so far as it serves as a non-violent and non-coercive

---

3 This is what Derrida calls the "law of iterability": "There is no more pure foundation or pure positing of law, and so a pure founding violence, than there is a purely preserving violence. Positing is already iterability, a call for self-preserving repetition. Preservation in turn refounds, so that it can preserve what it claims to found". Derrida 2002, p. 272.

technique of civil agreement.[4] However, Benjamin argues that pure means can also "under certain conditions" take the form of a revolutionary strike. Referring to George Sorel, he distinguishes between, on the one hand, a "political general strike", which uses the threat of violence as a means of forcing the state into accepting compromises, and, on the other, a "proletarian general strike", which categorically rejects the use of violence, and aims at the complete abolition of the state. Whereas, the first kind of strike is violent, "the second, as a pure means, is non-violent" (p. 246).

On Benjamin's view, then, the proletarian general strike promises to bring the dialectic of lawmaking and law-preserving violence to an end. Instead of positing new laws, it *de-poses* the laws; it rejects the manner in which legal subjects are coercively bound to the laws. In doing so, the proletarian general strike does not replace existing laws with new ones, nor does it introduce laws of its own. Although we tend to regard the strike as an "action", it is, as Werner Hamacher has rightly observed, essentially an omission, a non-action, an unconditional refusal to act.[5] It is a way of depriving the laws of their force and authority by refusing to instate or replace them. And, it is this very refusal to act, this non-action, which, according to Benjamin, severs the ties between law and violence; it interrupts all exploitive relations and the lawmaking and law-preserving violence on which they depend. For this reason, Benjamin believes the proletarian general strike is not only non-violent, but also "anarchistic" (p. 246): it temporarily cancels the force of law itself.

For lawyers and legal theorists, Benjamin's anarchistic solution to the problem of law and violence may seem a little disappointing. It is also deeply troubling if one considers the manner in which both Communism and Fascism would assault the rule of law and parliamentary institutions in subsequent years. In that sense, Judith Butler is probably right when she observes that:

> a general opposition to the binding, even coercive character of law seems less savory once we consider the rise of Fascism, as well as the flouting of both constitutional and international law that characterizes U.S. foreign policy in its practices of war, torture, and illegal detention.[6]

4 Axel Honneth has pointed out that Benjamin derives the idea and examples of non-violent alternatives to law from Rudolf von Jhering's influential book *Der Zweck im Recht* (1883). Like Jhering, Benjamin recognizes these non-violent alternatives in practices of voluntary altruism such as acts of courtesy and sympathy. A. Honneth, 'Zur Kritik der Gewalt', *in* B. Lindner (Ed.), *Benjamin Handbuch: Leben, Werk, Wirkung*, J.B. Metzler, Stuttgart/ Weimar 2006, p. 198.

5 W. Hamacher, 'Afformative, Strike', *Cardozo Law Review*, Vol. 13, No. 1, 1991, p. 1149.

6 J. Butler, 'Critique, Coercion, and Sacred Life in Benjamin's "Critique of Violence"', in H. de Vries & L.E. Sullivan (Eds.), *Political Theologies: Public Religions in a Post-Secular World*, Fordham University Press, New York 2006, p. 206.

Derrida is even more outspokenly critical when he suggests that Benjamin rode the same "antiparliamentary wave" upon which National Socialism would surface.[7] He suggests that Benjamin even shared with authors of the far right a fascination for a thematic of "destruction", a destruction of law, which, Derrida believes, should be rejected on both ethical and historic grounds.[8]

Yet, although Benjamin does indeed propose a general rejection of the violent and coercive character of law, there are passages in his text that suggest an alternative understanding of law. Indeed, nowhere in the text, does Benjamin argue that *all* legal systems should be opposed; nor does he explicitly reject the idea of law as such.[9] Instead, towards the end of his text, he sketches the vision of another law, another understanding of law, in which law is no longer fatally dependent on violence. In the next section, I will explore Benjamin's vision of this other law, a non-violent and non-coercive law, and examine what it may mean for critical legal thinking today.

BENJAMIN'S OTHER LAW

Interestingly, it is through a reconsideration of the biblical commandment 'thou shalt not kill' that Benjamin articulates his vision of this other law, a law that is no longer violent and repressive. As he explains, the commandment 'thou shalt not kill' is categorically binding, in the sense that it cannot be ignored under any circumstances. However, on Benjamin's understanding, the commandment does not take away the responsibility of persons and communities to engage with questions of life and death. Although it serves as a guideline for their actions, it cannot serve as a criterion for the deed itself (p. 250). This implies that one cannot know in advance how one should act on the basis of the commandment and how, or even on the basis of which criteria, the deed itself will be judged. Instead, Benjamin argues, one "has to wrestle with [the commandment] in solitude and, in exceptional cases, to take on [oneself] the responsibility of abandoning it" (p. 251).[10]

This is a remarkable phrase: the divine commandment would mandate only a solitary struggle, and leave open the possibility that it may have to be abandoned in exceptional cases. In her illuminating and engaged reading of the text, Judith Butler argues that Ben-

7 Derrida 2002, p. 259.
8 *Id.*, p. 261.
9 Butler 2006, p. 203.
10 Bullock and Jennings translate the verb "*absehen*" as "ignoring". However, I believe the meaning of this verb is more adequately rendered as "abandoning". Thus, in German, "*von etwas absehen*" does not mean that one ignores something, but rather that one consciously decides not to do something.

jamin here "figures the commandment as a kind of law that is neither binding nor enforceable in a way that requires legal violence".[11] This other law would still be binding in the sense that we cannot ignore it and that we are bound to struggle with it, yet it would not be dependent on violence in the sense that it would not be violently enforced. As Butler points out, Benjamin articulates a different Jewish tradition of understanding the commandment:

> Although we are accustomed to thinking of the divine commandment as operating in an imperative way, mandating action on our part and ready with a set of punitive reactions if we fail to obey, Benjamin makes use of a different Jewish tradition of understanding the commandment, which strictly separates the imperative that the law articulates from the matter of enforceability.[12]

According to this different understanding of the commandment, the imperative that is communicated in it – the imperative 'thou shalt not kill' – is not violently enforced; it is not forced upon us, and, therefore, does not reduce our responsibility to engage with it, to explain it, to either follow or abandon it in view of exceptional circumstances. As Butler points out, "this is an imperative that does *not* dictate, but *leaves open* the modes of its applicability, the possibilities of its interpretation, including the conditions under which it may be refused".[13] Thus, on Benjamin's understanding, the commandment 'thou shalt not kill' refers to a law that is radically open – a law that is open to future possibilities of interpretation, future conditions that may change the law's meaning, and even the possibility that it may have to be abandoned. In view of these possibilities, the commandment takes the form of an ethical address; it requires that each person and each community wrestles with the commandment in solitude without having any stable model of how it should be interpreted and under which circumstances it should be followed or abandoned.[14]

As an ethical address, it is characteristic of the commandment that it does not reduce, but enhances the responsibility of those subject to it. Benjamin emphasizes this responsibility, when he argues that, "in exceptional cases", we have to take on ourselves "the responsibility of abandoning it" (p. 251). The responsibility that one takes in relation to the commandment differs from legal accountability; it differs from the kind of duties and obligations that we are accustomed to associate with law, for, contrary to these, it does not dictate *how* we

11 Butler 2006, p. 204.

12 *Id.*, p. 204. Benjamin explicitly refers to this other Jewish tradition of understanding the commandment, when he notes that "Judaism (...) expressly rejected the condemnation of killing in self-defense" (250).

13 *Id.*, p. 205.

14 *Id.*, p. 212.

should act.[15] Instead, it presupposes our freedom to act in view of the commandment, a freedom that is lacking in the case of legal obligations and duties. The commandment, therefore, does not reduce us to legal subjects, upon whom the law is enforced, but, being a non-coercive, ethical address, it respects us as moral persons who are capable of responsible decisions. Still, the freedom we have in relation to the commandment is not unconstrained, because we are not allowed to ignore the commandment altogether. Instead, we are bound to struggle with it even if we decide to abandon it.

Both Butler and Derrida emphasize the anarchistic aspect of Benjamin's understanding of the commandment. On Butler's reading, the wrestling with the commandment is essentially "anarchistic", a "solitary coming to terms with the commandment", in which there is a "nongeneralizable moment that destroys the basis of law".[16] Similarly, Derrida links the responsibility to which Benjamin refers in relation to the commandment to the "absence of general criteria and automatic rules".[17] On his view, responsibility consists of an engagement with the unique, non-generalizable aspects of every situation, which suspends the applicability of general criteria and rules. He, therefore, suggests that, for Benjamin, justice can be attained only outside of law.[18] As the positing and application of law is always attended by violence – an exclusion of that which escapes the generalizing language of rules and norms – justice would consist of a deconstruction of law. Both Derrida and Butler, then, emphasize the anarchistic aspect of Benjamin's understanding of the commandment, arguing that justice can be attained only outside of law, in the very act that destroys the basis of law, that is, law's dependence on general criteria and rules.

By emphasizing the anarchism of Benjamin's approach to the commandment, Butler and Derrida effectively prevent it from becoming the model for another kind of law. Here, I tend to disagree with their otherwise persuasive readings. If Benjamin's approach to the commandment would be anarchistic, it would be incompatible with law; it would be unfit to serve as the model for another kind of law, a law less violent and more just. Yet, contrary to both Butler and Derrida, I believe a crucial aspect of Benjamin's notion of the commandment is that it implies the possibility of this other law – a law not dependent on violent positing and not reducing the responsibility of those engaging with it. On my view, Benjamin's notion of the commandment refers to the requirement of a responsive engagement with the law's imperative, in the sense that the imperative, though it may be abandoned, may never be completely ignored. This approach is not anarchistic, for it continues to

15 *Id.*, p. 213.
16 *Id.*, p. 214.
17 Derrida 2002, p. 288.
18 *Id.*, p. 286.

recognize the binding force of law, i.e., the impossibility to ignore the law's imperative altogether, while rejecting its coerciveness and violent enforcement.

Contrary to the readings of Butler and Derrida, then, I argue that Benjamin's notion of responsibility does not destroy the basis of law, but rather serves as law's presupposition, that is, the condition for its possible relation to justice. For Benjamin, justice cannot be realized through law. Nor can it be attained outside of law. Instead, it is possible only *before the law*; it becomes possible through a responsible engagement with the law's imperative, which always also includes the possibility of its refusal. By proposing a different understanding of the commandment, Benjamin opens up a whole new realm of legal thinking and acting, a realm of responsibility *before the law* which has remained largely unexplored. It is the realm of a responsive engagement with the law, an awareness that it might become necessary to abandon the law in exceptional cases, and that every case is, and must be, potentially exceptional. It is the awareness of the fact that justice, if it is possible at all, inheres in the decision on the exception, and that every legal decision, that is, every decision by which laws are made or applied, is always also a decision on the exception, and, therefore, an instance of our responsibility.[19]

Benjamin's alternative interpretation of the commandment not only enables him to develop a notion of responsibility – a responsibility before the law. It also enables him to criticize existing biopolitical approaches to law. Thus, the fact that one must be prepared to take responsibility for abandoning the imperative 'thou shalt not kill' in exceptional cases suggests that a legal order that is exclusively based on the preservation of life must be, necessarily, irresponsible and unjust. Benjamin rejects, more particularly, the "doctrine of the sanctity of life [*der Satz von der Heiligkeit des Lebens*]", which professes that the preservation of mere life is more valuable even than justice itself: The proposition that existence stands higher than a just existence is false and ignominious, if existence is to mean nothing other than mere life" (251). As Benjamin argues, it may well be true that the life of man is sacred, but there is "no sacredness in his biological condition, in his bodily life" (251). For Benjamin, then, what is sacred in life is not "mere life" but the possible righteousness of life, that is, the ethical task invested in life, the fulfillment of which is postponed to an unforeseeable future.[20]

---

19 In his reading of Kafka's parable *Before the Law*, Derrida refers to this notion of responsibility before the law. He relates it, more particularly, to revolutionary situations in which the law is suspended and a new law is not yet founded. Thus, on his view, it is a responsibility before a law that is not yet determined, a law still to come. *Id.*, p. 270. Compare also: J. Derrida, 'Before the Law', A. Ronell (Trans.), *in* D. Attridge (Ed.), *Acts of Literature*, Routledge, London/New York 1992, p. 181-220.

20 Referring to Benjamin's discussion of the sanctity of life, Giorgio Agamben introduces the notion of "bare life", a life that is stripped from legal and political qualifications, and thus directly exposed to state violence. As Agamben explains, bare life is produced by a sovereign power, by which it can be killed without committing

In a gesture that seems both bold and highly speculative, Benjamin relates this understanding of the commandment to the notions of a "mythic" and "divine violence": "Mythic violence", he explains, "is bloody power over mere life for its own sake; divine violence is pure power over all life for the sake of the living. The first demands sacrifice; the second accepts it" (p. 250). On Benjamin's understanding, mythic violence is exercised over life for the sake of mere life itself. It is a violence that seeks to preserve man's mere, bodily existence at any price, even if it requires the sacrifice of life itself. It is, therefore, said to be a bloody violence, not only because blood is "the symbol of mere life [*das Symbol des blossen Lebens*]", but also because mythical violence may demand a sacrifice of life – it may demand, for instance, a sacrifice of the lives of some to preserve the lives of the rest. Thus, on Benjamin's understanding, mythic violence is a bloody violence exercised over mere life, a violence that requires the sacrifice of life for the preservation of mere life itself.

By contrast, divine violence is said to be a "pure violence [*reine Gewalt*]" which is exercised "over all life for the sake of the living" and which does not spill any blood. It aims at preserving not mere life, but "the soul of the living [*die Seele des Lebendigen*]" (p. 250). The expression "the soul of the living" refers to Benjamin's idea that life is meaningful and sacred not because of its bodily condition, but because of its ethical task, the task of realizing justice before the law. It, therefore, appears to be connected to the notion of responsibility that Benjamin developed in relation to the commandment. This is also suggested by Benjamin's somewhat puzzling remark that divine violence does not "demand", but only "accepts" the sacrifice of life. This could be taken to mean that it does not enforce the sacrifice of life, but that it leaves the responsibility to decide questions of life and death to those subject to it. On this reading, divine violence does not *demand* the sacrifice of life, in so far as it has been enforced *under* the law, yet it does *accept* a sacrifice that originates from a responsibility *before* the law.[21]

homicide. Therefore, on Agamben's understanding, the doctrine of the sanctity of life directly relates to its opposite, the possibility of a politics of death: "The sacredness of life, which is invoked today as an absolutely fundamental right in opposition to sovereign power, in fact originally expresses precisely both life's subjection to a power over death and life's irreparable exposure in the relation of abandonment." G. Agamben, *Homo Sacer: Sovereign Power and Bare Life*, D. Heller-Roazen (Trans.), Stanford University Press, Stanford 1998, p. 83. In discussing Benjamin's critique of the sanctity of life, Agamben emphasizes the latter's objections against the biopolitical preoccupation with mere life. However, he does not explore Benjamin's alternative understanding of the sanctity of life, according to which the sanctity attaches not to mere life, but to the possible righteousness of life. Cf. *id.*, p. 65-67.

21 For a more comprehensive account of these theological motifs, compare: M. de Wilde, 'Violence in the State of Exception: Reflections on Theologico-Political Motifs in Benjamin and Schmitt', *in* De Vries and Sullivan 2006, p. 188-200 and M. de Wilde, *Verwantschap in Extremen: Politieke Theologie bij Walter Benjamin en Carl Schmitt*, Vossius Pers, Amsterdam 2008, p. 18-27.

In sum, Benjamin's understanding of the commandment 'thou shalt not kill' refers to the promise of another law, a law that is no longer violently enforced and that originates from the ethical responsibility of those engaging with it. It refers to a notion of responsibility that is not incompatible with law, but that can be taken only in relation to law; a responsibility *before* the law, taken in the awareness that even if the law is abandoned it cannot be ignored. Moreover, Benjamin's other law differs from the existing biopolitical approaches to law, in that it does not seek to preserve mere life at any price, but, instead, aims at saving the "soul of the living", that is, the ethical dignity of life. In doing so, Benjamin believes, it bears witness to a divine violence: it does not "demand", but only "accepts" the sacrifice of life as it originates from a responsible engagement with the law, a solitary struggle, in which it is recognized that life's dignity does not reside in its mere, bodily existence, but in its possible righteousness.

I would now like to illustrate the continuing relevance of Benjamin's approach to law with a contemporary example, the landmark judgment of the European Court of Human Rights in the case of *Pretty v. United Kingdom.*[22]

ILLUSTRATING BENJAMIN'S OTHER LAW: THE CASE OF *PRETTY V. UNITED KINGDOM*

Before analyzing the case of *Pretty v. United Kingdom* from the perspective of Benjamin's legal theory, let me begin by describing the facts.[23] Dianne Pretty was a 43-year old English woman who suffered from motor neuron disease. This incurable illness gradually weakens the muscles and usually ends in death through suffocation. When Mrs. Pretty brought her case to court, her disease was in an advanced stage. She was essentially paralyzed from the neck down, unable to speak, and fed through a tube. She was expected to live no longer than a few weeks or months. Faced with the prospect of a distressing and undignified death, Mrs. Pretty wanted to end her life. Being paralyzed and thus unable to take her life herself, her husband agreed to assist her. However, by doing so, he would risk being prosecuted, assisted suicide being a crime under English law (Section 2 of the Suicide Act of 1961). Therefore, Mrs. Pretty asked the Director of Public Prosecutions (DPP) to give her a written assurance that he would not prosecute her husband should he assist her in

---

22 *Pretty v. United Kingdom*, ECHR (2002), App. no. 2346/02.

23 On this case, compare: A. Mooney, 'Death Alive and Kicking: Diane Pretty, Legal Violence, and the Sacred', *Social Semiotics*, Vol. 18, No. 1, 2008, p. 47-60; B. Hale, 'A Pretty Pass: When Is There a Right to Die?', *Common Law World Review*, Vol. 32, No. 1, 2003, p. 1-14; S.B. Chetwynd, 'Right to Life, Right to Die and Assisted Suicide', *Journal of Applied Philosophy*, Vol. 21, No. 2, 2004, p. 173-182; H. Biggs, 'A Pretty Fine Line: Life, Death, Autonomy and Letting it B.', *Feminist Legal Studies*, Vol. 11, No. 3, 2003, p. 291-301; J.S. Nugent, '"Walking into the Sea" of Legal Fiction: An Examination of the European Court of Human Rights, *Pretty v. United Kingdom* and the Universal Right to Die', *Journal of Transnational Law and Policy*, Vol. 13, No. 1, 2003-2004, p. 183-212.

committing suicide. The DDP, however, refused to give her the assurance, arguing that he did not have the authority to grant immunities for future criminal offences. The DDP's decision was upheld by various domestic courts, including the House of Lords. Mrs. Pretty, thereupon, sought judicial review of the decision by the European Court of Human Rights, claiming that the prohibition in domestic law on assisted suicide violated her rights under Articles 2, 3, 8, 9, and 14 of the European Convention for the Protection of Human Rights and Fundamental Freedoms.

Before the court, Mrs. Pretty argued, among other things, that Article 2 of the Convention, which guaranteed the right to life, protected not only an individual's right to life but also his or her right to choose whether or not to go on living. On her view, the purpose of Article 2 was primarily to protect individuals from third parties, including the state and public authorities. She thus claimed that Article 2 essentially served to guarantee the individual's right to self-determination with regard to questions of life and death. It was for the individual, and not for the state, to decide whether he or she wanted to go on living or not. This interpretation, she argued, was acknowledged by law, as a person was legally allowed to refuse life-saving or life-prolonging medical treatment, or even to actively commit suicide. Therefore, the right to life of Article 2 had to be read as including the individual's right to choose death instead of life. "The right to die", she claimed, "was not the antithesis of the right to life but the corollary of it, and the state [had] a positive obligation to protect both" (para. 14, at 4, and 35).

The House of Lords had rejected Mrs. Pretty's argument. In formulating the majority opinion, Lord Bingham emphasized that Article 2 was framed to protect not the individual's right to self-determination, but the "sanctity of life". He argued that "the starting point must be the language of the Article. The thrust of this is to reflect the sanctity which, particularly in western eyes, attaches to life" (para. 14, at 5). He thus held that Article 2 could not be interpreted as including the opposite of what it was framed to protect, namely a right to die. Following Bingham's argument, the ECtHR indicated that it was not persuaded that the right to life of Article 2 could be interpreted as involving a negative aspect. Although it conceded that other Articles of the Convention allowed for some measure of choice and could, therefore, be read as involving a negative aspect,[24] the court noted that Article 2 was phrased in different terms. It was, more specifically, "unconcerned with issues to do with the quality of living or what a person chooses to do with his or her life" (para. 39). Therefore, the court argued that:

24 The court mentions the example of Article 11, which protects the freedom of association. As the court notes, the freedom of association involves not only a right to join an association but a corresponding right not to be forced to join an association. Therefore, this Article involves a negative aspect, which can be explained from a notion of freedom underlying the Convention.

> Article 2 [could] not, without a distortion of language, be interpreted as conferring the diametrically opposite right, namely a right to die; nor [could] it create a right to self-determination in the sense of conferring on an individual the entitlement to choose death rather than life" (para. 39).

The court thus concluded that Mrs. Pretty's claim had to be rejected. Shortly after its judgment was published, Mrs. Pretty died from the devastating effects of her illness.[25]

To understand what is at stake in the court's judgment, it is helpful to analyze it from the perspective of Benjamin's legal theory. More specifically, I argue that the right to life of Article 2 can be understood as one of the secular legal embodiments of the commandment 'thou shalt not kill'. Interestingly, like Benjamin, the judges relate this imperative to the doctrine of the sanctity of life.[26] It is this doctrine, which prevents them from understanding Article 2 as protecting an individual's right to assisted suicide. However, the court proposes an interpretation of the sanctity of life that differs significantly from Benjamin's. As the court suggests, it does not refer to a notion of self-determination or, more generally, to any beliefs about what may be judged a good life. What remains is the reference to life itself, that is, the reference to "mere life" in the sense of man's bodily existence. In the understanding of the judges, then, the sanctity of life stands for the sanctity of mere, biological life as opposed to a life that is freely chosen or believed to be worth living. It refers to the necessity of preserving life itself, independently of any beliefs of what constitutes a good life.

As we have seen, Benjamin explicitly rejects this interpretation of the sanctity of life. Although he allows for the possibility that the life of man is sacred, he finds that there is "no sacredness in his biological condition, in his bodily life" (p. 251). In sharp contrast to the courts, then, Benjamin argues that the sanctity of life attaches not to life itself, not to mere life, but to the possible righteousness of life, its ethical task. From this perspective,

---

25 In this analysis, I limit myself to the Court's decision with regard to Article 2, because it is the most relevant from the perspective of Benjamin's legal theory. However, the Court's judgment also dealt with Articles 3, 8, 9, and 14. Important questions were raised especially with regard to Article 8. Thus, the Court held that the DPP's decision interfered with Mrs. Pretty's right to respect for private life as guaranteed under Article 8 (1). However, it also concluded that the interference was justified under Article 8 (2), because it was "necessary in a democratic society" to protect the rights of others, *i.e.*, the rights of the "weak and the vulnerable and especially those who [were] not in a condition to take informed decisions against acts intended to end life or to assist in ending life" (para. 74).

26 The expression "sanctity of life" is mentioned six times in the Court's judgment, especially in the passages that quote the judgment of the House of Lords (para. 14). The ECtHR does not explicitly refer to the "sanctity of life" in relation to Article 2, but mentions it in relation to Article 8, when it considers that notions of the quality of life take on significance under Article 8 "without in any way negating the principle of the sanctity of life protected under the Convention" (para. 65).

Article 2 cannot be "unconcerned with issues to do with the quality of living or what a person chooses to do with his or her life" as the court claims it to be. Instead, it should allow for the possibility that one decides to end one's life when one has come to believe that it is no longer compatible with one's own understanding of what it means to lead a good life. By articulating a different Jewish tradition – one focused not on the necessity of preserving mere life, but on the possibility of leading a good life – Benjamin's approach shows that the judges' understanding of the sanctity of life is not a universally shared belief, and not even a shared Western belief. Instead, it is a particular Christian interpretation, at odds with other religious traditions that suggest that the sanctity of life protects not the right to mere life, but the right to a good life.[27]

Benjamin's other law enables us not only to criticize the court's judgment for depending on a particular interpretation of the sanctity of life. It also allows us to criticize, what Anabelle Mooney has identified as, a "legal religion" or "religion *of* the law", which can be traced in the judgment.[28] Characteristic of this legal religion is the close attention that is paid to language, and, more specifically, the belief in the truth and objectivity of the legal text.[29] This belief resurfaces briefly in the court's remark that "Art. 2 cannot, *without a distortion of language*, be interpreted as conferring the diametrically opposite right, namely a right to die" (para. 39, emphasis added), for it suggests that the language of the Article itself excludes a right to die. By contrast, Benjamin suggests that the law must always also allow for its opposite meaning, that is, the responsibility one may have to take for refusing its imperative in exceptional cases. For Benjamin, this is crucial: in figuring the commandment as the model for another kind of law, a non-violent and non-coercive law, he emphasizes the possibility of multiple, even conflicting interpretations. It is this possibility which shows that the law is founded upon the responsibility of those who are bound by

27 As Annabelle Mooney has noted in her brilliant analysis of the case, the phrase "sanctity of life" plays a key role in the arguments of both the Lords and the ECtHR. The word "sanctity", she explains, betrays the religious dimensions of the case, for "sanctity is not a synonym for secular respect. It is, quite literally, the *holiness* of life" (58). The religiosity of the phrase, however, is not made explicit; instead, it is related to a supposedly Western perspective. Article 2 is thus said to "reflect the sanctity which, *particularly in Western eyes*, attaches to life" (para. 14, at 5, emphasis added). The sanctity of life is not presented as a religious, or, indeed, a particularly Christian belief, but as a shared, secular conviction of the West. By relating the sanctity of life to a supposedly shared Western perspective, the courts prevent its Christian origins from being traced. Mooney 2008, p. 53 and 56.

28 *Id.*, p. 51-52.

29 The sources of this legal religion are probably age-old; they derive from the fact that Western legal thinking was developed from the Middle-Ages onwards in close relation to Christian theology, with which it shared, among other things, its exegetical method, *i.e.*, the word-for-word explanation of authoritative texts. What remains of this legal religion today, is a method of legal interpretation that presupposes the belief in the true and objective meaning of the legal text, a meaning that is believed to inhere in the text itself. Cf. R.C. van Caenegem, *European Law in the Past and the Future*, Cambridge University Press, Cambridge 2002, p. 54-55 and 62-63.

it. Thus, it is the very ambiguity of the legal text, the unavailability of a true and objective meaning, which makes the responsibility before the law possible.

However, Benjamin does not reject the religion *of* the law, to which the court's judgment testifies, altogether. Instead, he articulates a different religious tradition, emphasizing that the law's true and objective meaning cannot be known with certainty from the limited, historical perspective of man.[30] This implies that one has to take responsibility for one's own explanation of the law, allowing for the possibility of multiple interpretations, and proposing one's own in the awareness of this unavoidable uncertainty. On Benjamin's view, then, every interpretation of the law is, and must remain, one's own interpretation, not dictated by the language of the law itself, but stemming from the responsibility one takes for explaining the law. Therefore, deciding a case by noting that the legal text itself does not allow for a certain interpretation, as the court does in the case of Mrs. Pretty, can be criticized as a failure to take responsibility – a responsibility, which, Benjamin suggests, is involved in all interpretation of the law. Thus, the court's claim that the language of Article 2 would be distorted if it would be interpreted as conferring the diametrically opposite right, namely a right to die, can no longer be endorsed once one realizes that it is the very possibility of this opposite meaning, the very possibility that Article 2 does indeed confer a right to die, which constitutes our responsibility before the law.

I do not want to suggest that analyzing the case of Mrs. Pretty from the perspective of Benjamin's other law would have led to a different judgment. Nor do I claim that, in view of Benjamin's understanding of law, the possibility of assisted suicide should have been protected under Article 2. Rather, what I want to make clear is that the court's judgment in this case has been dependent on implicitly religious beliefs – beliefs that are not universally shared. These beliefs, a belief in the sanctity of life and a belief in the truth and objectivity of legal language, can be criticized from the perspective of Benjamin's other approach to law, which is based on a different religious tradition – a tradition that seeks

---

30 Brian Britt argues that, for Benjamin, sacred texts such as the biblical commandment paradoxically gesture to their true meaning through narratives of its loss. Britt refers to Benjamin's essay on Franz Kafka, in which the author suggests that the true meaning of the law has been lost to mankind. In a letter, Gershom Scholem had objected to this interpretation, arguing that the true meaning of the law had not been lost, but had merely become indecipherable, thus leaving open the possibility that it could be rediscovered. In a letter to his friend, Benjamin replied that the two interpretations amounted to the same thing: "whether the students have lost it or whether they are unable to decipher it comes down to the same thing, because, without the key that belongs to it, the Scripture is not Scripture, but life. Life as it is lived in the village at the foot of the hill on which the castle is built." Letter from Benjamin to Scholem, 11 August 1934, *in The Correspondence of Walter Benjamin and Gershom Scholem, 1932-1940*, ed. G. Scholem, G. Smith & A. Lefevere (Trans.), Schocken, New York 1989, p. 135. On this letter, compare: B. Britt, *Benjamin and the Bible*, Continuum, New York 1996, p. 13 and 29; Agamben 1998, p. 53; S. Mosès, *The Angel of History: Rosenzweig, Benjamin, Scholem*, trans. B. Harshav, Stanford University Press, Stanford 2009, p. 157-159.

to do justice to our responsibility before the law. From this perspective, it becomes possible to argue that, in view of Mrs. Pretty's exceptional circumstances, it was perhaps necessary to abandon the imperative 'thou shalt not kill', and to allow that her life was taken, not to protect mere life, but to protect her own understanding of what constitutes a good life. It is this possibility, I believe, that the court should not have categorically excluded by referring to a particular notion of the "sanctity of life" and a supposedly objective meaning of the law, but should have taken into consideration, as its responsibility before the law required it.

Conclusion

In this paper, my intention was to show how Benjamin, in his essay *Critique of Violence*, developed an alternative approach to law based on the idea that law should not be dependent on violent coercion, but on the responsibility of those bound to it. I began by describing Benjamin's critique of legal violence, explaining that it was directed not against law as such, but against certain conceptions of law. Thus, Benjamin criticized the mainstream theories of law of his day, legal positivism and natural law, for understanding violence instrumentally as a legal means to promote certain legal ends. As Benjamin explained, the legal order was dependent, instead, on a lawmaking and law-preserving violence that could not be adequately understood in terms of means and ends, and that could not be legally controlled. More particularly, Benjamin criticized the dialectic of lawmaking and law-preserving violence, arguing that it had led to a formless and unlimited kind of violence, which caused legal institutions to fall into decay. On his view, only the proletarian general strike's categorical refusal of law – a refusal to accept the authority of existing laws, as well as a refusal to impose new ones – could interrupt this catastrophic dialectic of lawmaking and law-preserving violence, thereby embodying the promise that law's dependence on violence would be brought to an end.

As we have seen, Benjamin's admiration for the revolutionaries' refusal of law has led some commentators to believe that, for Benjamin, law was inevitably tied to violence and oppression, and that justice could therefore be attained only outside of law. Contrary to these views, I argued that, for Benjamin, justice was necessarily related to law, and, more particularly, to a responsibility *before* the law. It consisted of the responsibility to engage with the law's imperative, to explain it, to follow or abandon it in view of exceptional circumstances. As we have seen, Benjamin developed this alternative understanding of law in the context of his discussion of the biblical commandment 'thou shalt not kill'. On his understanding, the commandment mandated only a solitary struggle, leaving open the possibilities of its interpretation and the conditions under which it could be refused. For Benjamin, the commandment thereby embodied the promise of another law – a law that would no longer dictate and that would no longer be violently enforced. As I suggested, Benjamin's notion of the commandment also enabled him to criticize existing biopolitical approaches to law, since it showed that the protection of mere life was not the ultimate purpose of the legal order. Thus, Benjamin related the commandment to a particular understanding of the "sanctity of life," according to which the sanctity attached not to mere life, not to man's bodily existence, but to the possible righteousness of life.

Finally, I examined the case of *Pretty v. United Kingdom* from the perspective of Benjamin's legal theory in order to show its continuing relevance. Following Mooney's analysis, I argued that the court's judgment was informed by two implicitly religious beliefs, a belief in the sanctity of life and a belief in the objective meaning of the legal text. As I suggested, both beliefs could be criticized from the perspective of Benjamin's legal theory. Thus the court's claim that Article 2 ECHR did not allow for a right to die, since it was framed to protect the sanctity of life, turned out to refer to a particular Christian understanding of the sanctity of life, which was not universal, nor even shared in the West. Articulating a different religious tradition, Benjamin suggested that the sanctity of life did allow for a deliberate taking of life in view of exceptional circumstances, because it protected not primarily man's bodily existence, but the ethical dignity of life. Moreover, as I explained, the court's belief in the objectivity of the legal text could be criticized from the perspective of Benjamin's alternative approach to law, as it could be viewed as a failure to take responsibility. Thus, on Benjamin's understanding, even if the law had a true and objective meaning, it could not diminish our responsibility for explaining it, and this required that other meanings had to be taken into consideration, including its opposite, that a right to die should be recognized in view of exceptional circumstances.

The question that remains is what *we* should think of Benjamin's law. How should we evaluate it? I am not the first to raise this question. As we have seen, authors such as Butler and Derrida already criticized Benjamin for his general opposition to the coercive character of law, pointing out that some level of coercion was necessary to prevent the kind of contempt for law that characterized Fascism and other systems of institutionalized violence. As I pointed out, however, Benjamin's opposition against the coercive character of law did not imply a complete rejection of law. Instead, it referred to the possibility of another kind of law – a law based not on violence, but on responsibility. Still, it is doubtful whether Benjamin's notion of a responsibility before the law suffices to prevent the violent refusal of law for which Butler and Derrida have warned. Although this would require a careful analysis – an analysis which falls outside the scope of this paper – my intuition is that it does not suffice. On my view, then, although the law should indeed be founded on the responsibility of those engaging with it, so that they cannot hide behind the rules or behind some supposed objectivity of the legal text, it should perhaps bind them in a manner that goes beyond its possible refusal, entailing the risk of coercion when the law is abandoned.

Does Carl Schmitt Defend a Critical Legal Indeterminacy Thesis?

Jeroen Kiewiet

Introduction

The recent interest of many critical legal scholars in the oeuvre of Carl Schmitt puts the following question to the fore: why is Schmitt's work relevant or interesting for Critical Legal Studies (CLS)? Prominent critical legal scholars like Giorgo Agamben, Jacques Derrida, Ellen Kennedy, Chantal Mouffe and Slavoj Žižek have analyzed Schmitt's work or have used Schmitt's insights for the benefit of their own work.[1] The interest of critical legal scholars in Carl Schmitt strikes on first sight as counter-intuitive, because of his conservative political views, which are *prima facie* in fierce contrast with the political beliefs of most critical legal scholars. Schmitt is known as a profound Catholic thinker, who even explicitly worked on the promotion of the position of the Roman Catholic Church in his 1923 volume *Roman Catholicism and Political Form.*[2] His criterion of the political, the distinction between friends and foes, in his famous work *The Concept of the Political,*[3] can only be traced back to a Christian stance: the existence of evil in the world after Adam and Eve left Paradise resulting in a state of chaos and the inevitability of a force strong enough to prevent that state of chaos.[4]

Despite the fact that Schmitt's anti-liberal stance stems from his Roman Catholic conviction, it has a significant resemblance with the position of many critical legal scholars. The critique of the modern liberal state constitutes a common denominator. In the left wing strand of thought of CLS, liberalism was understood as concealing society's real problems, i.e. class conflicts within society and society's power structures. CLS unmasked 'law as ideology': the ideological biases inherent in the, at first sight neutral, concepts and analyses. In Schmitt's analysis liberalism stands for neutralization and de-politicizations of the real issues. Liberalism obscures society's conflicts by moulding them into economic terms or

1 E.g. D. Dyzenhaus, *Hard Cases in Wicked Legal Systems*, Clarendon. Oxford 1991 and C. Mouffe(Ed.), *The Challenge of Carl Schmitt*, Verso, London 1999 and J.-W. Müller, *Ein gefährlicher Geist: Carl Schmitts Wirkung in Europa*, Wissenschaftliche Buchgesellschaft, Darmstadt 2007.

2 C. Schmitt, *Römischer Katholizismus und politische Form*, Klett-Cotta, Stuttgart 1985 (reprint 2nd ed. 1925).

3 C. Schmitt, *Der Begriff des Politischen*, Duncker & Humblot, Berlin 1996a (reprint 1932/1963).

4 H. Meier, *Carl Schmitt and Leo Strauss. The Hidden Dialogue*, Chicago University Press, Chicago 1995.

translating them into the human rights vocabulary.[5] According to Schmitt, political questions are de-politicized and no longer recognized as political problems. But no matter how hard liberalism tries to conceal or reject the political character of certain decisions, the political character of human society is unavoidable. This means, according to Schmitt's criterion of the political, that no ethical, religious, legal or economic analysis is capable to underpin final decisions. This is explicitly clear for warfare: no pious, moral or profit motives can provide a motivation for the decision of war.[6] But Schmitt's criterion of the political is not restricted to this: every religious, moral, economic controversy is to a certain degree a political controversy.[7] The political character lies not in the battle itself, but in the potential conflict between friend and foe, which does not run according to, for example, religious or economic criteria. Therefore, the Marxist class struggle (*Klassenkampf*) is not a purely economic struggle, as may be claimed by Marx, but essentially a political conflict.

The consequence of Schmitt's anti-liberal analysis of the unavoidable character of the political is his critique on the neutrality of legal positivism, understood as rule formalism. In this critique on liberalism legal positivism is understood as statuary positivism, used to conceal the real problems at hand. This critique comes very close to CLS' critique on liberalism and legal positivism. The question arises how far and in what sense the legal indeterminacy thesis of Schmitt and CLS are related. I will show that Schmitt's concept of legal indeterminacy can be traced back to his decisionism, which is in fact a three stage concept. In the subsequent paragraph I will investigate the precise extent of Schmitt's and CLS' legal indeterminacy theses. CLS' legal indeterminacy thesis must be split up into a critique on legal adjudication whose pretention of neutrality is contested, and a linguistic analysis critique. When discussing CLS' legal indeterminacy thesis I will make a direct comparison with Schmitt's conception of legal indeterminacy, to conclude finally if Schmitt defends a CLS-like indeterminacy thesis or not.

Carl Schmitt's Legal Indeterminacy Thesis

Determinacy in the context of this essay refers to the thought that the law is able to determine the outcome of particular legal disputes.[8] Schmitt deals with legal indeterminacy in a major part of his oeuvre. His first work after his PhD dissertation *Gesetz und Urteil* (*Statute and Judgment*) in 1912 is completely dedicated to legal indeterminacy and during

5 Schmitt 1996a, p. 55: 'Wer Menschheit sagt will betrügen' (Who says humanity intends to deceive).

6 *Id.*, p. 36.

7 *Id.*, p. 37-38.

8 L.B. Solum, 'Indeterminacy', *in* D.M. Patterson, *A Companion to Philosophy of Law and Legal Theory*, Wiley-Blackwell, Malden 1999, p. 488-509, at p. 488.

the 1920s and the start of the 1930s Schmitt returns on many occasions to the subject of legal indeterminacy. Conceptually, Carl Schmitt's and Critical Legal Theory's models of legal judgments are in close proximity. Because of this conceptual kinship it is necessary to draw a detailed comparison concentrated on three aspects. The first aspect concerns the *prima facie* radical legal indeterminacy thesis itself, which Schmitt seems to defend in *Gesetz und Urteil* in 1912. The second aspect concerns the personal aspect of the person who decides, which Schmitt unfolds mainly in his works *Die Diktatur* (*The Dictatorship*) and *Politische Theologie* [9] *(Political Theology).* [10] The third aspect concerns the lack of democratic legitimization of courts and especially constitutional courts, which Schmitt deals with in *Der Hüter der Verfassung* [11] *(The Keeper of the Constitution)*. To avoid any misunderstanding: these aspects cannot be considered separately, but are interwoven: Schmitt's criticism on the judges' lack of democratic legitimacy is already unfolded *inter alia* in *Gesetz und Urteil.* The kinship between Schmitt's conception of legal indeterminacy and Critical Legal Theory's legal indeterminacy thesis can be exposed more insightfully now. And this is necessary in order to conclude, in the following paragraphs, whether Schmitt's legal indeterminacy is a defendable thesis and whether Critical Legal Theory's indeterminacy thesis is affected by the critique which can be addressed to Schmitt's legal indeterminacy thesis.

First Stage: Rejection of Rule Formalism

In *Gesetz und Urteil* Schmitt rejects the positivist legal theory of rule formalism. This formalist legal theory is also referred to as rule formalism (‘*Gesetzespositivismus*’). His criticism on this rule formalism is that it presupposes the legal system to be a closed system. The legal system equals the statutes. There is no law beyond or before the codified collection of statutes. This is in Schmitt's opinion a ridiculous claim. A legal system is more and something different than a mathematical system. The judge cannot draw a solution in a court case upon the axioms that rule the system. Judicial decisions are not like mathematical equations: there is *always* room for interpretation. [12] Statutes never completely dictate the outcome. [13] The binding force of precedents is not under discussion as a determining factor: statutory rules equals law in this rule formalistic view on law.

---

9 C. Schmitt, *Politische Theologie. Vier Kapitel zur Lehre von der Souveränität,* Duncker & Humblot, Berlin 1993a (reprint 1922, 6th ed.).

10 C. Schmitt, *Die Diktatur. Von den Anfängen des modernen Souveränitätsgedankens bis zum proletarischen Klassenkampf,* Duncker & Humblot. Berlin 1994.

11 C. Schmitt, *Der Hüter der Verfassung,* Duncker & Humblot, Berlin 1996b (reprint 1931).

12 C. Schmitt, *Gesetz und Urteil. Eine Untersuchung zum Problem der Rechtspraxis,* C.H. Beck, München 1969 (2nd ed.), Chapter 1.

13 *Id.*

Even the promoters of rule formalism and the claim that the law consists only out of statutes must admit that sometimes there is a doubt concerning the right application of a statutory provision. It cannot be completely ruled out that the unhindered application of a statutory provision is always the case. In general, not every case can be foreseen by the legislator; the language of the provision is ambiguous or the outcome if the rule would be applied is not acceptable. But even in cases in which rule application is problematic the formalist legal positivists claim that all legal decisions can be traced back to statutes. The focus, then, is shifted towards the ambiguity of the rule, which, in Schmitt's analysis of the 'statutory positivists', was overcome with an appeal to the intention of the legislator: to rule out the ambiguity of a statutory provision a research of what the legislator intended suffices. [14] Including the legislator's intention, the claim of a completely determined legal system could be attained.

According to Schmitt, this is the traditional rule formalist vision. [15] Critique on this rule formalist position is obvious. The intention of the legislator and the sources in which this can be found, like the framer's memorandum, are not part of the actual statute. The opinion of the framer of the legislation has no legal status. The main point of criticism, though, pertains to the required psychology necessary to operate the concept of intention or will. In the first place it must be clear whose will is meant. The framers of an act are not one person with one will but in general a body or different bodies existing of a certain number of members. It is not unthinkable that during the legislative process several members of different government or parliamentary bodies are involved. Are all these 'wills' subjected to investigation? And if these wills are conflicting, are there any conflict rules giving priority to some wills over other wills? A more fundamental critique is that psychology should be avoided in legal argumentation. Psychology is as such irrelevant for the meaning and scope of legal provisions: a psychological argument is not *per se* legally relevant.

Schmitt's critique on a rule formalist concept of law must be put into perspective. Schmitt holds on to this view on formalism, [16] without critically reviewing his own critique. His anti-formalist critique can be traced back to the Free law movement (*Freirechtsbewegung*) of Eugen Ehrlich and Hermann Kantorowicz. Both authors criticized legal formalism from a sociological point of view. Kantorowicz's analysis suggests that rule formalist legal posi-

14 *Id.*

15 Cf. R. Dworkin, *A Matter of Principe*, Harvard University Press, Cambridge (Ma.) 2000, p. 33-71.

16 E.g. C. Schmitt, *Verfassungsrechtliche Aufsätze aus den Jahren 1924–1954. Materialien zu einer Verfassungslehre*, Duncker & Humblot, Berlin 1958, p. 346.

tivism ignores the fact that the judge is not a kind of machine,[17] who, in the famous words of Montesquieu, acts like "*la bouche de la loi*".[18] Max Weber gives a compact summary of this "present-day legal science" in a few postulates. Most importantly, concrete legal decisions are the application of an abstract legal proposition to a concrete fact situation (*Tatbestand*), the law is a "gap-less" system, and it must be possible to reach in every concrete case a decision from abstract legal propositions.[19] This understanding of "present-day legal science" by Kantorowicz is in fact an ideal and not the reality of the practice of legal adjudication. The claim that a legal system is 'gap-less' and that judges do nothing else than applying abstract propositions to concrete fact situations has nothing to do with the reality of legal adjudication. The Free law movement takes this ideal as the reality of legal adjudication.[20]

The critique that can be raised against the Free law movement can be directed against Schmitt's criticism on the rule formalist concept of a completely determined legal system and the role of the judge reduced to a 'mechanical judge'. On itself the rejection of Kantorowicz's and Schmitt's critique directed against the rule formalist conception of a closed legal system operated by a mechanical judge is correct. But was this rule formalist conception ever claimed by anyone? Schmitt is very scarce with references to 'formalists'; Carl Friedrich von Gerber and Paul Laband show up as "formalists" and "statutory positivists".[21] The attacks of Kantorowicz and Schmitt seem to be essentially attacks on a rule formalist straw man. Why is the opposition against a formalist concept of law as vehement as presented in Kantorowicz's and Schmitt's work? A reason lies in the rejection of the primary focus on the legislator in the first years after the enactment of the German private law codification in 1900,[22] and a rehabilitation of the position of the judge since the strong emphasis in German jurisprudence at the end of the nineteenth century on the legislator. Schmitt does not abandon his anti-rule formalist position, despite the obvious critique from a socio-historical point of view.

---

17 H. Kantorowicz, 'Der Kampf um die Rechtswissensenschaft' [reprint of 1907 version], *in* Th. Würtenberger (Ed.), *Rechtswissenschaft und Soziologie. Ausgewählte Schriften zur Wissenschaftslehre*. Müller, Karlsruhe 1962.

18 Montesquieu, *De l'esprit du loi*, XI, 6: '*Mais les juges de la nation ne sont [...] que la bouche qui prononce les paroles de la loi [...].*' <www.efm.bris.ac.uk/het/montesquieu/mindex1.htm> (last accessed: 6 June 2011).

19 B.Z. Tamanaha, *Beyond the Formalist-Realist-Divide. The Role of Politics in Judging*, Princeton University Press, Princeton 2010, p. 25.

20 Cf. Kantorowicz 1962, p. 38.

21 E.g. Schmitt 1994; Schmitt 1958, p. 263-350.

22 R. Ogorek, *Richterkönig oder Subsumtionsautomat? Zur Justiztheorie im 19. Jahrhundert*, Klostermann, Frankfurt 1986, p. 56. Regarding the American Legal Realists: Tamanaha 2010.

Second Stage: The Coordination Function of Law

According to Schmitt, it is sometimes more important that a decision be made, regardless of the exact content of the decision. The decision itself must be seen as separate from the norm and its content.[23] Schmitt claims that in a modern society the coordinating function of law is predominant. In *Gesetz und Urteil* and *Politische Theologie* Schmitt uses the example of the railway timetable to illustrate that it is more important that something be decided upon than the content of the decision.[24] Strangely, Schmitt picks the non-legal example of a railroad timetable to stress the importance of legal decisions. The example does not illustrate Schmitt's point that it should be more important that a decision is taken than the content of the decision. It is obvious that law should be effective and that the law should be predictable, but is not clear why legal certainty should be so important in contrast to the substance of the decision itself. Schmitt overstates the importance of the coordinating function of law. That in a modern society coordination of traffic is important simply ignores too much the importance of the substance of decisions. Imagine the daily practice of lawsuits: in almost every case it is the substance of the decision – do you get your defective television repaired at the cost of the manufacturer or can you force your landlord to get entrance to your rented apartment – which is of interest and not that just the simple fact that a decision is taken. It is not coordination, as Schmitt claims with his decisionism, but certainty that a relevant decision can be produced within the legal system.

The coordination argument by itself is an interesting point: it might be plausible that in Western society at the beginning of the twentieth century the need for social and economic coordination by law was getting stronger. In a society getting more complex, coordination by formal institutions, like law, might be more important than in less complex societies. In fact, almost every important sociology of law theory, e.g. Émile Durkheim's sociology of the stages of mechanical and organic solidarity and Donald Black's relational distance proposition, is based mainly on society's complexity and the need for law as a co-coordinating instrument to 'manage' this complexity. Thus, Schmitt's claim that there is an increased need for law as a coordinating instrument seems to be plausible. Nevertheless, the question is whether his decisionist concept of law can supply such a coordinating function. In fact only in very few cases it is as trivial as Schmitt describes in his examples of travelling at the right or left hand side of the road and his railroad timetable example. As already argued, the timetable example partly fails its purpose: Schmitt overstates the coordinative aspect. The traffic regulation example is in fact more clarifying: it is indeed morally neutral which side of the road the traffic uses, as long as it is the just the same

23 Schmitt 1993a, p. 37.

24 Schmitt 1969, p. 48; Schmitt 1993a, p. 36-37.

side.[25] It is possible to see the need of traffic regulations as a second order moral requirement: the decision may be highly contingent, but the need for a well-regulated traffic serves in itself a moral purpose.

The most surprising aspect of the coordination argument is that Schmitt contradicts this argument in his warning for so-called motorized legislation.[26] Schmitt criticises in his 1932 volume *Legality and Legitimacy* delegation from the formal legislator as designated in the constitution hierarchy to lower legislative bodies. His critique is a recurring question of constitutional law: is there a sufficient legal basis for government actions? The limits of delegation should be clearly demarcated. And in line with the limitation of delegation, Schmitt claims that statutes are not any longer used to regulate general classes of cases but are enacted on an *ad hoc* basis to regulate concrete cases instead of giving general rules. This practice conflicts with the legal principle of *quod raro fit, non observant legislatores* (legislators do not enact laws to deal with concrete cases). In a formal conception of rule of law the principle of legality serves as the ultimate safeguard against unlawful government actions.[27] The tension between Schmitt's coordination argument and his delegation critique concerns the following: if Schmitt's warning against unbridled delegation should be taken seriously, it is not at the same time possible to claim an unlimited form of the coordination argument. The law fulfils its coordinating role with as many rules as possible: if it were a rule for each case specifically coordination would be optimal. But at the same time this 'motorized legislation' threatens the interests at stake of the concept of formal legality, which demands that statutes regulate general categories and not specific cases.

Third Stage: Who Decides?

Schmitt complains in the preface of the second edition of *Gesetz und Urteil*, in October 1968 that his legal theory of decisionism has been turned by his opponents into a 'fantastic voluntaristic act, decisionism as a dangerous perception of the world and the deformation of the word decisionism to a slogan and an invective'.[28] It is true that decisionism has often been interpreted as voluntarism,[29] or arbitrariness[30], and hence as something condemnable. The following passage from *Political Theology* illustrates the close relation

25 Cf. H.L.A. Hart, *The Concept of Law*, Oxford University Press, Oxford 1994 (2nd ed.), p. 229.

26 'Die Lage der europäischen Rechtswissenschaft', Schmitt 1958, p. 386-429; 'Legalität und Legitimität', *in* Schmitt 1958, p. 263-350; W.E. Scheuerman, 'Motorized Legislation? Statutes in an Age of Speed', *Archiv für Rechts- und Sozialphilosophie*, Vol. 88, No. 4, 2002, p. 379-397.

27 B.Z. Tamanaha, *On the Rule of Law*, Cambridge University Press, Cambridge 2004, p. 91-101.

28 Schmitt 1969, p. VII.

29 Tamanaha 2004, p. 114 ff.

30 P. Westerman, *The Disintegration of Natural Law Theory*, Brill, Leiden 1998, p. 259-285.

between Schmitt's decisionistic stance and the legal 'bindingness' of a *prima facie* arbitrary will of the person or legal instance that decides:

> That it is the instance of competence that renders a decision makes the decision relative, and in certain circumstances absolute and independent of the correctness of its content. This terminates any further discussion about whether there may still be some doubt. The decision becomes instantly independent of argumentative substantiation and receives an autonomous value. [31]

Decisionism has been identified in the legal theoretical context with voluntarism, [32] which is identification deemed objectionable because the law is no more than the arbitrary will – *voluntas* – of the person or legal instance that decides. Understood thus, it goes against the grain of the modern ideal of the rule of law, advocating the opposite: the idea of 'government of laws and not of men'. [33] Schmitt's position in *Gesetz und Urteil, Der Wert des Staates und die Bedeutung des Einzelnen, Die Diktatur* and *Politische Theologie* is essentially that of a legal positivist. Stanley Paulson describes the core of legal positivism forcefully:

> 'Legal positivism in the jurisprudential tradition of the European Continent is characterized by what might be called the facticity thesis: the law is ultimately explicable in terms of, or "reducible to", a concatenation of fact – whether it be power, the will of the sovereign, or the community's acceptance of the legal system.' [34]

Or in John Griffiths' words: "It is the factual power of the state which is the keystone of an otherwise normative system, which affords the empirical condition for the actual existence of 'law'". [35] Kelsen and Hart are prominent representatives of this 'facticity thesis'. The question is whether Schmitt can be considered to belong to this legal positivist tradition. How close is Schmitt's legal theory to the 'facticity thesis' which characterizes legal positivism? The question whether a specific legal theory should be labeled 'legal positivist' or 'natural law' is certainly one of the most confusing questions in modern legal theory. There is no overlapping consensus concerning the concepts of legal positivism and natural law. It is much more useful to compose a set of criteria by reference to which different legal

31 Schmitt 2005, p. 31.

32 A.G.G. de Groot. *Der skandinavische Realismus und seine Bedeutung für die rechtliche Grundlagenforschung*, Thesis, Amsterdam 1997, p. 302-304.

33 J. Locke, *Two Treatises of Government*. New Haven & London: Yale University Press, New Haven/London 2004, § 202: 'Wherever law ends, tyranny begins (...)'; Massachusetts Constitution, art. XXX.

34 S.L. Paulson, 'Hans Kelsen's Earliest Legal Theory: Critical Constructivism', *Modern Law Review*, Vol. 59, No. 6, 1996, p. 797-812.

35 J. Griffiths, 'What Is Legal Pluralism?', *Journal of Legal Pluralism*, Vol. 24, 1986, p. 1-55, at p. 3.

theoretical stances can be reviewed. Criteria such as the facticity thesis, the separation of law and morality, and the inclusion or exclusion of legal principles as part of a concept of law.

Schmitt expresses a fierce criticism of rule formalistic legal positivism, as being empty and formalistic, ignoring society's substantive values. This criticism *prima facie* comes very close to Critical Legal Theory's critique on 'the poverty of legal positivism'. [36] In Critical Legal Theory legal positivism stands for a concept of law that ignores the political nature of law. Law is presented as objective and neutral, but the concepts and analyses are not neutral but always used for certain political interests. The ideal of rule of law is used as a dress to cloak the real interests and conflicts in society. In doing so, it suppresses (racial) minorities, women, and other group interests that fall outside the fold. [37] In short, Critical Legal Studies accusations amount to ideology critique: the Western liberal ideology conceals the real interests and conflicts because that is beneficial for a bourgeoisie minority.

It must be kept in mind that Schmitt envisages a very specific concept of legal positivism, namely legal positivism as rule formalism statutory positivism, as set out above, referring to his view on decisionism. His rejection of a rule formalistic legal positivism does not automatically imply that he adheres to H.L.A. Hart's separation thesis, which claims that there is no necessary connection between law and morality. [38] There is a clear tendency in Schmitt's work to stress the morality of law. His decisionistic stance at the start of his work is directed at the morality of the judges, to be found in the judge's professional ethics. But still, Schmitt underlines the importance of the decision, contingent in terms of content as it may be, as illustrated by his 'traffic cases' ('*Bedürfnisse des Verkehrslebens*'). As mentioned before, it is possible to see the need of traffic regulations as a second order moral requirement: the need for a well regulated traffic serves in itself a moral purpose.

As mentioned in *Der Wert des Staates und die Bedeutung des Einzelnen*, *Die Diktatur* and *Political Theology*, Schmitt sticks to a position which is really close to Paulson's the facticity thesis. [39] The state, designated in *Political Theology* as sovereign, is there to actualize the law. Only by its actualisation does the law receive its legally binding force. Schmitt nuances this position strongly in his famous *Verfassungslehre*. There, he argues that the ethical substance of a presupposed people is the constituting will, giving binding force to the

36 Cf. Dyzenhaus 1991, p. 268.

37 Tamanaha 2004, p. 89; D. Kennedy, 'A Left Phenomenological Alternative to the Hart/Kelsen Theory of Legal Interpretation', *in Duncan Kennedy. Legal Reasoning, Collected Essays,* Davies Book Publishers, Aurora 2008, p. 167.

38 H.L.A. Hart, 'Positivism and the Separation of Law and Morals', *Harvard Law Review,* Vol. 71. 1958, p. 593-629.

39 Schmitt 2004; Schmitt 1994; Schmitt 1993a.

constitution and with it (as the normative top of the legal order) to the legal order itself. In *Der Hüter der Verfassung* this position culminates in the assertion that the state leader needs a special kind of authority.[40] Finally, Schmitt's decisionistic legal theory is partly rejected by himself as only being one type of legal thinking next to statutory positivism and concrete order thinking, which is Schmitt's concept of institutional legal theory.[41] Thus, the 'emptiness' of the decisionistic decision, in the sense that it is more important that a decision is taken than its content, is relativized by the quality of the person or legal instance that takes the decision and by the introduction of the 'concrete order', viz. institutions like family, army, marriage, that provides the 'ethical substance' of the decision.[42]

CLS' Legal Indeterminacy Thesis

A general characterization of CLS' indeterminacy thesis is problematic: there is probably much disagreement within CLS on this topic. Regardless, I believe that CLS' indeterminacy thesis boils down to two distinctive branches of argumentation that can be distinguished within CLS' concept of legal indeterminacy. The first branch concerns the gap between moral and political principles that exists because of legal indeterminacy. I will discuss this first point with the help of Duncan Kennedy's contribution to CLS' legal indeterminacy thesis. I will discuss Kennedy's critique and compare it with Schmitt's view. Therefore, I will have to give a summary of Kelsen's and Hart's thoughts on legal indeterminacy because Kennedy's position is a reaction on Kelsen's and Hart's conception of legal indeterminacy. The second branch of critique focuses on a linguistic analysis, viz. the semantic scepticism associated with Wittgenstein and Derrida.[43] This linguistic critique maintains the idea of rule following and boils down to the thesis that nothing in language compels a particular result. This critique will be discussed in the final section. I will start this section with a short introduction to the context in which CLS' thoughts on legal indeterminacy originated and with some remarks concerning the differences between the civil and common law system, relevant to understand properly the different environments in which the ideas on legal indeterminacy of Schmitt and CLS originated.

40 Schmitt 1996b.

41 Schmitt 1993a, p. 8.

42 C. Schmitt, *Über die drei Arten des rechtswissenschaftlichen Denkens*, Hanseatische Verlagsanstalt, Hamburg 1934, p. 44.

43 B. Leiter, *Naturalizing Jurisprudence. Essays on American Realism and Naturalism in Legal Philosophy*, Oxford University Press, Oxford 2007, p. 99.

Different Context: Civil and Common Law

American Critical Legal Studies developed its critical view on the US Supreme Court in the 1970s. The main criticism was that the court decided on essentially political issues without being politically responsible. In the US constitutional practice the court in fact is legitimized to judge on political issues.[44] It does because the US Supreme Court does not limit itself to a pure procedural role. Such a role means that the Court only checks whether the procedural rules in the legislative process are respected. Instead, the Court also checks the compliance of statutes with the US Constitution's substance, including the Bill of Rights. To fulfil this task the Court has to interpret these fundamental rights. This substantial interpretative activity of the Court has led to an extensive interpretation of several such rights, for example the Court's decision that the claimed right of abortion in the case of Wade v. Roe was in accordance with the Constitution's text. The court decided that the right to privacy extends to the woman's decision to have an abortion, whereby that right must be balanced against that of protecting prenatal life and the mother's health.

The Court's extensive interpretative activity raises the question, from a critical legal perspective, on what grounds individual members of the court, each being appointed by the US president, decide upon highly controversial matters. Predicting what these members would decide could be easily done by looking what their shared socio-economic background is.[45] Especially Critical Legal scholars criticized the lack of democratic legitimacy of the Court's *de facto* political judgments. A majority of conservative Court members could easily block the wish for social change by society's majority. The final decision on controversial political issues is effectively in many cases with the US Supreme Court instead of the US legislator. Difficulties with organising majorities may lead to inertia concerning politically controversial matters. At the same time the US Supreme Court cannot refuse to judge in cases which ought to be decided by Congress, which gives the Court *de facto* power to decide in political controversial matters. Critical Legal scholars actually broadened their criticism to judicial decisions in general. Not only the US Supreme Court's decisions are in many cases disputable because of their lack of democratic legitimacy – being effectively the exercise of power by some men over society – but legal judgments in general are in fact undemocratic exercise of power by some men. Duncan Kennedy summarizes this critique: 'it is a premise of the liberal democratic theory of the separation of powers that ideology is *not for the judiciary (or for the jurist)*, but rather for the democratically elected legislature.' A theoretical assumption is necessary to make this claim plausible: legal

44 K. Langenbucher, 'Das Dezisionismusargument in der deutschen und in der US-amerikanischen Rechtstheorie', *Archiv für Rechts- und Sozialphilosophie*, Vol. 88, 2002, p. 398-406.

45 Tamanaha 2004, p. 89.

judgments are not completely determined by statute or precedent. A statute or precedent may affect a judgment in certain respect but that does not rule out that there is always the judge who is a determinant of the legal decision.[46] But despite this claim, Critical Legal scholars do not defend a radical indeterminacy thesis, which would mean that it is inconceivable that a legal judgment is completely determined by statute or precedent: sometimes the law is determinate and sometimes indeterminate.[47]

The difference between the civil and common law systems explains the kind of criticism that is exposed against a formalist claim of a determinate legal system. In the civil law system the claim was made in the view of the critiques of the Free law movement that statutes provide under every circumstance a sufficient determining factor. By contrast, American Legal Realists, being in this respect CLS' intellectual forerunners, criticized a formalist approach of the existing precedent system at the American courts. According to Max Weber's analysis of the difference between civil and common law systems: 'In civil code countries (…), legal formalism was the product of systematic rationalization in the universities – academic jurists controlled legal education and legal development. In common law countries, by contrast, lawyers were trained mainly by practitioners (as apprentices), and judges developed the law in a piecemeal fashion.'[48] Despite the rise of law schools in America and the rise of legal science the unsystematic development of the common law and its distinctive method of operation remained. This difference between common and civil law systems is nowadays only a matter of degree, as the systems seem to converge,[49] but the conceptual analysis of legal determinacy is still interconnected with the differences between the prominence of the legislator and the courts. It is important to take this difference into account because a substantial part of the criticisms directed at law's indeterminacy is still determined by the legal system most familiar to the critic. A similar provincialism in the current debate is the rather exclusive orientation to the US Supreme Court among American scholars. Exemplary is the work of many American scholars, notably Ronald Dworkin, who focuses entirely on the US Supreme Court and the specific problematic matter of legal indeterminacy concerning that court. This kind of generalizing the critique on the US Supreme Court constitutes a danger for a correct analysis of the judging and legal indeterminacy, as Tamanaha summarizes:

> The greatest error committed in perceptions of judging, a mistake that fans unwarranted skepticism today, is to extrapolate from the U.S. Supreme Court

46 Kennedy 2008, p. 159.
47 Kennedy 2008, p. 160. Cf. Solum 1999.
48 Tamanaha 2010 p, 26 (Max Weber, *Wirtschaft und Gesellschaft*, Mohr (Siebeck), Tübingen 1947 (3rd ed.), p. 397).
49 J.P. Dawson, *The Oracles of the Law*, Greenwood, Westport 1978, p. 505.

> to judging on other courts. The Supreme Court is a court unto itself. The factors identified above that enhance the potential influence of political views do not operate to the same extent on the lower federal courts (state high courts share some of these characteristics but not others).[50]

The US Supreme Court is, compared to many other highest courts in the Western legal systems, a highly political court. A great deal of the analysis of legal indeterminacy is simply connected with the Court's position as the ultimate decision-making institution on many highly political controversial topics. This is not true for countries in which the highest court does not have the status of a constitutional court, as for example in Germany when Schmitt developed his decisionism, or in the Netherlands still today. Here the highest court is not allowed to review legislation on substantive or formal grounds.[51]

CLS' Critique on the Debate's Starting Point

Prominent CLS scholar Duncan Kennedy starts elucidating CLS' view on legal indeterminacy by criticising *in extenso* Kelsen's and Hart's views on indeterminacy. To get a grip on CLS' views on legal indeterminacy it is important to first give a brief sketch of Kelsen's and Hart's conceptions of legal indeterminacy. In their views, a legal norm can be more or less determined. For Kelsen, the aspect of abstraction of the legal norm depends on its place in the dynamic conception of the *Stufenbau*. In Kelsen's *Pure Theory of Law* law is a set of binding legal norms.[52] Legal science is the study of these legal norms. Kelsen drew on Hume's – and Marburg's Neo-Kantian – distinction between is (*Sein*) and ought (*Sollen*). To claim that the complete legal system exists of legal norms which all express a normative ought means that the highest norm of the system – the basic norm (*Grundnorm*) – must be a legal norm too, but cannot be a norm itself. The basic norm is necessary to provide the legal system's normative aspiration; it is the ultimate normative acceptance of the legal system. The collection of legal norms forms in Kelsen's concept of law a *legal system*. This legal system is differentiated into different aspects of legal norms. The legal system is pyramid-shaped: the highest norm of the legal system is the most abstract norm; the lowest legal norm is the most concrete legal norm. Typically, the basic norm is the highest norm and an executive order the lowest and most concrete legal norm. Kelsen took this pyramidal

50 Tamanaha 2010, p. 198.

51 Article 120 Dutch Constitution.

52 H. Kelsen, *Reine Rechtslehre. Mit einem Anhang: Was ist Gerechtigkeit*, Franz Deuticke, Wien 1960, (2nd ed.).

conception of a legal system from his pupil Adolf Merkl, who destined this conception of a legal system as *Stufenbau.*[53]

As a consequence, this state of affairs requires controlling the correct application of legal norms. For this reason, Kelsen promoted in the 1920 Austrian Constitution constitutional control as a way to supervise the right application of constitutional norms and their congruence with lower legal norms, mainly to safeguard the lawful use of competences. Hence, constitutional judicial review or control exists to safeguard the coherence of the legal system ensuring the proper distribution of competences (which the application of legal norms brings along) rather than to safeguard the protection of fundamental or civil rights against state infringement. This objective is markedly different form that of the US Supreme Court since the 1970s, or *in extremis* the European Court of Human Rights (ECHR). These courts do exist for the protection of civil and fundamental human rights. Although the US Supreme Court still serves to protect and control competences of legal authorities and coherency within the legal system. The tendency – especially in the public opinion – is now to ensure the essential protection against state power of civil and fundamental human rights. This tendency is similarly visible in respect of the German constitutional court. The idea of Rule of Law or *Rechtsstaat* is nowadays directly centred on the idea of a constitutional civil and human rights court as an essential organizational back-up.

H.L.A. Hart's views on the application of legal norms (in Chapter VII of his *The Concept of Law*, on formalism and rule-skepticism) is still matter of debate today.[54] Hart advocates a position beyond formalism and rule-skepticism, which to him are the Scylla and Charybdis of legal theory.[55] Hart first sketches cases in which rule application is non-problematic. If a rule prohibits vehicles in the park a motor-car most certainly is not allowed to drive in the park.[56] However, it is not these clear-cut cases that make up the core of the rule. Rather it is the penumbra of a legal norm that causes uncertainty about its application. Is a bicycle, an (model) airplane or a set of roller skates a 'vehicle' in the terms of the legal norm, stating that vehicles are not allowed in the park? Hart describes the uncertainty about the application as the 'discretion thus left to him [typically the judge] by language' causes vagueness.[57] This 'discretion' renders the decision a choice, but a choice under the condition that 'it may not be arbitrary or irrational'.[58] This choice implies

53 *Id.*, p. 228ff.
54 Hart 1994, p. 124-154; Leiter 2007, p. 100.
55 Hart 1994, p. 147.
56 *Id.*, p. 126.
57 *Id.*, p. 127, 132.
58 *Id.*, p. 127.

adding a case to a class of cases, which it resembles, for which the outcome is clear. Decisive is whether the resemblance is legally relevant and sufficiently comparable.

Kennedy's criticism is that Kelsen and Hart's views blend out the role of the interpreter of the law. Kelsen and Hart claim that indeterminacy is not always the case: for Hart there exists a core within each legal norm (the motor-car driving through the park), in which interpretation is determinate.[59] Kelsen claims, according to Kennedy,[60] the same: there is a frame of indeterminacy, but beyond that frame the legal norms are determined. Confronted with an interpretative gap something more than mere application of the legal norm is required.[61] It is, according to Kennedy,[62] that because of the 'work' of the interpreter a gap is signalized: gaps do not exist independently from the interpreter. In legal practice it is pretended that the 'facts will be understood to establish guilt or innocence "of their own accord", as the norm "applies itself" seemingly without any agency of the interpreter'.[63] This, as Kennedy calls it, 'work' of the interpreter is what Schmitt means with stressing the importance of the decision and its 'autonomous value'.[64]

Language as Source of Legal Indeterminacy

Jacques Derrida's defence of indeterminacy is based on his techniques of deconstructivism.[65] Derrida claims that the indeterminacy of rules is, in Solum's summary, 'the function of deep contradictions within liberal society, or the failure of liberal society to reconcile or mediate a deep contradiction within the individual'.[66] In Derrida's analysis the contradiction between 'self' and 'others' is the main current that underlies all aspects of law.[67] This analysis is in fact the opposite of what Schmitt claims. For him the rule formalist's claim that the law is completely determined by statutes is a folly. Indeterminacy is a necessary component of a legal system described in realistic terms. By contrast, Derrida only focuses on the problems regarding the justification of the legal system which in reality is the battleground between individualism ('self') and altruism ('others'). For Schmitt rule formalism and the 'determinacy claim' is the product of liberal ignorance.[68] Rather than,

59 Kennedy 2008, p. 154.
60 *Id.*
61 Kennedy 2008, p. 157.
62 *Id.*, p. 158.
63 *Id.*
64 Schmitt 1993a, p. 31.
65 Solum 1999, p. 495.
66 *Id.*
67 Kennedy 2008.
68 Schmitt 1958, p. 496.

as Derrida claims, legal indeterminacy being a function of the contradiction of liberal societies.

In essence, Schmitt's idea of the rule not applying itself, as demonstrated above, especially in the quoted passage of *Political Theology*, shows a clear resemblance with the radical indeterminacy concept. The latter concept is based on a rule sceptic argument, which holds that because legal rules cannot determine their own application there is no such thing as following a rule. [69] The argument is based on Saul Kripke's interpretation of Ludwig Wittgenstein's discussion of teaching mathematical series. [70] A general rule scepticism would imply that there are no rules for the application of language to any situation. Although the idea that legal rules cannot determine their own application, which is in line with Schmitt's thoughts, it is important to mark that Schmitt is not following the rule skepticism's contention that there is no such thing as following a rule. There is no indication with Schmitt that he would agree with such a radical thesis. In fact, the following of rules itself is not subject of discussion in Schmitt's work. For example, in *Gesetz und Urteil* the legal profession itself can be interpreted as a type in the sense of Max Weber's ideal type, providing a set of rules for judges on how to decide, [71] and in *Political* Theology it is not under discussion that the sovereign enacts statutes that can be followed without completely abstracting from the social context and of the meaning of language. In short, there are no indications that Schmitt would agree with rule scepticism's contention that there are no rules for the application of language.

Reasons versus Causes of Indeterminacy

Critical Legal scholars focus on factors like wealth, gender, race, culture and ideology as determining the outcome of cases. This is a clear focus on reasons. [72] By contrast, Schmitt is not interested in these motivations. In his earlier work, like *Gesetz und Urteil*, Schmitt's focus is on the causes of indeterminacy, viz. that a statute does not dictate one outcome, but can be interpreted on several ways. Coleman and Leiter note that American Legal Realists were clearly focused on this causal factor too when they criticized the use interpretation methods, which can in fact legitimize many outcomes, and not, as sometimes by courts pretended, only one outcome. [73]

---

69 Solum, p. 493.

70 Solum, p. 493-494.

71 Schmitt 1969, Chapter IV, p. 71-119; Schmitt 1993a, p. 43ff.

72 J.L. Coleman & B. Leiter, 'Determinacy, Objectivity, and Authority', *University of Pennsylvania Law Review*, Vol. 142, 1993, p. 549-637; Solum 1999, p. 496, 497.

73 Coleman & Leiter 1993, p. 581-582; Tamanaha 2004, p. 78; Leiter 2007, p. 20.

Schmitt's claim is that next to statutes the type of the other judge is the causal factor in the determination of legal outcomes.[74] The judicial profession itself is in this way the factor that *legitimizes* the outcome of legal adjudication. The 'type of the other judge' as introduced by Schmitt comes close to CLS' idea of conventionalism as explanation for the predictability in law. A crucial difference is that Schmitt acknowledges the shared legal culture as a way of legitimatising the judge's decision given the fact that a stature does not provide in full determination of a decision. This is true for Ehrlich and Kantorowicz's Free law movement; they do not focus on the reasons for deciding like the judge's socio-cultural background or ideology are not in their focus.

Despite their shared conceptual aspects concerning the radical indeterminacy thesis and the problem of lacking democratic legitimacy of the one who decides, Schmitt and CLS differ on one important issue: the determining factor of legal judgments. Critical Legal scholars conclude that the socio-cultural person of the judge is determining legal judgments. Schmitt does not completely agree with this. In *Gesetz und Urteil* the type of the other judge is the standard which transcends the arbitrariness of the individual judge's will. In *The Dictatorship* and culminating in *Political Theology* Schmitt poses the question that if the decision is normatively born out of nothingness who will decide on the exception, suggesting that it would be the person of the judge. But this is only a single fragment in Schmitt's oeuvre. Schmitt fills the gap of the emptiness of the decision with the ethical substance provided by the people in *Constitutional Theory* (1928) and *The Concept of the Political*. The problem which was signalled clearly in *The Dictatorship* and *Political Theology* of the impossibility of the people to act, to apply rules concretely,[75] explains Schmitt's interest for representative theories, seeking an answer to the question of how to overcome the impossibility of the people to effectively rule whilst being the ultimate source of legitimization of these rules at the same time.

Conclusion

Schmitt defends a particular type of indeterminacy thesis. His concept of indeterminacy oscillates between the search for substantive quality of the law and the assertion that the law is radically indeterminate when viewed from a rule formalist point of view. Schmitt's attacks at the rule formalist position and the necessary replacement of rule formalism because of its inadequacy for jurisprudence are not entirely convincing. At the beginning of the twentieth century many voices, notably Kantorowicz's Free law movement, objected against rule formalistic legal positivism. Schmitt's portrait of liberal legal positivism that

74 Schmitt 1969.

75 Schmitt 1969, p. 29.

would defend rule formalism boils down to an attack on that ideal of rule formalistic positivism. But Schmitt's critique was not a reflection on the actual practice of legal adjudication in Germany in the first decades of the twentieth century, but a mere theoretical critique. CLS shares this formalist critique partly, but from the American Legal Realist's perspective: a formalistic style of legal reasoning avoids the political dilemmas which judges face in legal practice.[76] This American Legal Realist's attack on formalism cannot hold because the image of legal practice in which judges do not make law but merely discover and apply pre-existing law has no connection with the reality of legal adjudication.[77]

The 'type of the other judge' as introduced by Schmitt to legitimize the judge's position comes close to CLS' idea of conventionalism as explanation for the predictability in law. A crucial difference is that Schmitt acknowledges the shared legal culture as a way of legitimatising the judge's decision. The second stage of Schmitt's legal indeterminacy thesis, the coordination function of law, bears similarity with American Legal Realists' emphasis on legal certainty,[78] but is not very prominent in CLS. The third stage of Schmitt's thesis, the emphasis on the person who decides, shows similarity with CLS' claim that the legal work of the judge decides if a legal rule is determinate or not. Determinacy or indeterminacy of a legal rule is not a given fact but depends on the 'legal work' of the person who decides.[79]

CLS has a clear focus on the reasons of legal indeterminacy, viz. the ideological preferences of the judge. This attention for the reasons of legal indeterminacy can be explained by the prominent political position of the US Supreme Court in the American legal system, compared with other highest courts. Schmitt's focus is neither on the reasons or on the causes of legal indeterminacy, in contrast with the Free law movement and American Legal Realism who are concerned with the causes of legal indeterminacy. Only at the start of his oeuvre does Schmitt explicitly state why statutes can never be assumed as dictating an outcome and can be interpreted with the help of methods of interpretation in different ways. Schmitt shifts his critique from the causes of indeterminacy to emphasize the autonomous value of the decision and the person or legal instance that takes the decision. Kennedy's notion of 'work' of the interpreter can be translated with Schmitt's stress on the importance of the decision and its 'autonomous value'.[80] But finally Schmitt does not share the explanation of the way in which legal indeterminacy is explained by means of CLS' contention that there is no such thing as following a rule. Despite their shared anti-

76 Kennedy 2008, p. 162; Tamanaha 2010, p. 58.
77 Tamanaha 2010, p. 13.
78 *Id.*, p. 33-37.
79 Kennedy 2008, p. 160.
80 Schmitt 1993a, p. 31.

liberal stance Schmitt cannot be interpreted as defending a Critical Legal indeterminacy thesis.

Four and Half Centuries of New (New) Law and Economics

Legal Pragmatism, Discreet Joint Regulation, and Institutional Capture at the Commercial Court of Paris[1]

Emmanuel Lazega

The 'Consular' Model for Social Control of Economic Activity[2]

Social oversight and regulation of entrepreneurial and commercial activities have always involved an unbalanced three-way competition for influence between the State, the business world (companies and their institutional representatives) and consumers. This struggle is growing more intense in a market society centred around organizations. External (i.e. State) regulation and market self-regulation (primarily by the business world) are usually studied separately in the social sciences, and this leads to a grossly oversimplified understanding of the social organization of business, and hence of market society as a whole.

---

1 A first version of this paper was published in French in the *Revue française de socio-économie* in 2009. Potentially controversial positions taken in this article are mine alone. They developed out of empirical research conducted with Lise Mounier and funded by the Mission de Recherche *Droit et Justice* of the French Ministry of Justice, by the *Cognitique* program of the Ministry of Research, and by the Institut Universitaire de France. I thank Sophie Harnay, Lyana Francot-Timmermans and Bald de Vries for constructive criticism.

2 An explanation of the term consulaire is in order. The *consulat* was a mode of urban government practiced in the Middle Ages in the southern part of the Kingdom of France by cities with a right to self-administration and self-defense. 'Consulatus' is formed from 'consul', meaning 'council'. The word referred to a community's ability to deliberate together in an assembly likewise called the consulat. Urban communities governed by a consulat could call themselves cities. All had markets and many had fairs. In a *'régime consulaire'* the community governed itself by way of consuls, who varied in number and by qualifications. Merchants organized into socially distinct guilds occupied an important place in the régime consulaire. On the basis of the lex mercatoria, they managed to negotiate with the State a kind of joint regulation of their business activities within the consulat framework: their local self-regulation was to be founded on the State's sanctioning power. The State, meanwhile, whose own administration was as yet embryonic, may paradoxically have seen this cooptation by local merchants as a means of further extending its central control over the country. A major component of the 'consular regime' is the *tribunal de commerce* or commercial court, whose content evolved over time.

Jean-Daniel Reynaud's notion of "joint regulation",[3] here extended to a larger context,[4] together with study of specific institutional forms of joint regulation – e.g., specialized professions,[5] or the 'responsive self-regulation' studied by Ayres and Braithwaite – help correct this oversimplified view.[6] France offers its own example of joint regulation, a complex system of cooperation between the State, local intermediate meso-level bodies and individual members of civil society, a system that has given rise to particular institutions such as chambers of commerce and two so-called consular judicial institutions, i.e. first level labour relations courts and first level commercial courts. These consular institutions involve specific ways of sharing the costs of control and regulation of markets and of using the experience and knowledge of work and the economy that lay judges possess.

Existing institutional solutions for social control of markets often differ by country and even within single countries. France's specialized commercial courts are partially in charge of settling disputes between economic actors and imposing a degree of discipline in matters of market entry, activity, and exit; they are the first judicial level for commercial litigation and bankruptcy cases. The longevity and resilience of this so-called consular institution – it has existed in France for four and a half centuries – makes it of particular interest for the study of joint regulation of markets. It is one of the only institutions to have come through the French Revolution virtually unchanged, while being regularly subjected – since its inception – to thoroughgoing critiques that threaten its existence. It is the perfect example of an intermediate institution whose existence is difficult to justify in theory – classic legal and political theory, that is – but that has always held its own in practice due to demand from both the State and at least some of the interested parties.

The French State has long shared its judiciary power with local business communities.[7] From its inception, lay commercial court judges have been called '*juges consulaires*'

---

3 J.-D. Reynaud, *Les Règles du Jeu*, Paris: Armand Colin 1989.

4 E. Lazega & L. Mounier, 'Interlocking Judges: On Joint External and Self-Governance of Markets', *in* V. Buskens, W. Raub & Ch. Snijders (eds.), *Research in the Sociology of Organizations*, Vol. 20, p. 267-296, Elsevier, Den Haag, 2003a; E. Lazega & L. Mounier, 'Lorsque l'Etat se Retire du Contrôle de l'Économie, qui Prend le Relais?', *in* J. Crête (Ed.), *Hommage à Vincent Lemieux: La science politique au Québec*, Presses de l'Université Laval, 2003b, p. 155-178; E. Lazega & L. Mounier, 'La Régulation Conjointe des Marchés: Le Cas du Tribunal de Commerce de Paris', *in* B. Convert (Ed.), *Repenser le marché*, Cahiers Lillois d'Economie et de Sociologie, n° 41, L'Harmattan, Paris, 2003c.

5 E.g., business lawyers; but also professions such as accountants, consultants and *notaires*, E. Lazega, *Networks in Legal Organizations: On the Protection of Public Interest in Joint Regulation of Markets*, Inaugural lecture (Wiarda Chair), Faculty of Law, Utrecht University, 3 December 2003; E. Lazega, 'Les conflits d'intérêts dans les cabinets américains d'avocats d'affaires: concurrence et auto-régulation', *Sociologie du Travail*, Vol. 35, 1994, p. 315-36.

6 I. Ayres & J. Braithwaite, *Responsive Regulation: Transcending the Deregulation Debate*, Oxford, Oxford University Press, 1992.

7 *Supra*, note 1.

reflecting the fact that their power was granted by the State (historically, the king) and is founded on State sanctioning power. Commercial court judges, who readily identify themselves as representatives of 'economic civil society', are not paid for their services. Would-be candidates for the position must be sponsored by an employers' association and, in Paris, preselected by a committee composed of members of the city's chamber of commerce. Once selected, these voluntary, lay and truly judicial judges are elected by a body composed of sitting judges and employer association delegates to the local chamber of commerce, for a two- or four-year term (for a maximum total of fourteen years). In theory, the two consular economic institutions – chambers of commerce and commercial courts – are supposed to maintain close ties and refer to each other's decisions. [8] This institutional solution allows for three-way sharing of control costs by the State, industries and businesses, and the individual judges. However, the theoretical understanding also holds that each judge acts as an individual, without a specific mandate from any economic sector.

Commercial court judges and the other actors attach considerable value to their experience and knowledge of the economy in their task of implementing this form of social control. This understanding goes hand in hand with their *claim to make pragmatic legal decisions*. One of my concerns in this contribution is to relate this claim to Richard Posner's theories (1993 and 1995) on the 'experiential' or 'everyday' pragmatism of judges – what could be called the (New) New Law & Economics or (N)NLE. [9] I show that beneath 'individual' legal pragmatism, rooted in a judge's everyday experience, there is a 'collective' legal pragmatism that carries with it neo-corporatist values and interests. This observation raises political issues that extend beyond the nature of the pragmatism operative in social control of markets and social control of business itself; namely, the issue of redefining the role and structure of intermediary bodies and the issue of the consequences of extending the consular model – i.e., delegation of State power – to semi-private institutions or independent administrative authorities, as the French State has shown itself increasingly inclined to do with its own version of New Public Management. In this sense, this contribution suggests

8 For a historical contextualization of this intermediate institution, see J. Hilaire, 'Perspectives Historiques de l'Élection du Juge Consulaire', *in* J. Krynen (Ed.), *L'Élection des Juges, Etude Historique Française et Contemporaine*, Presses universitaires de France, Droit et Justice, Paris, 1999; J.-P. Hirsch, *Les Deux Rêves du Commerce. Entreprise et Institution Dans la Région Lilloise (1780-1860)*, Éditions de l'EHESS, Paris, 1985; R. Ithurbide, *Histoire Critique des Tribunaux de Commerce*, LGDJ, Paris, 1970; J, Lafon, *Juges et Consuls à la Recherche d'un Statut dans la France d'Ancien Régime*, Paris, 1981; C. Lemercier, *Un Si Discret Pouvoir. Aux Origines de la Chambre de Commerce de Paris, 1803-1853,* La Découverte, Paris, 2003, among others. On lay judge identity construction, see E. Lazega & L. Mounier, 'Quête de statut social, partage des compétences et néo-corporatisme au Tribunal de Commerce de Paris', *in* H. Michel & L. Willemez (Eds.), *La justice au risque du profane*, Paris, Presses Universitaires de France 2008.

9 R.A. Posner, *The Problems of Jurisprudence*, Harvard University Press, Cambridge (Mass.), 1993; R.A. Posner, *Overcoming Law*, Harvard University Press, Cambridge (Mass.), 1995.

the relevance of rethinking public action on the basis of a critique of the French consular system.

A Pragmatic Institution for Joint Regulation of the Markets

Private-sector business lawsuits in France are handled by courts of various sorts located in different cities, each with a clearly defined geographical jurisdiction.[10] Article L.411-1 of the *Code de l'organization Judiciaire* defines commercial courts as specialized first-level courts whose specific jurisdiction, as established by the *Code de Commerce* and the *Nouveau Code de Procédure Civile* (NCPC), is to rule on commercial disputes between merchants or companies, persons or legal entities – that is, between companies, but also for example between a company and an individual consumer engaged in contractual activity. Articles 631 and following of the *Code de Commerce* determine what kinds of disputes are to be brought before the commercial court (in cases where parties have not previously signed an arbitration clause). In general terms, the main types of suits covered by commercial court jurisdiction concern commitments and transactions between merchants or various kinds of businesses, commercial transactions of any sort between individuals, and disputes between partners in a company.[11] Furthermore, commercial courts are competent in bankruptcy proceedings (restructuring, liquidation) and more recently became so in bankruptcy prevention. Some restrictions apply to Commercial court jurisdiction with respect to work accidents, commercial property leases, brands and patents.[12] Many of the disputes handled by this court are quite routine; the largest mass of commercial court litigation in France, and perhaps in all countries, is made up of contract-related cases and debt collection. However, commercial court judges' work, though strictly defined and framed by procedure, can quickly become extremely complex due to conflicts between existing norms, instrumentalization of the court by business people who use the judges decisions to renegotiate their deals, and a fairly high incidence of litigant 'bad faith'.

The Law of 16 July 1987, stipulates that judges are to be elected by an electoral college made up of consular delegates,[13] sitting judges at the current commercial court, members

10 It should be recalled, however, that a disagreement can be settled by means other than a legal ruling: legal mediation, arbitration, out-of-court settlement and transaction, etc.

11 M.-F. Coutant, *Les Tribunaux de Commerce*, Presses universitaires de France, coll. QSJ, Paris.

12 There is little systematic information available at the national level on French commercial courts, their work and the kind of cases they handle. Unaggregated statistical data are not available because they are the property of the commercial court administration (the *greffe*), itself a private business whose official status goes back to the time of the Ancien Régime. Official statistics for each commercial court in France primarily concern number of disputes and bankruptcies handled, as well as time taken to expedite them.

13 'Consular' delegates are representatives of the *Chambre de Commerce et d'Industrie* for the districts they belong to. Candidate lists are drawn up by professional category and sub-category. Eligible voters include

of the chamber of commerce, and former members who have requested to participate. The official candidate list is established by a committee headed by a sitting judge. Judges have to be at least thirty years of age, registered to vote in the jurisdiction of the given commercial court and have either been registered for at least five years with the *Registre du Commerce et des Sociétés* (official registry of companies) or have worked as a senior manager for five years (CEO, general administrator, or other). Applicants who have themselves filed for bankruptcy or already served continuously as commercial court judge for fourteen years are ineligible. As mentioned, commercial court judges work on a voluntary basis; they are not paid by the State. They may be, at the same time, magistrates at the court and regular company employees. A judge's first term is for two years; subsequent terms are four year terms. Consular judges have the same powers and prerogatives as career magistrates. They must also comply with the conflicts of interests rules of the *Nouveau Code de Procédure Civile* or NCPC (Art. 339 to 341).

Consular judges justify this joint regulation system in several ways. First, it is claimed to be a faster, less costly means of rendering legal judgments than an arrangement using career judges. The business world incurs a greater part of the cost of settling its own disputes than it would in the traditional judicial system, and delays and waiting time are shorter than in France's regular first level courts. Speed is certainly an essential value in the consular regime. [14] Second, career judges – State civil servants in France – are often thought of as inexperienced, not trained to grasp business problems and unable to oversee and, when necessary, sanction entrepreneurs' behaviour in an appropriate way, particularly where bankruptcies are concerned. [15] Third, commercial law often pays no attention to the idiosyncratic traditional and customary practices known in French commercial courts as 'usages', i.e. practices based on the customs and culture of a particular industry or economic sector. Consular judges think that effective dispute resolution has to take into account these rules and conventions, [16] which structure business practices differently in each traditional sector. Commercial court judges, understood to be experienced business men and women, are thought of as specialists in their professional area and therefore more likely (than permanent civil servants) to be familiar with such customs, know how to adapt them

businesses registered with the chamber of commerce in the given district, business owners registered with the *Répertoire des Métiers* and the chamber of commerce, etc.

14 The perverse effects of speed are hard to measure without access to un-aggregated docket data. Moreover, speed is particularly likely to be promoted as a value given that the commercial court is instrumentalized by companies for renegotiation of their contracts (as much as to obtain 'justice').

15 B.C. Carruthers & T. Halliday, *Rescuing Business: The Making of Corporate Bankruptcy Law in England and the United States*, Oxford University Press, Oxford, 1998, p. 431 report on similar ideas elsewhere.

16 O. Favereau, 'organization et Apprentissage Collectif: Un Paradigme non Standard pour Trois Théories Hétérodoxes', *in* A. Orléans (Ed.), *Analyse Économique des Conventions*, Presses universitaires de France, Paris, 1994.

quickly to the unstable, shifting world of business, and therefore how to innovate in matters of regulation.

French commercial courts thus give some visibility to certain aspects of the relationship between (exogenous) legal mechanisms and (endogenous) social mechanisms for social control of markets. Here the State does not sanction alone. It delegates to trade associations, companies, as well as private citizens – that are willing to incur part of the costs of control. In fact, these elected judges fulfil what is usually considered one of the core functions and prerogatives of the State. This rather special case of joint regulation may be thought of as an extreme form of 'co-regulation', [17] understood as self-regulation by State-recognized industrial associations. Judges at the Commercial Court of Paris do not seem to think that taking account of business world 'usages' is the equivalent of representing corporatist interests. The media, the public, and even Senate committees, [18] on the other hand, have long suspected that cooptation in the judge nomination process leads to the electing of judges who cannot then distance themselves appropriately from their initial professional milieu (e.g., the sector that sponsored their candidacy) and thus cannot detach themselves from particular interests. Litigants, meanwhile, are likely to think that decisions by such lay commercial court judges cannot be fully impartial, especially in small town courts. Their fear is that judges in these small courts will use their position to exert control over their own competitors. [19]

Generally speaking, the business world has certain expectations of modern commercial courts: speed and firmness, few appeals, a clean separation between personal patronage and legal decision-making, and as much neutrality as possible. In the case of France it is

---

17 P. Grabosky & J. Braithwaite, *Of Manners Gentle: Enforcement Strategies of Australian Business Regulatory Agencies*, Oxford University Press, Melbourne, 1986, p. 83.

18 A. Montebourg & F. Colcombet, *Les Tribunaux de Commerce: Une Justice en Faillite ?*, Rapport n° 1038, Commission d'enquête parlementaire de l'assemblée nationale, Michel Lafon, Paris, 1998.

19 This deficit in legitimacy results in endless attempts to redesign this institution, attempts that are in turn used by this institution itself to adapt to societal evolution – perhaps one of the reasons for its resilience and longevity. The French commercial justice system is thus evolving; the State has tried to be more present at the *tribunal de commerce*. Since 1981 the attorney general has had an office at the court and can partake in judges' deliberation, particularly in the case of bankruptcies (which are heard in closed chambers and may have a criminal dimension with important social consequences). In 2001 and 2002, attempts by the Socialist government to convince Parliament and the Senate to include permanent career judges on the court failed. Reformers presented this 'mixing' (of lay and career judges) as a means of improving control over controllers and thereby reassuring foreign businesses involved in lawsuits. It is interesting to notice that this reform actually produced a paradoxical situation: when the French State was more active and interventionist in the business world, the commercial justice system was not really supervised by the Ministry and its *Chancellerie*. In the 1980s, when the State began withdrawing from direct control of the economy it also began increasing its presence in the commercial courts and slightly the degree of oversight it had on these judiciary processes. To justify this change, the State declared that its primary goal was to reassure European and international investors who were demanding equitable treatment in the French system.

in the interest of entire sectors of the business world (represented by their employers' associations) to be represented at the courts, namely in order to defend the customs linked to their particular activities or professions. This means that, at least for some economic sectors, consular judges are more than judges; they are judicial, institutional entrepreneurs who represent the sensitivity of the employers' association that initially helped them get a seat on the court by endorsing their candidacy.[20] The judges themselves do not all share this view. In interviews with them they officially declare that once appointed they are independent, have no mandate from the sector they came from, are totally impartial. However, each judge is often consulted in connection with a particular profession or activity, making it difficult to fully dissociate competence from representativeness. They nonetheless see the system as a typical joint regulation regime where public institutions, business, and private citizens agree to share the costs of control.

The Commercial Court of Paris is significantly larger than other similar courts in France. The number of specialized chambers (nine out of twenty-one) is higher,[21] as is the number of cases handled. Alone it handles 10% to 12% of all commercial litigation in France (not including arbitration). In 2002 it ruled on 101,201 cases. It is also different in terms of the variety of economic sectors its judges come from, and the economic importance of the parties (large companies with their headquarters in Paris). Commercial Court of Paris judges are almost all very highly educated (trained at the prestigious *Ecole Polytechnique (X), Ecole Nationale de l'Administration (ENA), Hautes Etudes Commerciales (HEC),* or *Institut d'Etudes Politiques* (*Sciences Po*), or sometimes have a PhD in law), but only half have had any legal training. The diversity of their business experience forms a kind of 'competence capital' that the institution seeks to make use of by way of a 'consulting culture' in which judges seek advice from each other intensively. Most judges are no longer working as business people or entrepreneurs in the traditional sense, but are instead senior managers or former senior managers of major companies. As one judge put it: 'This is the age of managers'.

Our empirical research consisted in three waves of in-depth interviews with all consular judges on the Commercial Court of Paris.[22] The interviews made possible at least a partial

20 W.V. McIntosh & C.L. Cates, *Judicial Entrepreneurship: The Role of the Judge in the Marketplace of Ideas*, Greenwood Press, Westport (Ct.), 1997.

21 Specialized Commercial court chambers include, for example, Business law, International law, European Union law, Multimedia and new technologies, Unfair competition, Counterfeit products.

22 The first survey wave was conducted in fall 2000 using the list of 157 judges who had attended hearings during the second quarter of 2000; to this list another 10 persons were added: 'wise men' (retired judges advising sitting judges) and association heads. The second wave was conducted in 2002 on the basis of a list of 197 judges, including those from the first wave (either still on the courts or not) and all judges elected in fall 2000 and fall 2001. The third wave of interviews took place in fall 2005 and involved 234 judges, including

assessment of the transversal legitimacy constructed by this contemporary consular institution.

PRAGMATISM, CUSTOMS AND FAIRNESS-BASED JUDGMENT

With respect to procedure, consular commercial courts comply with general requirements of the NCPC (Art. 12). However, certain features of 'practical' commercial court procedure, observed ethnographically and taught by experienced business lawyers at the *Ecole de Formation du Barreau de Paris,*[23] allow for defining the legal context in which 'pragmatic reasoning' comes to acquire some of its meaning. 'Consular' judges reason a great deal in terms of precedent, but case law in these courts is actually quite opaque (as in all first-level jurisdictions in France). Very often, commercial litigation is not first and foremost a matter of justice but rather a means of renegotiating contracts, a process that instrumentalizes the court by seeking a decision that will later serve to restart these renegotiations. Commercial court judges therefore do not look well on lawyers who file suits without first having tried to settle the conflict out of court. These magistrates feel close to the parties: they like business people to come to the court in person, especially for the defence plea, as opposed to just sending in the lawyers. They prefer to avoid legalese and ask questions in ordinary, non-technical language; one effect of this is that lawyers are often quite concerned about their clients' uncontrolled reactions during interaction with the judge. Commercial court judges also look for alternatives: they like accessory claims to be presented that will help them help the parties reach a compromise; they like finding that both parties are right, and explaining to the losers why they have lost.

That commercial court judges make extensive use of precedent renders their practice somewhat similar to that in Common Law. In practice, judges define their pragmatism as a particular attention paid by their decisions to their effects on the economy. What counts most, according to them, are the consequences that legal rules, precedents, decisions, and institutions have on the world of facts. Their decision-making is pragmatic in that it combines knowledge of the economy and management on the one hand, law and jurisprudence on the other. In practice this results in judgments that have produced their own synthesis of law, management and economics, further informed by common business-world customs, common sense, and a sense of fairness (*équité*). It is not easy to determine

166 who had participated in hearings in 2005 and judges from the previous waves, as well as all judges elected since 2002. With an average response rate of 90%, more than 500 interviews, including qualitative interviews, were conducted over time. Research reports are available at the Justice Ministry's *Mission de Recherche 'Droit et Justice'*.

23 School of the Bar Association of Paris.

the degree to which French commercial court judges rely on positive law compared to other decision-making criteria when passing judgment. Assuming it were possible to do so, it would be impossible here because there are no available docket data and unaggregated trial statistics available for this court. Still, these judges reserve the right to synthesize in this way, in the name of their 'experience' and 'pragmatism'. And in their syntheses, we find at least two normative but non-legal components: reference to *usages* and a concern for fairness or equity (our translation of équité).

In speaking of their non-routine work, many commercial court judges stress the importance of equity-based judgment. Taking into account experience and custom in their deliberations is part and parcel, as they see it, of equity-based justice. Interestingly, the relative weight of equity-based judgments compared to law-based judgments seems to vary from one judge to another. For some it is obvious that judges should learn *not* to practice equity-based justice, *as* equity presupposes the use of reasoning and arguments that offer a foothold to external influences that reduce judges' independence. For others, the specificity of the commercial court is precisely its inclusion of equity thinking: fairness can legitimately be taken into account despite the problems it raises. In the work of a pragmatic judge, decisions and rules have to be found that will produce relatively desirable outcomes. Those outcomes may be short or long term, systematic or singular. Pragmatizing law can mean all sorts of things, and efficiency can have all sorts of meanings. What counts is that criteria be practical and their specific content malleable.

The following quotations, all from interviews conducted with Commercial court of Paris judges, illustrate the importance many attach to reasoning in terms of equity:

> You've got civil courts that have career judges who apply the law stricto sensu. For our part, we have to look into law and its economic effects. So you can't have judgments that run entirely counter to the law, of course, but you do have to find an intermediate term. … We're judges, but commercial court judges, and we have to have a more economic view than a purely legal one. (Judge no. 72).
>
> Justice must be rendered and we render law-based justice. We try to base it on law and equity, but that isn't always easy to do. It's obviously at the commercial court that you've got a better chance of getting justice based on law and equity. I think that point is increasingly likely to get lost, and with the reform they're talking about, we're moving away from many of the reasons commercial courts were set up to begin with. (Judge no. 101, interviewed in 2000).

> One very important quality is good common sense – actually, that may be the most important quality. You've got to have a minimum of competence – if you're not a jurist, you acquire it – but you've got to use good sense and be impartial. You have to forget equity somewhat, because it's a natural tendency to judge in terms of equity. There's an article in the Code that allows it when you don't know what else to do. But you often have an equity-based opinion, and you try if possible to justify it. If you can't, never mind. Sometimes we start drafting a ruling and we change the conclusions because the reasoning doesn't hold up. I'm telling you, more than legal qualities – which you do need – what you need is a certain bent for analysis and synthesis, to be able to simplify the jumble of lawyers' files – I once had them piled up as high as this table. You need jurist qualities, but in fact, often, it's not a matter of finding legal arguments but arbitrating between the litigants' own legal arguments. (Judge no. 97).

> I think you have to know business to be able to sense where the real dispute lies, not the one they present to you. [...]I think that to be at ease in the circumstances you're presented with, the circumstances of a legal dispute, you have to have lived through business life intensely. And at all levels. Not just at the level of CEO. You have to have experienced it, you have to have had a true business life. And that's the strength of the tribunal de commerce: having people in it who are business people. (Judge no. 158).

Clearly we would need a greater number of respondent statements to conclude that commercial court judges systematically rule on the basis of equity,[24] especially in routine cases that require nothing more than a writ of execution. It seems reasonable to assume that unpaid bills are ordinary problems as they raise no legal issues and do not give any discretion to the judge; he or she has no choice but to make a law-based decision. Nonetheless, a simple unpaid bill can require complex interpretive work. And it may involve other problems of the sort pragmatic judges are ready to lend an ear to, thus resulting in a reading less committed to law. One lawyer admiringly relates the work of a presiding judge for whom he was clerking in one of the chambers in 2005:

> A company was having leases of its closed-circuit surveillance equipment paid over a three- to four-year period. A small company leasing this equipment was paying quarterly. It forgot to pay. The surveillance company laid low for one, two, three, four payments, then sent notice: 'Pay the four lease payments or contract terminated and summons to appear in commercial court'. At court it

24 J. Hilaire, 'Grandeur ou Servitude de la Justice Consulaire: La Controverse de l'Équité', *Justices*, No. 1, 1998.

> demanded that the small limited liability company pay the rent for the entire duration of the contract. In this kind of case, it's David against Goliath. And the closed-circuit surveillance company comes back all the time with the same suit. I had to deal with that company five times in four months. The Goliaths win because they make sure they've got an armour-plated contract. Especially at the commercial court, where it's fairly simple, they just apply the contract, period: 'These are two professionals. They signed'. Even when the small company is very small. Consumerist thinking on consumer protection has not yet reached the commercial court. But it made the president mad. He said, 'I see you here all the time with the same old refrain, the same excuses for letting the lease run unpaid, then clobbering the small companies'. He brought in special arguments via moderation of the penal clause and managed to moderate the penalties initially provided against the party that isn't paying. A professional judge can do that by following jurisprudence, but he found a legal argument here against the standard solution, a solution he didn't approve of. The commercial court judge has his solution in his mind first, then he writes up his ruling. Only later do they find the famous syllogism! I don't see anything wrong with that.

As the judges see it, pragmatic judgment often involves individual sensitivity and experience. However, the second non-legal feature that commercial court judges are likely to take into account, namely the idiosyncratic conventions and customs referred to as 'usages', shows that pragmatism is not only an individual trait but is also associated with more fully collective business-world norms. The standard expression '*Usages* are a source of law' (*Les usages sont sources de droit*) is cited so often by these judges that it could be engraved on the pediment of the commercial court. As mentioned, French business law often does not acknowledge these *usages*, that are based on traditional industry or commerce subcultures. *Usages* also serve as guidelines for business operations, particularly in contract matters, and they are recognized by the commercial courts. The *Guide Pratique du Magistrat Consulaire* (2001) defines a *usage* as 'a practice that, for a given profession and region, has obligating power for contracts'.[25] Usages may be local, national, or international (e.g., general sales rules for foundries based within the European Union). Some customs have been incorporated into law (e.g., commercial *usages* regarding sales); others into standard contracts (e.g., the York-Antwerp rules on ordinary losses in overseas transportation). While commercial usages may not run contrary to fundamental French business law, they may be exempted from compliance with *Code Civil* rules that do not pertain to public order (e.g., presumption of creditor or debtor solidarity in business operations and quarterly

25 At p. 134.

interest capitalization on standard bank accounts). Usages that are not common knowledge have to be proved by the party citing them. A certificate delivered by the *Chambre de Commerce* or a recognized professional organization such as the *Association Française des Banques* validates a *usage* as common knowledge.[26]

Usages in the sense thus defined are sectorial norms and recognized, technical specifications officially listed with the commercial court registry. Despite the fact that commercial activity is now highly formalized (written contracts) and that the afore-cited recognized but less formal norms are only exceptionally cited, the Commercial Court of Paris considers reference to norms outside positive law both valid and of value. And those recognized norms and specifications are not the only non-legal conventions and criteria that commercial court magistrates make use of in their legal decision-making, namely when they have a great deal of discretion for assessing the situation.

COMPARISON WITH POSNER'S LEGAL PRAGMATISM

One of the main arguments used to legitimate this consular institution, is pragmatism based on the combined competence and experience acquired by lay judges in the course of careers as entrepreneurs or senior managers. Interestingly, this type of pragmatism and its implications raise issues very similar to those being discussed, debated and theorized in the Anglo-Saxon legal worlds. Thinking of the French commercial court as a particularly interesting and paradoxical illustration of this Anglo-Saxon pragmatism sheds light on certain aspects of the French consular institution while clarifying some of the implications of the way it operates. Anglo-Saxon legal pragmatism, particularly the American variety, is a theory with a critical view of traditional definitions of law and judicial decision-making.[27] The classic understanding of law, especially in common law countries, is that it is based on *jurisprudence* or case law analysis; i.e., an analysis of universal, abstract legal fact, precedents, and rigorous argumentation that makes use of analogy in what are purely legal disputes. For many sociologists of law and legal pragmatists this approach is overly legalistic, naively rationalist and based on a misapprehension of how judicial institutions actually work. In legal pragmatism – because of law's eclecticism, which is in turn the consequence of its multiple objectives – the emphasis is on the need to take into account more than purely legal facts and on the understanding that law is an instrumental practice situated in an economic, political and social context, a practice with no immutable abstract,

26 Since 1982, the expert evaluation office the Commercial court of Paris has a section for registering professional usages. Professions have been called upon to register their usages and rules with this office. On 31 October 2000, 275 usages had been registered.

27 M. Brint & W. Weaver, *Pragmatism in Law & Society*, Westview Press, Boulder (Co.) 1991.

universal foundation, a practice linked to at least one and often several different perspectives. According to partisans of legal pragmatism, *jurisprudence* and case law analysis itself is characterized by pragmatism. Under these circumstances – the legal pragmatist argument runs – judges themselves cannot be thought of as purely rational individuals capable of foreseeing all the consequences of their decisions. To reach those decisions – to render justice – they make use of their personal abilities and sensitivities. Judicial decision-making thus seems rooted in the judge's experience and his or her attention to the given context, attention thought of as free of false *a priori* beliefs in universal legal foundations or bases. This is empirical *jurisprudence*: application of the experiential method to complex, uncertain contexts.

In a way, no one has better expounded the pragmatism to which commercial court judges in France lay claim than Richard Posner, judge and professor at the University of Chicago and a decidedly complex figure.[28] As a leading New Law & Economics (NL&E) thinker early in his career,[29] Posner endorsed the radical version of this school,[30] where the understanding was that (neo-classical) economics should dictate law. Utility maximizing became a synonym for justice. Econometric efficiency measurements were to replace the traditional legal principles that served as a foundation for judicial decision-making. Judgment was identified with – reduced to – a kind of calculation which, framed by restrictive formulas, would suffice to settle legal disputes.

Law, this argument ran, should draw closer to the demands of the economy as defined by neo-classical economists. However, over the 1990s, Posner shifted from radical positivism, for which economics should dictate law, to 'softer' pragmatism. It is this second Posner that can be used as a reference point here. We can characterize the shift toward pragmatism

28 This excessively brief overview of pragmatism and the evolution of Richard Posner's conception of judges owes much to S. Harnay & A. Marciano, *Posner et l'Analyse Économique du Droit*, Collection Le Bien Public (Editions Michalon), 2003; E. Krecké, 'Economic Analysis and Legal Pragmatism', *International Review of Law and Economics*, Vol. 23, 2003. p. 421-437; E. Krecké & C. Krecké, 'The anti-foundational dilemma: Normative implications for the economic analysis of law', *in* E. Krecké, C. Krecké & R. Koppl (Eds.) *Cognition and Economics*, Vol. 9, Elsevier, New York, 2006; and N. Mercuro & S.G. Medema, *Economics and the Law: From Posner to Post-Modernism and Beyond*, Princeton University Press, Princeton, 2006. These texts have guided me in my exploration of this literature.

29 The Law & Economics approach appeared in the late 1950s at the University of Chicago with the *Journal of Law and Economics*; it is generally referred to as 'old law and economics'. At the outset the main focus was areas of law explicitly linked to economic issues and research topics, e.g., competition, industrial concentration, tax and industrial property law. What is called 'new law and economics' in basic textbooks (an extension of economic logic to other legal areas) began in 1972 with the publication of Richard Posner's *Economic Analysis of Law*.

30 R.A. Posner, *Economic Analysis of Law*, Boston/Toronto, Little, Brown and Company 2003 ((6th edition, original: 1977); R.A. Posner, 'The Ethical and Political Basis of the Efficiency Norm in Common Law Adjudication', *Hofstra Law Review*, Vol. 8, No. 3, 1980, p. 487.

found in some of Posner's 1990s works as new (new) law & economics or N(N)L&E. Though the distinction is an oversimplification, one can call the Posner of the first (positivist, neo-classical) period Posner I, and distinguish those views from the thinking of the second-period Posner, the author of *Problems of Jurisprudence* and *Overcoming Law,* [31] whom I will call Posner II. This distinction between the two Posners is not a 'registered' one.[32] Posner's about-face (his straying from the path, some would say) is sharply contested in current economic analysis of law, including at times by Posner himself – a kind of Posner III. This is not to claim that N(N)L&E marks the beginning of an entirely new approach or movement. Rather it is a critical source for understanding how economic analysis of law is applied in such courts as the Commercial Court of Paris. Richard Posner belongs to a rich, heterogeneous tradition of American pragmatists, the most recent being, among others, Daniel Farber, Thomas Grey, and Margaret Radin;[33] a tradition whose philosophical genealogy (Charles Pierce, William James, John Dewey and more recently Richard Rorty) and legal genealogy (Holmes, Brandeis, etc.) need hardly be retraced.[34] In his 1993 and 1995 works, Posner II stressed 'the primacy of consequences in interpretation'.[35] The main principle continued to be judges' evaluation of the effects of their decisions on the functioning of the economy. What counts most in this view are the consequences of legal rules, decisions and institutions on the world of facts (close econometric measurement of efficiency is no longer the point).

Posner II regrets that economic analysis of law seems to have eschewed legal formalism only to apply neoclassic economics principles that are just as formal and artificial – in sum: to have taken mathematical calculation for its foundation and dismissed the world of experience just as fully as legal formalism had done, no longer providing accessible instruments for judges or lawyers, no longer guiding them in their everyday decision-making. This positivist approach has not won much credence among judges. It has also been sharply criticized on theoretical grounds by, for example, Sunstein.[36] Posner II shifted

31 *Supra*, note 9.

32 Posner II had several purposes in writing *Overcoming Law*, among them defining common law against the European tendency to regulate by law and codified legislation. I am more interested here in his critique of neo-classical positivism – a kind of self-critique.

33 D. Farber, 'Reinventing Brandeis: Legal Pragmatism for the Twenty-First Century', *University of Illinois Law Review,* 1995, No. 1, p. 163-190; T.G. Grey, 'Holmes and Legal Pragmatism', *Stanford Law Review*, Vol. 41, 1989, p. 787 and T.G. Grey, 'Freestanding Legal Pragmatism', *Cardozo Law Review*, Vol. 18, 1996, p. 21; M.J. Radin, 'The Pragmatist and the Feminist', *Southern California Law Review*, Vol. 63, 1990, p. 1699.

34 On this subject see also M. Dickstein, *The Revival of Pragmatism: New Essays on Social Thought, Law, and Culture,* Duke University Press, Durham 1998 and B.Z. Tamanaha, 'Pragmatism in U.S. Legal Theory: Its Application to Normative Jurisprudence, Socio-legal Studies, and the Fact-Value Distinction', *American Journal of Jurisprudence*, Vol. 41, 1996, p. 315.

35 Posner 1995, p. 252.

36 R.C. Sunstein (Ed.) *Behavioral Law and Economics*, Cambridge University Press, Cambridge (Mass.) 2000.

the foundation for 'pragmatic' legal decision-making toward the judge as a person and his or her everyday experience, a form of legal pragmatism that relies heavily on the more general American pragmatism of the early twentieth century by scholars like John Dewey.[37] Posner II continues to favour legal theory that will serve as a framework for judges called upon to make law-based decisions and apply the law. He has not given up on the idea of positive jurisprudence.[38] It is just that legal decision-making in this understanding is no longer based on either scientific or legal logic but on the judge's experience. For Posner II, a judge's reasoning – good reasoning – is necessarily subjective, tacit, based on convictions derived from routines or personal experience (practical wisdom) acquired in the course of his or her career.[39] Indeed, pragmatic reasoning requires an ability to adapt to ever-changing materials (either legal or another kind, namely economic), a quality that knowledge and familiarity with the law does not develop and that seems to require a mixture of judgment and intuition, as well as prudence, detachment, imagination and common sense. So judges' reasoning, in this understanding, is no longer founded on positivist economic science. In *Overcoming Law,* Posner claims that pragmatism is the best normative *and* positive theory of the judiciary role. The theory of pragmatism rejects the idea that law is anchored in fixed, permanent principles and applied through logical operations based on those principles, asserting instead that it should be used as an instrument to social ends. Pragmatism amounts more to common sense and an everyday sense of what is reasonable than to a body of doctrine.

For Posner II, judging implies both a sense of logic, such as when the judge takes the economy into account, and common sense, which encompasses norms, customs and beliefs. Economic science in this understanding is not the normative instrument to be used in the field of law but rather one source among others of legal learning. Posner II rejects the idea of a complete, self-contained explanatory system – i.e., what he claimed economic analysis of law to be when NL&E was first developed. Though in this theory a veil is thrown over the utilitarian criterion of maximizing wealth, efficiency remains an implicit value. Calculation is still in part the relevant mode for pragmatically apprehending the law. It is not because Posner II no longer openly declares that the effects of legal rules should be assessed in terms of efficiency that the efficiency criterion – albeit a different type of efficiency criterion, a subdued one, from the perspective of Posner I and NL&E, a criterion that absorbs components of limited rationality and legal subjectivism, with experimental pragmatism becoming another name for, or an ersatz of, the 'efficiency' of the wealth-maximization criterion – has disappeared. The shift from Posner I to Posner II cannot be

37 A. Ogus, *Costs and Cautionary Tales – Economic Insights for the Law*, Oxford, Hart Publishing 2006.

38 Krecké 2003.

39 Posner 2003.

understood to undermine or disqualify all of Posner I's prior works; i.e., all of standard NL&E, including the economic analysis of law idea. [40]

Posner II's legal pragmatism is of interest precisely because it remains economic, that is, implicitly founded on efficiency logic, despite the fact that this may no longer be the efficiency logic operative in the wealth-maximization criterion. Comparing the N(N)L&E approach with the approach of French commercial court judges is therefore heuristically relevant because there is obviously an economic dimension to French commercial court activity. Underlying commercial court decision-making is an 'efficiency' criterion in that in the experience of commercial court judges, pragmatism involves adding economic and management competence to law. [41]

I take responsibility for this debatable comparison while acknowledging the 'novelty' of Posner II. The shift from Posner I to Posner II is of interest here because it represents a change in the author's understanding of judicial pragmatism. That change seems to have led to his notion of 'experiential' pragmatism, which is quite similar to the notions of pragmatism expressed by the judges observed here at the Commercial Court of Paris. The French commercial court overtly makes use of a kind of pragmatism in socially controlling markets and dealing with disputes between entrepreneurs. Indeed, certain characteristics of the way this legal institution operates suggest that it makes widespread use of N(N)L&E-type pragmatism. Though Posner II is from a very different legal background than French commercial court judges, his thinking corresponds closely to the 450 years of consular, lay judge experience: judges in this institution have always sought to bring together law and the demands of the economy and management as they define those demands in their role as business practitioners. French commercial court judges are business men and women sponsored, as explained, by employers' associations and paid nothing for their services, men and women who pride themselves both on their beliefs in the vital importance of markets and entrepreneurship for society as a whole, and about their legal pragmatism, i.e., applying their knowledge of the economy and management (first-hand knowledge that career judges do not have, they say) and business world usages, common sense, and a sense of fairness in their task of rendering justice. In theory, these magistrates simultane-

---

40 Harnay & Marciano 2003.

41 Harnay & Marciano 2003. For them, Posner's shift from Posner I to Posner II is perhaps not so fundamental or radical. Specifically, it would seem that 'soft' Posner (II) is in fact a 'hypocritical' version of 'hard' Posner (I), the Posner of standard NL&E. This is consistent with the idea the Posner I and Posner II are continuous, an idea that sociologists of economics and law would need to examine with respect to judges' practice rather than exegesis of NL&E or N(N)L&E texts. One obvious example is an economics of law analysis of bankruptcy in which economic calculation would clearly have an important role (despite the fact that different aims may be involved).

ously take into account law, efficiency (as defined by economists and managers), the consequences of their decisions, and the satisfaction and support of their particular public.

If Posner II's 'experiential' pragmatism can be considered an approach to judicial decision-making or justice-rendering, and if responses from representatives of France's system for jointly regulating markets – that is, commercial court judges – resonate with this approach, then the French commercial court logically becomes an institution emblematic of both the joint regulation specific to consular regimes and the 'experiential' legal pragmatism operative in the work of economic judges, a pragmatism in which the value of efficiency has not necessarily become obsolete. For consular judges – judges who, clearly, have been practicing and exploring the principles of N(N)L&E for the last 450 years – usages are a source of law when chosen by an experiential judge who wishes to go beyond routinely applying decisions reached in earlier cases or strictly applying existing legislation. As Krecké sees it, [42] the more modest vision of Posner II represents a gain in realism and common sense yet also results in a loss of NL&E theory consistency and assumed predictive ability.

From a sociological perspective, the detour by way of Posner II pragmatism sheds light on the main limitation of consular judges' pragmatic theory, namely that it is defined as purely individual. In fact, as already suggested by the inclusion of usages and sectorial norms, these judges' individual pragmatism and experience are rooted in decidedly *collective* representations. If we examine the attributes, careers, reasoning and motivations of French commercial court judges we find that they reach their decisions within an *institutional context* that values their pragmatic reasoning, or certain dimensions of it, to varying degrees. [43] Whereas a N(N)L&E judge is an individual who decides alone, the judges observed at the Commercial Court of Paris act within a context of conflicting conventions and collective representations.

As soon as we take the organizational apparatus and institutional framework of these judges' work seriously, their pragmatism takes on a new, collective dimension. In the next section I present characteristics of the social control of markets in France that illustrate

42 Krecké 2003.

43 E. Lazega & L. Mounier, 'Polynormativité et contrôle social du monde des affaires: le cas de l'interventionnisme et de la punitivité des juges du Tribunal de Commerce de Paris', *Droit et Société*, Vol. 71, 2009, p. 103-132 ; E. Lazega & L. Mounier, 'La rhétorique des professions libérales au service de la privatisation de l'État: le cas des juges consulaires du Tribunal de Commerce français ', *in* D. Demazière & Ch. Gadéa (Eds.), *Sociologie des groupes professionnels: Acquis récents et nouveaux défis*, Paris, La Découverte 2010 ; E. Lazega & L. Mounier, 'Le régime consulaire de contrôle social des marchés et ses soutiens institutionnels: Le cas du Tribunal de Commerce de Paris au début du XXIe siècle', P. Fridenson (Ed.), *Marché et concurrence: droit et institutions*, Paris, IGPDE 2011, in press.

the importance of analyzing legal institutions' *collective* actors and *collective* pragmatism. Comparing Posner II attitudes to French commercial court judges' makes it clear that pragmatism without a theory of organizational and social structures and of representations and conventions cannot stand as a convincing theory of social control of markets, particularly when it comes to accounting for the neo-corporatism and institutional capture that may be observed in consular institutions. 'Institutional capture' is meant here from the perspective of a neo-structural approach to the social control of markets: as an extreme form of joint regulation. It could also be understood from the perspective of many career judges (who push for radical reform of this specialized consular court).

THE PRAGMATIC INSTITUTION AS A TARGET FOR LEGAL ENTREPRENEURS

Courts are not static institutions that make a-temporal, purely rational decisions.[44] They are highly valued territorial institutions that generate much in the way of competition and conflict outside the courtroom.[45] This is particularly true of courts whose judges are themselves business men and women sponsored by employers' associations, selected to represent extremely diverse sectors of the economy, and elected by the chamber of commerce of their jurisdiction. Given that this form of joint regulation – by the State, intermediate bodies and private citizens – presupposes the coming together of heterogeneous actors from different milieus, it can reasonably be seen as a kind of 'governance' of the market with business as the key player.

In the case under study here, a case of structured interests trying to shape the consular commercial court, judges can be thought of as both official third parties who represent the general interest and apply legal rules and procedures in dispute settlement processes *and* non-official potential surveillance and influence 'levers', who represent their economic sector and are likely to advocate settlements that will not hurt those particular interests. As levers they can have either a direct effect on legal decisions or an indirect one should they succeed in influencing other judges on the court. Under these circumstances, one implication of pragmatism as defined by N(N)L&E – and regardless of the consistency of its positions – is to make this institution for social control of markets even more sharply contested a territory than usual. Collective sensitivity and corporate interests borne by individual sensitivity can be expressed legitimately thanks to the notion of pragmatism;

44 W. Heydebrand, & C. Seron, *Rationalizing Justice: The Political Economy of Federal District Courts*, SUNY Press, Albany 1990; S. Wheeler, K. Mann & A. Sarat, *Sitting in Judgment: The Sentencing of White Collar Criminals*, Yale University Press, New Haven, 1988.

45 R.B. Flemming, 'Contested Terrains and Regime Politics: Thinking about America's Trial Courts and Institutional Change', *Law & Social Inquiry*, Vol. 23, 1998, p. 941-965.

pragmatism, then, serves as a kind of 'foot in the door' for the collective and the corporations. The most clearly visible example of this strategy is *domination by banker-jurists* (i.e. bankers with a law degree). According to standard justifications of this joint regulation system, judge selection should produce widely diverse representation of existing economic sectors, particularly in major commercial courts such as Paris's. At the time of the study, the sectors represented by the judges, sectors in which they were working or had worked, were indeed highly diverse. And in complex cases, the court might indeed access information on a particular area of the business world by turning to judges from that particular area. Some sectors and/or companies, however, invest more than others in legal entrepreneurship and take on a greater part of control costs because it is in their interest to do so. In theory, any employers' association can present candidates for consular judge positions to fill the vacancies left by 10% annual turnover. Analyses show that while not all these associations present candidates, some do so more systematically than others: 29% of judges were from the banking/finance sector. Every year this sector puts up several candidates to the commercial court.[46]

The financial sector is clearly overrepresented at the Commercial Court of Paris, in both absolute and relative terms. In 2000 it seems to have accounted for 3% of the occupied population in France,[47] and 5.1% in Paris, where service industries are overrepresented relative to the provinces.[48] That year, financial services accounted for 5.3% of the total value added to the French economy.[49] These descriptive indications suffice to show that the 29% of judges from the finance sector are indeed potential levers for that industry and that the influence they may exert on other judges represents a threat to the court's independence.

Traditionally, this is a highly litigious sector.[50] For obvious reasons, a significant proportion of commercial court work concerns the financial sector, and this motivates that sector to

46 For example, in 2003, 21 of the candidates were sponsored by the *Association Française des Banques* and 5 by the *Association Française des Sociétés Financières*. The financial institutions employing active judges in the Commercial Court of Paris included BNP-Paribas, 7 judges; Suez, 4; Société Générale, 4; Crédit Lyonnais, 4; and Crédit Commercial de France, 4.

47 Source: *Enquête Emploi 2000*, Institut National de la Statistique et des Etudes Economiques (INSEE), CD-ROM version.

48 Source: INSEE, monthly journal No. 202 (Oct. 2001), *Ile-de-France à la Page*; 'Gros plan sur l'emploi francilien en 1999'.

49 Source: INSEE, Comptabilité Nationale 2001. In 1998 there were 1,237 lending institutions in France, for a total of 25,428 cashiers and 714,730 clerks.

50 R.E. Cheit & J.E. Gersen, 'When Businesses Sue Each Other: An Empirical Study of State Court Litigation', *Law & Social Inquiry*, Vol. 25, 2000, p. 789-816.

invest in legal entrepreneurship – e.g., to limit its risks in cases involving high credit levels.[51] The following example illustrates the sector's interest in assuming a larger-than-average part of the costs of control of the French business world. In 1985, the Socialist government changed bankruptcy laws to give priority to the battle against unemployment, a change obviously consistent with the interests of employees rather than creditors. The new law required judges to rule on whether the companies in question could survive if they were better managed.[52] If the judges decided that a company – and its jobs – could be saved, they were to appoint an administrator to manage it. If they decided it could not be saved, they were to order its liquidation. Banks and financial institutions were often creditors in these cases and so risked losing enormous sums as soon as the new law was passed. For nine years, the French financial sector pressured politicians to change the law.[53] In 1994 a lost vote in Parliament seems to have moved the sector to switch strategies and to try instead to increase the number of 'its' consular judges in charge of making insolvency-related decisions. In 2006, 21 years after passage of the bankruptcy law, the banking sector finally managed to get it changed in its favour.

Collective Pragmatism and Institutional Capture by a Discreet Co-Regulator

The financial sector expends great quantities of resources in commercial litigation and bankruptcies. Consequently, it is willing to invest in the regulatory process and it is in its interest to try to structure the court in a way that will increase the influence of its norms and practices rather than those of other sectors. Its priorities (e.g., keeping the value of assets high or low depending on its position and exposure, eschewing both excessive financial support and sudden breaks in lines of credit, high sensitivity to the repercussions of business failures on the economy at large) are therefore likely to be promoted with insistence as ready-made solutions in this kind of commercial courts, to be permanently taken into consideration there in connection with all kinds of legal disputes and bankruptcy cases.

51 Here is where the lack of non-aggregate statistical data on commercial court rulings becomes an impediment to research into the consular system for social control of markets. More generally, the Ministry of Justice has very few figures on the work of commercial court judges.

52 A. Guérault, H. Lamotte & B. Du Marais, *Les Garanties et le Crédit aux Entreprises* (Rapport du Conseil National du Crédit), Éditions de la Banque de France, Paris 1993.

53 On the position of the *Conférence Générale des Tribunaux de Commerce* on the law of 1985, see Rey (2001), to be read from the distanced perspective of Commons (1924). A recent President of the Commercial Court of Paris from the banking world, she had decisive impact in shaping France's new bankruptcy and business insolvency prevention bill (2007) – just as the President of the Commercial Court of Paris wrote the French Code of Commerce in 1807.

The fact that this pragmatic institution is a target for legal entrepreneurs creates a risk that, in the consular context of joint regulation of markets, Posner II and (N)NL&E's 'experiential' pragmatism will be informed by collective pragmatism and permeated with corporate norms. In (N)NL&E, learning and experience are necessarily purely individual. But as Durkheim showed as early as 1898, individual representations are structured by collective ones, especially when reframed in institutional contexts where authority arguments are carefully distributed. [54] When judges share their experience and skills, when they follow rules, they make use of collectively constructed foundations. The problem thus exceeds that of purely individual reasoning about fairness (*équité*). When French consular magistrates explain that their discretion (for example their *pouvoir souverain d'appréciation*) and their moral duty to judge are legitimately grounded in their individual experience and knowledge of the economy and management, not exclusively in the law, their 'individual sensitivities' are in fact echoing collective, sectorial criteria and norms, and using them to adapt codified law to ever-shifting economic and business realities. Efficient dispute settlement cannot ignore the entire world of informal conventions that variably structure business practices. [55] Clearly we are back to the 'collective sensitivities' – i.e., shared conventions – that underlie individual ones, [56] sensitivities that characterize not merely isolated individuals but all individuals from a given occupational and economic sector.

Institutions of joint regulation thus appear to be the locus of a struggle to exert influence upon the construction of their shared frame of reference, which is required if their members are to be able to describe and interpret facts in a stable way. In this 'epistemic' and regulatory competition between sectors, the banking and finance sector (often, but not always formally organized to do so) is in a position to promote its own, readily identifiable occupational sensitivities, its own collective representations, customs, justice criteria and conventions. Empirical research brings to light a relationship between career, sector, and the sensitivity commercial court judges draw upon in deciding cases in which they have a great amount of discretion. For example, judges who are both legally trained and members of the banking and finance world tend to be more interventionist than all commercial court judges taken together in cases of conflicts between boards and minority shareholders. [57] In such disputes

54 E. Lazega, *Micropolitics of Knowledge*, Aldine-de Gruyter, New York 1992.

55 E. Lazega & O. Favereau, 'Introduction, *in* O. Favereau & E. Lazega (Eds.), *Conventions and Structures in Economic Organization: Markets, Networks, and Hierarchies*, Edward Elgar Publishing, Cheltenham 2002, p. 1-28.

56 Lazega & Mounier 2009.

57 E. Lazega, 'Disciplining a combat tank manufacturer? A tale of lay judges handling punitive claims for moral damages in business', *in* N. Doornbos, N. Huls & W. van Rossum (Eds,), *Liber Amicorum Prof. Dr. J.F. Bruinsma. Rechtspraak van buiten: Negenendertig door de rechtssociologie geïnspireerde annotaties*, Amsterdam, Kluwer 2010, p. 169-176; E. Lazega, L. Mounier & P. Tubaro, 'Norms, advice networks and joint economic governance: the case of conflicts among shareholders at the commercial court of Paris', *in* M.Ugur &

they are more inclined than other judges to decide in favour of the board. They are thus less hostile than other respondents to judicial intervention in the internal affairs of a company. On the other hand, they tend to be much less interventionist than their colleagues in disputes between parties to a contract on a given market, i.e., inter-organizational cases. Lastly, they are less 'punitive' than their average colleague with respect to awarding so-called 'moral' damages resulting from unfair competition of the sort that may disrupt (supposedly natural) market operations.

In contrast, the reverse is observed for judges coming from the building sector. The latter are likely to be less interventionist than their colleagues in intra-organizational cases opposing the board to minority shareholders. They are much more interventionist than the other judges in inter-organizational litigation between parties to a contract on a given market. This contrast is confirmed by banker-jurists' less punitive attitude (compared to judges form the building sector) concerning claims (by companies) for punitive damages, for example in connection with bidding processes in public works. Moreover, young judges tend to be more interventionist and punitive than older ones with regard to markets and companies alike.

By systematically sending high numbers of senior managers with legal training to the Commercial Court of Paris, the financial sectors have achieved epistemic domination of that court. The simultaneously individual and collective sensitivities of judges from these sectors who hold a law degree (banker-jurists) are of particular interest in this study because they are key players in the skill- and experience-sharing that characterizes the community of commercial court judges. For example, in our examination of the advice network among judges, exchanges of ideas and opinions that may be assumed to shape judicial decisions, the influence of banker-jurist judges was indeed measured and established. The advice network developed by these lay judges and its effectiveness in setting the premises of decision may be said to reflect strong coordination between organization structure and organization member rationality.[58] Observed regularities in advice seeking and exchanges

D. Sunderland (Eds.), *Does Economic Governance Matter? Governance Institutions and Outcomes*, Cheltenham, Edward Elgar 2011, in press.

58 Lazega 1992 and E. Lazega, *The Collegial Phenomenon: The Social Mechanisms of Cooperation Among Peers in a Corporate Law Partnership*, Oxford University Press, 2001. See also E. Lazega, C. Lemercier & L. Mounier, 'A Spinning Top Model of Formal Structure and Informal Behaviour: Dynamics of Advice Networks in a Commercial Court', *European Management Review*, Vol. 3, 2006. p. 113-122; E. Lazega & L. Mounier, 'Networks of institutional capture', *in* B. Vedres & M. Scotti (Eds.), *Social Networks and Public Policy*, Cambridge University Press 2011, in press; E. Lazega, L. Mounier, T. Snijders & P. Tubaro, 'Norms, status and the dynamics of advice networks', *Social Networks.* 2011 in press. Electronic version <http://dx.doi.org/10.1016/j.socnet.2009.12.001>.

among commercial court judges show 'who is ready to listen to whom' when problems have to be framed and a decision reached.

Domination by bankers with a legal education is not necessarily well tolerated at this court; banker-jurists' social integration into the court is weaker than that of judges coming from other sectors, precisely because the banking sector has so many representatives: having such a strong presence or 'position' (in Flemming's sense) may be resented by others, and even sometimes prove counterproductive in terms of influence. At the time of our study, the financial sector was indeed perceived by judges from other sectors to be either defending its own corporatist interests or trying to replace the State once the latter began withdrawing from direct control of the economy [59]. As a response to this reaction, one judge, himself a former banker, dismissively declared: 'shopkeepers hate bankers'. Another indicator of this tension between representatives of the finance sector and the others was the fact that the former were nearly systematically elected with the smallest number of votes at the Chamber of commerce. [60]

Rethinking Public Action on the Basis of a Critique of the Consular Regime

The Commercial Court of Paris, a consular but truly judicial first level court, is an institution of joint regulation of markets – joint in the sense that the State delegates and works together with business, its representatives (in the chamber of commerce) and members of civil society. Business world experience and economic expertise, two characteristics of the consular regime for the more than four centuries it has been in existence, have proven a strong argument in favour of having consular judges render justice in commercial matters. The complexity of the tasks performed by commercial court judges, as much in matters of insolvency as in general or specialized litigation areas, points to the considerable skills and variegated experience – legal, economic and managerial, among others – applied in this type of institution.

Commercial court judges do use a great variety of means for finding the information and advice on which to base their arguments and decisions. But one argument cited by judges in major commercial courts to justify the traditional *consular* operation of commercial

59 A trend related to the rise of neo-liberalism and New Public Management in France in the 1980s.

60 The judge elected with the fewest votes is called the '*culot*' (cul means ass in French *argot*). Until very recently the 'culot' was subjected to ritual hazing from his peers during his first year (made to carry the chamber president's briefcase, to remain silent at the weekly meeting of his particular chamber, to try to amuse the colleagues during meals, etc.). Since recent 'culots' were all bankers, this ethnographic detail gives an idea of how they are sometimes perceived by non-bankers.

justice in France is that extremely diverse kinds of competencies are thus represented in these institutions: judges are in a position to draw on the experience of colleagues in different specialties from all the sectors of the economy. Court judges are identified within the institution by their specialized knowledge and expertise, so that their colleagues know who to consult on what. Knowledge is thus 'distributed', and shared. From this it follows apparently fairly 'naturally' that the consular institution should make use of the varied experience of its judges and should attach value to pragmatism in justifying its existence.

In sum, studying cooperation at the Commercial court of Paris, a consular, pragmatic institution for jointly regulating markets, brings to light close ties between (New) New Law and Economics 'experiential pragmatism' and 'everyday pragmatism' theses and French commercial court judges drawing on their knowledge of the economy and management to make equity-based rulings on economic disputes and bankruptcies. However, exposing how this pragmatic institution is remote-controlled by the financial sector and its criteria likewise exposes the fact that beneath 'individual' pragmatism anchored in the individual judges' everyday experience there is a 'collective' pragmatism permeated with neo-corporatist values and interests. This, then, is the nature of the legal pragmatism characterizing the French consular regime for social control of markets. It raises questions on how to protect the general interest,[61] how legal pragmatism becomes operative, and how N(N)L&E thinking relates to the work being done in the rising number of institutions to which the French State has begun delegating its powers.

The pragmatism put forward approvingly by actors in this institution and by the N(N)L&E is individual pragmatism. However, at the scale of a consular institution such as this commercial court, pragmatism acquires a political dimension. Given commercial court judges' identity; given the way they are recruited and how they learn on the 'job'; given the existence of interests, customs and collective representations that are characteristic of the specific professions and industries those judges come from; given the processes for resolving normative divergences and controversies within this institution; pragmatism in it is necessarily permeated by neo-corporatism whose existence and power threaten court impartiality. Moreover, as attested by the socially constructed resilience and 'irreversibility' of the Paris Commercial Court's institutional design, that neo-corporatism extends beyond mere promotion of collective pragmatism and sensitivities. Once collective pragmatism has been instituted, once it has opened the door to exogenous influence from sectorial norms, it becomes difficult to separate the pragmatic judgment of an individual judge from the corporate regulatory interests he or she necessarily represents to some degree. And

61 E. Lazega, *Networks in Legal Organizations: On the Protection of Public Interest in Joint Regulation of Markets*, Inaugural lecture (Wiarda Chair), Faculty of Law, Utrecht University, 3 December 2003.

what of the astounding longevity of an institution for jointly regulating markets where business directly participates in running a part of the State apparatus? Clearly that longevity cannot be fully explained by the individual pragmatism of its judges and its willingness to accept the neo-corporatism of individuals seeking to exert influence in it. Observation of how this institution operates and its relations with its environment shows that (1) it provides services to the public authorities (commercial court magistrates are not paid; they process bankruptcies without compromising politicians in case of mass lay-offs; [62] they implement industrial policy that the Ministry of the Economy does not wish to implement openly; [63] they train young graduates of the *Ecole Nationale de la Magistrature* in the intricacies of the business world; etc.); (2) it is supported by a highly integrated inter-organizational system (made up of the *Chambre de Commerce et d'Industrie* and employers' associations); 3) it is subjected to no more than superficial (statistical) monitoring by the Ministry of Justice, and this state of affairs allows it and its administration, the *greffe*, to maintain the opacity of its decisions and the ways in which it handles conflicts of interest.

Moreover, the institution can only be captured by a discreet co-regulator because it has been supported for centuries by the social milieu that has been constructed around it: commercial court judges are the primary recruiters of new judges; they are also often likely to be candidates' relatives or friends. [64] Lastly, legal pragmatism goes together with a professional rhetoric that proves extremely useful in conveying the notion that 'consular' judges and the institution as a whole are independent, [65] a rhetoric that includes (a) emphasizing the complexity of the tasks to be performed and the management of uncertainty that is involved; (b) developing an elitist approach to cooptation in the election of the judges; (c) claiming that working as a lay judge for the consular commercial court is a disinterested public service; (d) pointing to collegial competence sharing; and (e) ensuring that the organization (*Conférence Générale des Tribunaux de Commerce*) is perceived as an organization that represents and oversees its members, i.e., an organization that for the judges themselves fulfils practical and symbolic functions very similar to those of an official professional association, such as the Bar; when in fact their activity does not actually correspond to a profession.

---

62 In a way, consular judges do the 'dirty work' of both public authorities and the market economy. By putting their expertise and experience in the service of the general interest, they put to sociologists a very specific variant of the general question raised by Everett Hughes (1962), that of 'good people and dirty work'.

63 Lazega & Mounier *in* Fridenson (Ed.) 2011.

64 A.M. Falconi, K. Guenfoud, E. Lazega, C. Lemercier, L. Mounier, 'Le Contrôle Social du Monde des Affaires: Une Étude Institutionnelle', *L'Année Sociologique*, Vol. 55, No. 2, 2005, p. 451-484.

65 E. Lazega & L. Mounier, 'Polynormativité et Contrôle Social du Monde des Affaires: Le Cas de l'Interventionnisme et de la Punitivité des Juges du Tribunal de Commerce de Paris', *Droit et Société*, Vol. 71, 2009, p. 103-132.

In the different legal systems, where the appearance of a conflict of interest is taken as seriously as a full-blown conflict of interest, this type of institutional capture can be avoided. In a legal culture where situations that look like conflicts of interest are always blamed on individuals, not on the institution and its structure, this kind of neo-corporatism raises political problems. But the consular model and pragmatism constitute a political option that is never debated in the public arena. In this regime for social control of markets, a part of the State administration – and hence of government – operates in pragmatic mode, self-perpetuates in neo-corporatist, elitist fashion. Viewed this way, the existence of this kind of institution itself begins to seem incompatible with the definition of impartiality in Article 6 of the European Convention on Human Rights. The consular regime of joint regulation of markets involves appropriating the power of part of the State apparatus in a way that exceeds simple privatization of public services. In this sense, the issues it raises amount to new questions, to be added to those raised by political sociology and political science in the 1980s. Consular-type public action is spreading today. It is now operative in arbitration and is affecting the 'regulatory State' that has already gone some way to have independent administrative authorities carry out some of its own core functions. Research on this kind of institution suggests that the field of critical legal studies might benefit from more systematic research into organization and structure of such institutions, namely by paying more attention to the complex balance of 'joint regulation' that they advocate, to the complex forms of State privatization that they represent, and to who wins and who loses in each kind of 'balance' of power that is achieved in them.

Lastly, these observations strongly suggest that privatization of State functions is not 'disinstitutionalization' but rather a gradual replacement of statutory institutions with institutions that operate on the consular model. This points to the importance of rethinking public action on the basis of a critique of such consular regimes, as much as on the basis of a sociology of professions.[66] Furthermore, sociologists of the economy and the law are much more attentive today to the norms surrounding institutions such as commercial courts than are specialists in law and economics.[67] It is important to mention that in this sociological approach research on the notions such as self-regulation, co-regulation and joint regulation in connection with the economics of institutions, conventions, and regulation, goes far beyond the usual divide between hard law and soft law. Hypotheses and methodologies that can be promoted by such an economic sociology of law have yet to be further developed. In this area much remains to be done.

---

66 Lazega 1994; Lazega 2001.

67 Ayres & Braithwaite 1992; Lazega 2003; and R. Swedberg, 'The Case for an Economic Sociology of Law', *Theory and Society*, Vol. 32, 2003. p. 1-37.

Justice Unbound

Responsibility in the Second Modernity

Lyana Francot & Ubaldus de Vries[*]

Introduction

Contemporary Western society is boundless. Many socio-structural developments cause scholars to speak of society as a "world society".[1] This world society seems to usurp other, state-defined, societies. In all domains of sociality, live seems to have become unlimited and borderless. Modern transport leaves no place undiscovered and social relations are within reach by a few mouse clicks. Romantic relations start in airplanes, our kitchen cupboards are full of exotic spices and other ingredients, and in our gardens exotic plans and flowers emerge. Contemporary society offers endless options and opportunities. At the same time, we see how 'smart' investment firms cut the roots of national companies to become part of global corporates with increasing political power. We also become aware that decisions made here, for example about consumption, affect the lives of people elsewhere. Industrialization and capitalism have brought wealth – if not to all – but is now disclosing its many side effects for humans and the natural environment. World society is not merely a world society in economic terms, although we like to think of globalization mostly in economic turns. Contemporary society is boundless also in a political sense, where political movements have a global impact and are developing before the eye of the world, to which the spring revolt in Egypt in 2011 attested. And Academia too cherishes its global playing field with many cross border research networks and student exchange programmes. Modern law has seen the introduction of global aspects too, although termed internationally, such as the International Criminal Court and other (ad hoc) tribunals and courts, transcending the traditional jurisdiction of the nation state.

* This contribution is based and builds upon a previous publication of the authors; see: Lyana Francot & Ubaldus De Vries, 'No Way Out. Contracting about Modern Risk', *ARSP,* Vol. 95, No. 2, 2009, p. 199-215.

1 N. Luhmann. *Die Gesellschaft der Gesellschaft,* Suhrkamp, Frankfurt am Main 1997; A. Schütz, 'The Twilight of the Global Polis: On Losing Paradigms, Environing Systems, and Observing World Society', *in* G. Teubner (Ed.), *Global Law without a State,* Dartmouth, Aldersot/Brookfield (USA) 1997; R. Stichweh, *Die Weltgesellschaft: Soziologische Analysen,* Suhrkamp, Frankfurt am Main 2000; H. Wilke, *Supervision des Staates,* Suhrkamp, Frankfurt am Main 1997, p. 228.

All these developments transform individuals to world citizens, whether they like it or not, whether by choice or default, negative or positive: to both the tourist and the immigrant the world has become their oyster.[2] Home to the world citizen, this globe is not a safe haven *per se*. The individual, moreover, has become detached from ties that have been instrumental to his identity: nation-state, religion, language, currency, to name but a few.[3] It indicates that a world society has not only advantages but also has to deal with its specific problems. To wit: we suggest that this world society constitutes its unity and identity by and through these problems.

Exemplary are environmental problems and ecological disasters. The recent three-fold disaster in Japan – earthquake, Tsunami and nuclear threat – and the oil spill in the Gulf of Mexico in 2010 are central topics on the political agenda and in the global media. Catastrophes of this magnitude instil a sense of immediate urgency, duly emphasized by politics and 24/7 coverage by the global media networks – 'solutions' must be found, here and now. This experience of urgency renders almost any ecological problem a problem with a global impact. Although environmental disasters take place locally, their consequences carry with them a global effect and not merely in terms of physical damage to the environment and individuals but also in terms of political, economical and cultural damage. The Japan disaster causes stock markets to plummet, makes politicians elsewhere decide to put on hold the development and building of nuclear power plants, sees the destruction of villages and towns and their cultural heritage, uproots people and so on. Or, to say it differently, following Beck & Grande, environmental risks (which constitute the problem) "universalise the probabilities of disaster".[4]

In this contribution we argue that if contemporary law is to deal with world society problems effectively, it can do so only if it can take issue with its changing environment and the organising principles (or meta-rules of justice) that can be deduced from within this environment. The environment of contemporary law is global now and no longer limited to the nation state or international and supranational alliances. We do not seek to catalogue all problems with a global impact. Rather, we focus upon those problems that are conceptualized, in the social theoretical literature, as 'modern risks'. We seek to analyse how these modern risks confront contemporary law with unexpected problems. Western society has been preoccupied, throughout its modern development, with the problem of the just distribution of wealth. This distribution problem is compounded now by a second problem: modern risks. It necessitates legal-theoretical considerations, about a possible just distri-

---

2 See also: Z. Bauman, *Wasted Lifes. Modernity and Its Outcasts,* Polity, Cambridge 2004.
3 L. Heidbrink, *Handeln in der Ungewissheit – Paradoxien der Verantwortung,* Kadmos, Berlin 2007, p. 9.
4 U. Beck & E. Grande, *Cosmopolitan Europe* (Tran. Ciaran Cronin), Polity Press, Cambridge 2007, p. 198.

bution of these risks. Is it possible to devise a just distribution key that can deal with the *responsibility* for these risks, as a meta-rule of justice, which allows for the formulation of enforceable legal rules?

This contribution seeks, tentatively, to devise such a key. It draws upon the work of Ulrich Beck. His theory of reflexive modernization allows, in our view, for an inventory of social developments. Such an inventory contributes to the analysis and formulation of the main problem with which world society confronts contemporary law and, subsequently, makes it possible to formulate solutions for the distribution problem from a legal-theoretical perspective. In the second paragraph the theory of reflexive modernization is introduced. Its essence is constituted by the idea that our world society enters a new phase in the process of modernization, in which it is confronted with the side effects of its successes. These side effects radicalize, according to Beck, the processes of individualization and democratization, and are conceptualized in the notion of modern risks: world society is a risk society. The third paragraph takes issue with these risks and how Beck conceptualizes them. This analysis reveals that the problems of the risk society are linked with the unequal position of individuals in a globalising world. These positions transcend the classical, socio-economic, unequal positions in the nation state. This suggests that the nation state is no longer exclusively able to fulfil its distributing role. This conclusion sets us up to formulate, in paragraph four and five, the contours of a distribution key which focuses on the distribution of the responsibility for risks at a global level. Finally, in the sixth paragraph we explore what is demanded from contemporary law in teasing out the key in hard and fast rules.

First Modernity's Heritage

Beck's social-theoretical analysis centres on the ongoing process of modernization, albeit under different conditions and circumstances, rather than implying a post-modern phase as if there is a radical break with the past.[5] Indeed, Beck presents his findings under the heading of the theory of *reflexive modernization*. Stripped to its bare essence, the theory boils down to the thought that contemporary word society is confronted with the negative side-effects of the successes of the process of modernization. The theory seeks to explain the nature and scope of this confrontation of society with itself and the side effects it created – side effects that are global in their social reach and factual impact.

To elucidate this societal self-confrontation, Beck's distinguishes between two phases in the process of modernization: the 'first modernity', followed by the second phase – the

5 Cf. J.-F. Lyotard, *The Postmodern Condition: A Report on Knowledge* (Trans. G. Bennington and B. Massumi), Manchester University Press, Manchester 1984.

'second modernity'.[6] The first modernity is characterized by the central problem of scarcity and the search for rational (economic) solutions.[7] Industrialization and the development of technology can be seen, in this view, as processes that enabled the efficient and sufficient provision of human's material essentials. It enabled a large part of the population to attain a level of wealth over and beyond the means of subsistence, at least in Western-styled society. Scarcity changed from an absolute problem to a relative one and the focus on Progress, in the terms of wealth and later of wellbeing, became the norm – a state of being, instrumental to our life biographies. The processes not only changed the material conditions of living substantially but also re-shaped our attitude towards our natural environment and life as such. We are 'programmed', so to speak, towards Progress and we expect nothing less: life becomes better and longer. This attitude also translates into our attempts to control, or domesticate, nature, which also confronts us now with all kinds of side effects.[8] If we want better and longer, this will come at higher costs, which we 'encrypt' in our distribution key.

The production of wealth went hand-in-hand with the distribution of wealth. This caused, in fact, the second problem that characterized first modernity: what constitutes a just distribution of wealth? As much as industrialization captured the problem of scarcity and wealth, the process of democratization captured the problem of just distribution. Society in first modernity was an industrial society with the nation-state as the primary and exclusive unit of ordering social relations pertaining to the production and distribution of wealth. Its ideal is a free democratic and industrialized nation-state, bound by law in which those who participate in the production of wealth can claim a part of this wealth.[9]

Beck argues that society has now entered a second phase: second modernity. This suggests, at least, that Beck does not say farewell to modernity and modernization; the second phase is not a radical departure or break with that what preceded it. Rather, second modernity is a progression of the process of modernization but under different circumstances and new conditions. Second modernity sets the scene for a full-blown confrontation with the unwanted side-effects that resulted from solutions to first modernity's problems. These

---

6 Or solid modernity versus liquid modernity, according to Zygmunt Bauman; see: Z. Bauman, *Liquid Modernity,* Polity, Cambridge 2000.

7 First in an absolute sense and later also in a relative sense, during the triumph of the Welfare State.

8 See also: H. van der Loo & W. van Reijen, *Paradoxen van Modernisering,* Coutinho, Bussum 1997, p. 233-275.

9 See also U. de Vries & L. Francot-Timmermans, 'As Good As It Gets: On Risk, Legality and the Precautionary Principle', *in* L. Besselink, F. Pennings & S. Prechal (Eds.), *The Eclipse of the Legality Principle in the European Union,* Wolters Kluwer, Alphen aan den Rijn 2011, p. 1. The rule of law, as an aspect of the process of democratization, is also under siege by the problem of risks and how society has responded to them, for example, through the precautionary principle.

side effects see the light of day in the radicalization of the processes of industrialization and democratization into processes of "multidimensional globalization" and "forced individualization".[10] The process of forced individualization denotes the insight that individualization is not, or at least no longer, an individual choice but brought about by developments and decisions elsewhere and by others, which are beyond the control or reach of the individual. Multidimensional globalization embodies the idea, in Beck's view, that globalization is not limited to the economic dimension, even though globalization is most visible and, arguably, successful in this dimension. Globalization is more than the creation of a worldwide free market of money, goods and services. It also refers to other dimensions: globalization is also inherently political, cultural and social, tying individuals across borders and nationalities. Society in second modernity has become a post-industrialized society or, even more so, a risk society. In the theory of reflexive modernization, 'risk society', as the locus of second modernity, is made up, as it were, of the effects and results of forced individualization and multidimensional globalization. Beck refers to these effects and results as modern risks. The second modernity, hence, has its own distribution problem that does not substitute but accompanies the distribution problem of first modernity which still demands constant care and attention, but now on a global scale. This recent and global distribution problem concerns the distribution of the unwanted, *abundant*, side-effects; the distribution of modern risks. The upshot for this analysis of the consequences of the risk society, Beck has described in his *Risikogesellschaft* in 1986,[11] followed, in 1999, by the *World Risk Society.*[12]

The Problems of Second Modernity

The previous paragraph showed that first modernity's heritage includes more than the achievements of democracy, wealth and individual autonomy. Modernity's heritage also includes unwanted side-effects, which second modernity makes visible: modern risks. Initially, in *Risk Society,* Beck restricted himself to a theoretical analysis of the societal effects of ecological risks. In his later work the catalogue is extended to include risks that are political, economical and individual in nature.[13] The essence of what these risks constitute of has remained the same. A further analysis of modern risks is, hence, relevant for

10 Beck & Grande 2007, p. 29.

11 U. Beck, *Risikogesellschaft: auf dem Weg in eine andere Moderne,* Suhrkamp, Frankfurt am Main 1986. Translated in 1992: U. Beck, *Risk Society: Towards a New Modernity,* Sage, London 1992.

12 U. Beck, *World Risk Society,* Polity Press, Cambridge 1999.

13 U. Beck, *The Reinvention of Politics: Rethinking Modernity in the Global Social Order,* Polity Press, Cambridge 1997. On p. 12 Beck argues that '[n]ew insecurities are infiltrating the secure milieu of the welfare state and erupting there. These may involve the loss of formerly secure benefits, threats to health or life itself from toxins, criminality and violence, or the loss of such certainties as the faith in progress, science and experts'.

two reasons: First, such a description discloses the precise nature of the current distribution problem and the consequences for global justice. Second, such a description enables mapping out possible solutions in the light of the processes of forced individualization and multidimensional globalization.

Aspects of Modern Risks

Since modern risks are to be understood as side effects of first modernity, in which the process of industrialization played a key role, the first aspect Beck ascribes to modern risks is that they are self-produced and, consequently, self-inflicted. [14] Modern risks are not incidental risks. Rather, they constitute, as a negative side-effect, a structural part of contemporary society as they are the mirror image of structural wealth production. This means, in the first instance, that modern Western societies are themselves responsible for the production of these risks. But the consequences of risk production (including those in the shape of a disaster (the manifestation of a risk)) are not limited to these societies: they are instead inherently global and future oriented, tying in present and past generations across the globe.

The second aspect is this global character of modern risks. [15] Although modern risks are produced locally (worldwide), their consequences are both local *and* global. So, if globalization points, among other things, to the free movement of products worldwide, it implies, by necessity, the worldwide movement of modern risks as the latter is intricately bound to the former. Illustrative, here, is the spread of disease through the worldwide movement of livestock, such as BSE, avian flu and foot-and-mouth disease.

The third aspect, one that follows from the global reach of modern risks, refers to the existence of social risk positions. [16] People are exposed to risks in many different ways. Some are able to limit the possible manifestation of risks or to limit the consequences of such manifestation. A large group though is at the mercy of the manifestation and consequences of modern risks. [17] These social risks positions – contrary to class positions – are not limited to the borders of the nation state. These positions are both global and international. What is meant here is that on the one hand there are states that are either more or less exposed to risks and their consequences. Thus, Western states, through better econom-

14 Beck 1992, p. 21.
15 *Id.*, p. 21-22.
16 *Id.*, p. 35-36.
17 The phrase 'consequences of risks' is not, in the view of the authors, elegantly put but serves a purpose: Beck does not distinguish between risks and the manifestation of risks in the shape of disasters. These disasters (and *their* consequences) are what is referred to here.

ical, technological and scientific development, are better able to protect themselves against risks than states in the developing world. On the other hand, social risks positions also refer to individuals or groups of individuals across states and the extent to which these groups are able to protect themselves against risks and their consequences. These groups are not necessarily limited to groups within states but exist globally, for example all those who work in sweatshops – who work in pitiful conditions in either Manila or New York,[18] and who struggle with the problem of wealth as well as of risks. Beck considers however these positions to be temporary – in time we all are exposed to risks equally. The global character of risks has a 'boomerang effect': everyone, including those in the West, will be exposed to risks in like fashion. There is no way out.

The fourth aspect is the 'invisibility' of risks. What is meant here is that risks cannot be perceived sensory. Modern risks are constructions of scientific knowledge and exist in mathematical or chemical formulas. It also means that individuals or groups of individuals in scientific and political key positions can determine when what is a risk. The ability to formulate risks does not mean that one is able to predict when and how risks manifest themselves in the shape of disasters and catastrophes. Such knowledge exists merely in probability and educated guesses – in other words, such knowledge exists in terms of uncertainty. In the here and now, risks are formulas and they may become events in the future when they loose the characteristic of 'risk', i.e. if and when the uncertainty of their manifestation becomes a certainty, in a yet unknown future. Risks bind the future and the present, as they force us to look forward, making us conscious of a future which may be unfavourable (or not) but without us being able to determine cause and effect.

Increasing social complexity, arguably, contributes to this.[19] Complexity, here, refers to the endless horizon of options and possibilities from which we must choose. All of these options and possibilities cannot be realized, at least not at once and not by one actor. Furthermore, making a selection may be an onerous task. We may often not be able to foresee or anticipate the intended and unintended consequences of selections and choices we have made. In addition, it leads to the observation that society is characterized by the experience of contingency: everything could be different.[20] Complexity, thus, entails a

18 N. Klein, *No Logo*, Picador, New York 1999, in particular ch. 9-11.

19 See: L. Francot-Timmermans & U. De Vries, 'Normativity in the Second Modernity', *Rechtstheorie*, Vol. 39, No. 4, 2008, p. 477-494. Illustrative too, is: Heidbrink 2007.

20 Contingency refers to the modal logical concept of "*Auch-anders-möglich-Sein*" or "neither necessary nor impossible": "A fact is contingent when seen as a selection from other possibilities which remain in some sense possibilities despite a selection"; see: N. Luhmann, 'Generalized Media and the Problem of Contingency', *in* J. Loubser, *et al* (Eds.), *Explorations in General Theory in Social Science – Essays in Honor of Talcott Parsons*, The Free Press, New York 1976, p. 507-532, at p. 50.

quantitative (the amount of options) as well as a qualitative aspect (how to choose).[21] The perception of this social complexity has lead to the insight that it has become increasingly more difficult to judge the effects of one's own actions (effects that can also manifest themselves outside the actor's field of action) and the effects of others upon our decisions and subsequent actions.[22]

The last aspect Beck ascribes to modern risks follows from this and concerns the problem of responsibility and causality. A central notion of responsibility is the possibility to attribute an effect (or consequence) to an actor, whose actions caused the effect. In other words, the attribution of responsibility is conditioned by this notion of (linear) causality.[23] As it becomes increasingly more difficult to detect causal connections in the production of risks (and in their consequences), it becomes also more difficult to determine who is or can be held responsible for what. Beck concludes:[24]

> Corresponding to the highly differentiated division of labor, there is a general complicity, and the complicity is matched by a general lack of responsibility. Everyone is cause and effect, and thus non-cause. [...] This reveals in exemplary fashion the ethical significance of the system concept: one can do something and continue doing it without having to take personal responsibility for it.

Some Notes on Beck's Concept of Risk

Beck's view on modern risks invites at least three critical comments. The first comment deals with 'what' actually must be distributed. The problem is that Beck fails to make a clear distinction between risks on the one hand and the manifestation of risks in the shape of disasters and other catastrophes on the other. Damage, dangers, disasters: Beck considers all these phenomena as appearances of modern risks. But in our view there is a crucial difference between situations where one realizes that there is a risk which could manifest itself in the future and situations where an actual disaster has happened with real damage. Essentially, the difference is between that what lies in the future and that what lies in the past. To be more precise, the difference is between the uncertainty inherent in risks (as risks are future-related) and the certainty of the manifestation: the disaster has struck and the uncertainty of risk is replaced by the actual event; the certainty of a manifested risk. The manifestation of a risk does not necessarily mean, though, that we know what we are

21 L.M.A. Francot-Timmermans, *Normativity's Re-entry: Niklas Luhmann's Social Systems Theory: Society and Law*, Wolf Legal Publishing, Nijmegen 2008, Ch. 4.

22 Heidbrink 2007.

23 Much of the civil liability regimes in the world are based on this notion of causality.

24 Beck 1992, p. 31 (emphasis in original).

dealing with, in the sense that it is immediately clear who or what is responsible and what is cause and effect. The distinction is important also, when we consider the role of contemporary law which struggles with the notions of causality and responsibility under the conditions of the second modernity.

Furthermore, and this is the second comment, Beck seems to limit his concept of risks to those that are systematically and structurally produced, in particular industrialization risks. However, in addition to these risks there does exist all kinds of other uncertain but probable threats, such as epidemics, natural disasters (earth quakes, tsunamis, volcanic eruptions) which are not necessarily *modern* risks but are of all times. But what these risks have in common with modern risks is the extent of the consequences and how we seek to deal with these consequences and the loss they cause: we want all loss, whatever its nature, to be prevented or if this is not possible remedied. To this end, we look to an earthquake in a highly industrialized society in a similar way as to the (subsequent) nuclear disaster in that same society. It shows that modernization has weaved a web, so to speak, of modern risks, literally: we live our lives for the most part in such a dense and interconnected way that risks are not clustered in a few locations but are located everywhere. Even if a more traditional risk manifests itself it often causes a chain reaction of modern risks materialising. Again, Japan is a case in point. Second modernity discloses the advent of 'hyper risks': we are not merely confronted with self-produced, modern risks but also with the risk that these materialize in disaster through traditional risks – risks over which we have no control whatsoever.

The third comment pertains to Beck's view on the equalizing effect of modern risks. This may be true in abstract terms: when we understand risks as uncertain, invisible, future events presented as formulas, we are all subjected to them in a like manner. But this is different when we consider manifested risks such as disasters and the like. At first sight, it seems plausible to suggest that, sooner or later, we all will be confronted with risks and their consequences equally. Nuclear fall-out is democratic, to paraphrase Beck.[25] Epidemics such as caused by avian flu like diseases could be another example. The world trade in poultry could lead to a world-wide epidemic from which it may be difficult to escape. However, the question is whether the *effects* of modern risks are actually as equalizing as Beck suggests. Are Western societies not far better equipped to deal with these risks and their consequences? Can they not fall back upon vast resources of money, expertise and advanced technology within a well-organized infrastructure of transportation, health services and rescue services, even if this infrastructure is (partly) destroyed? Furthermore, even if risks produced elsewhere boomerang back, are the consequences merely or only

25 Beck 1992, p. 36.

physical (in terms of physical damage) or rather economical, political and financial? In our view, the equalising effect is not of such a nature that we're all in the same boat. On the contrary, we believe that modern risks radicalize social risk positions, strengthened by the existing global and international institutional order of dependency relations. The poorest regions of the world still struggle with the problem of scarcity (however this scarcity is 'produced') and are now also confronted with the problem of risk. It seems likely that this double problem exacerbate global social risk positions. Risks have a discriminatory effect. Perhaps a parallel can be drawn with Manuel Castell's view of society as a network society. Social risk positions pertain to the extent people are included or excluded from "the global networks that accumulate knowledge, wealth, and power". [26]

To sum up: the five aspects Beck ascribes to risks are interrelated. Modern risks, which are by their nature systematically man made and self-inflicted, are global in their reach and sensory invisible, *leading to* unequal social risks positions and *result both in and from* organized irresponsibility due to a weak causality. One final characteristic of risks is the magnitude of their manifestations in the shape of disasters, catastrophes and calamities.

Modern risks escalate the global relationship between rich and poor, North and South, deepening the gap and put into focus the injustice of it. We share Beck's view that dealing with the distribution problem of risks, formulating solutions, cannot take place within the confines of the nation state. Instead, it demands a global or in Becks words, a cosmopolitan perspective that transcends the perspective of methodological nationalism. [27] The distribution of risks is a global problem and this problem is a descriptor of a new *Verelendung*, [28] this time at a global level. It is this discriminatory effect that shapes the discussion on global justice, puts it into focus and makes it urgent.

The Central Problem

It is now possible, and necessary, to refine the distribution problem in second modernity at least for the benefit of a legal perspective.

---

26 M. Castells, *The Rise of the Network Society. The Information Age: Economy, Society, and Culture*, Vol. 1. (2nd ed.), Wiley-Blackwell, Oxford 2010, p. xvii.

27 The cosmopolitan methodology, developed over and beyond methodological nationalism is addressed by Beck in U. Beck, *The Cosmopolitan Vision*, Polity, Cambridge 2005 and criticized by, among others, R. Fine, *Cosmopolitanism*, Routledge, London 2007, p. 9-14. t is beyond the scope of this contribution to deal with it, but see, for example, Francot & De Vries 2008.

28 Pauperization, the term with which to describe the awful situation of the proletariat in the industrialized cities in Europe.

To argue that the distribution pertains to risks per se is not sufficient for the current discussion as to if and how law may play a role. Modern risks are uncertain future events, merely visible in mathematical or chemical formulas and as such difficult if not impossible to distribute. Another option is to look at the redistribution of the *production* of risks. This could take place within the domains of the economy, science and politics. It would pertain to a factual redistribution, re-allocating factories and the application of new (no or low risk-producing) technology. Law can fulfil a function here, providing rules to facilitate technological innovation or risk-preventing policies. The precautionary principle is perhaps an illustration of this. But, it is also an illustration, as we have argued elsewhere, that the principle cannot be cast in a hard-and-fast legal rule.[29] Law operates *ex post facto*. Only after the event, modern law seems able to offer certainty. It allocates, within a national setting only, responsibility in terms of civil liability, providing remedies for (financial) loss, but stumbles upon all kinds of problems, including the magnitude of loss, problems concerning causality and the notion of several liability). Prior to the event, at the stage of risk, law seems at a loss in respect of risks themselves. If we want distribute risks, it really means that we seek to distribute uncertainty, in a double sense: in respect of the manifestation of a risk (if and when), its consequences and for whom.

We focus, instead, on the distribution of *responsibility* for the production of modern risks. The central problem in the risk society is not the distribution of risks per se or their production but their organized irresponsibility in respect of those who produce, spread and consume these risks, and contribute to their manifestation. It is this insensitivity towards responsibility that must be halted. Hence, the distribution of modern risks lies in the attribution of responsibility for them and their manifestations against the background of global justice.

Towards State-Transcending Solutions

The kernel of the problem in the second modernity concerns in our view the global injustice that emanates from modern risks. The poorest countries and individuals not only struggle with the problem of (absolute) scarcity but are also burdened with the problem of modern risks, in all its aspects. This is ironic and bitter as these risks follow from wealth production to which the poorest do have little or no access at all.

29 De Vries and Francot-Timmermans 2011.

Insufficient Alternatives

The characteristics ascribed to modern risks constitute in themselves specific but interrelated problems which must be taken into account when formulating suitable solutions.

The first characteristic referred to risks as systematic and structural side-effects of wealth production. We produce risks ourselves. Beck's argumentation, then, seduces us to conclude that the production of risks would end if there is an end to (technological) progress or at least when progress is put in check. In other words, the production of risks would stop if we stop producing wealth in the manner we do. Although it seems like the quickest solution to the problem of unwanted abundance, it obviously is an oversimplification of the problem and hardly realistic. It would demand a change of mentality which cannot be realized in a short time and on a global scale. Whatever the other consequences of a 'return to nature', one can at least surmise that it would see the resurfacing of the problem of scarcity (world wide) and perhaps leading to a truly Hobbessian state of nature. The solutions will double the problem. It would be more realistic to focus technological progress, not on wealth production (progress rationalization) but on risk reduction (welfare or sustainability rationalization). Hence, one could plead for a change of perspective as to the goal of the processes of modernization: not wealth (and the typical material connotation the word accompanies) but welfare in terms of sustainability as desirable outcome of modernization. This perspective is by no means a new one and features prominently in the discussions about the welfare state. Nowadays, though, welfare is also understood globally and environmentally, in terms of sustainability.[30] Talk is about sustainable development (sustainable wealth production) that incorporates concerns for the environment and labour conditions, human rights and poverty, etc. demanding a fresh perspective on the role of politics, law, economy and technology. These two possibilities illustrate a mental and factual change but require time and are not necessarily global as the problem of scarcity remains a real problem locally still. They are really solutions that, in practical terms, only the West can afford, notwithstanding the fact that such solutions should be promoted and sustained whenever possible.

Modern risks do have a global impact, as Beck convincingly illustrates. This second aspect of risks – their globality – demands a global response. Response limited to the nation-state level or the individual level cannot and will not suffice. It goes without saying that individuals (and states) play a crucial role here (in respect of the individual responses they can make). But, in addition to these efforts, the global reach of the problem necessitates also

30 Consider the discussion about "ecological modernization"; see: R. Lee and E. Stokes, 'Ecological modernization and the Precautionary Principle', *Ethics, Law and Society,* Vol. 4, No. 1, 2005, p. 103-113.

formal organizations and institutions at the global level.[31] IGOs such as the IMF and the World Bank, NGOs like Greenpeace, global corporates, states, cities and other regional actors have a role to play here, in particular to the refocusing of technological progress and the ending of poverty/scarcity.[32]

The third aspect – the existence of social risk positions – takes a central position in the search of global, state-transcending just solutions. This is so, because we argue that risks (if and when manifested) have a discriminatory rather than, as Beck argued, an equalising effect. It leads to the conclusion that any solution must *strife* at legitimising differentiations between social risk positions. The existence of different social risk positions is accentuated by the fourth aspect: the non-sensory character of risks and their existence in formulas. It implies that those in key positions in politics and science determine in the end what is and what is not be presented or perceived as a risk. Considering the state of knowledge and the availability of the means to expand upon this knowledge in the developed, networked, world,[33] it has an advantage in determining risks and in calculating or evaluating the uncertain but possible consequences and how to respond to them. With this advantage comes the responsibility to share this knowledge in a way similar to how informational technology knowledge is shared for the purpose of its constant regeneration and expansion.[34] Knowledge breads knowledge and this is fundamental in dealing with the problem of modern risks, to which we are all subjected.

Responsibility

We are mostly concerned with formulating a possible solution for what we perceive as the central problem: the distribution of the responsibility for risks. In the first instance, one could argue that distribution follows from actually *taking* responsibility based on a moral duty. However, we believe that a mere moral dimension is insufficiently effective in a globalized world, considering, among other things, the improbability of a universal morality, at least in terms of content. It could be seen, though, as an approach to provide, following Pogge, "necessary, not sufficient, conditions for the acceptability of a moral conception".[35] Although a moral dimension is a necessary element and contributes to formulating a shared perspective of the central; problem, it is insufficient. The moral duty to take responsibility is a first step but we must be realistic in that not everyone (perhaps

31 We have addressed the role of organizations in more detail in: Francot and De Vries 2008.

32 See also Thomas Pogge and his arguments pertaining to the global resource dividend and the borrowing and resource privilege; in: Th. Pogge, *World Poverty and Human Rights,* Polity, Cambridge 2002.

33 Castells 2010.

34 Castells 2010, Ch. 1.

35 Pogge 2002, p. 94.

even most of us) is willing or able to take on a duty merely on moral grounds, based on self-discipline and self-regulation. Morality falls short in respect of the execution and enforcement of distribution and responsibility decisions; morality lacks an 'organizational back-up'. Were the formulation of a shared perspective upon distributing responsibility for risks possible, it should be a matter of politics and law to tease out the details.

Formulating a Distribution Key: an Upbeat

Law by and in itself is unable to offer direct solutions for the central problem at this general level. There is no global law, or regulatory framework, about which there is general agreement and subject to enforcement. International law consists, on the whole, of general guidelines and where it does provide detailed rules, it is on the whole in bi-lateral or multilateral treaties pertaining to the first modernity problem of the nation state system and wealth production and distribution. [36] And where law does take issue with the central problem, in does so in a haphazard way, devoid of a solid foundation. [37]

What is necessary is to develop a shared point of departure, or, if one likes, an organising principle or maxim. This principle, then, can be worked out legally, in hard-and-fast rules. The organising principle, as it is aimed at a distribution problem takes the shape of a distribution key. In doing so, we must take into account a number of considerations. First, modern risks, within the contemporary context, are a given. Only if we forego the production of wealth risks will not be an unavoidable side effect of this wealth. Second, we are not concerned with the distribution of modern risks themselves but with the responsibility for them. First modernity was concerned with the distribution of wealth (wanted but scarce resources) and demanded the formulation of rights (and corresponding duties). Now, we are concerned with an, in principle, [38] unwanted abundance, requiring the formulation and attribution of duties (and corresponding rights). The question, then, becomes: who can and must these duties be attributed to? [39]

The global reach of risks and the fact that they are products of the processes of modernization have the consequence, as discussed above, that they lead to different social risk positions

36 Is EU law, for example, not about economic integration and the creation of a common market in which persons, services, products and capital can freely roam?

37 Here, again, the precautionary approach is illustrative.

38 Modern risks, too, create their own market. Beck: 'Demands, and thus markets, of a completely new type can be created by varying the definition of risk, especially demand for the avoidance of risk'; Beck 1992, p. 56.

39 And a similarly important question is: who can attribute these duties? To deal with this question demands the formulation of the distribution key, and is outside the scope of this article.

– risks discriminate, as we argued above. And only *some* have actually benefited from the fruits of these risks, i.e. the 'modernized' part of the world. Those parts of the world that are not (yet) modernized,[40] still struggle with the problem of scarcity and are confronted now also with the problem of risk, also because these parts are attractive and cheap places for risk producing industry. As Beck states: "extreme poverty [attracts] extreme risks".[41]

When we take these considerations into account, a risk calculus becomes essential. In this calculus a number of factors are balanced. The point of departure is that everyone is subjected to modern risks and that everyone contributes, in many different ways, to the production of risks. Risks are to be considered as the unwanted side-effects of wealth. This must be balanced against the fact that, although everyone contributes to the production of risks and, hence, the production of wealth, not everyone shares in the enjoyment of and access to this wealth. Furthermore, those who do enjoy access to wealth are less subjected to the risks, whereas those who have no or limited access to wealth are much more exposed to risks. The degree in which people are exposed to risks is inversely proportional to which people have access to wealth, or so it seems. It is reasonable, therefore, to consider these aspects and to argue that responsibility is not to be distributed in proportion to the production of risks but in proportion to the consumption of wealth (from which these risks originate). In a supply-and-demand world economy this is even more so, considering that the demand is instrumental to the production (supply) of risks. It leads to the following two-folded distribution key:

1. Those who do not participate in the production of risks (in the production *and* consumption of goods) are not attributed responsibility for these risks.
2. Those who do participate in the production of risks are attributed responsibility in a measure equal to the access of goods corresponding with these risks.

The key excludes the possibility to burden people (in groups or organizations) who in fact cause the actual production of risks if they do not have access to the corresponding goods. Such a distribution strategy would probably be justified in a modern liberal theory based upon the maxim: "the polluter pays". But it is not an option that can feasibly be maintained from the perspective of global social justice. On the contrary, responsibility ought to be placed on those who enjoy unbridled access to and consumption of wealth and goods,

40 To be clear: when the problem of *absolute* scarcity is resolved, a country can be said to be modernized – at least, in the Beckian sense.

41 Beck 1992, p. 41.

causing others to suffer.[42] Indeed, in second modernity, the maxim ought to be: 'the consumer pays'. The distribution key counters the harm principle as an organising principle in first modernity. The harm principle allows for (state) intervention when one's actions cause or threaten to cause harm to others. Usually this is based on a direct form of causality. The distribution key safeguards those who actually produce the risk (the potential harm) of being exposed to this direct causality and be imposed responsibility. Rather, the key implies an indirect form of causality, based on consumer demand, so to speak.

THE ROLE OF LAW: A REFLEXIVE APPROACH

The distribution key is a meta-principle and forms the upbeat for further elaboration in hard-and-fast rules. Law in particular, is deemed more than suitable for the task of redistributing responsibilities. This is what it is geared to do: to distribute among, and attribute to, us duties, obligations and responsibilities which we favour not to have. Usually these duties are formulated in response to rights and entitlements, for example, in relation to property. The focus, here, is on how law can play a role in the distribution of responsibility for risks as future events, striving towards an *ex ante* distribution of responsibility. Modern law is not geared towards such a distribution *ex ante*. Understanding first modernity society suggests considering society as based upon the fundamental belief of Progress through Reason, culminating in the belief of the *Machbarkeit* of society, guided by certain fundamental organising principles, or values, such as democracy, rule of law, freedom, equality, solidarity, sovereignty, capitalism, etc.[43] Risks illustrate the changing conditions modern law is confronted with, demanding a reflexive approach and this implies, first and foremost, taking into account the changing global condition of the second modernity. This global condition makes also visible the blind spots, limitations and failures of modern law.[44]

---

42 Cf. Pogge 2002, who argues that the affluent West violates its negative duty not to cause harm to the global poor and suggests institutional reform to stop this violation.

43 The Rawlsian interpretation would be societies geared towards cooperation for mutual benefit within a given jurisdiction, i.e. nation-states circumscribed by the notion of freedom, equality and difference; see: J. Rawls, *A Theory of Justice*, Harvard University Press, Cambridge (Mass.) 1971:
"A set of principles is required for choosing among the various social arrangements which determine this division of advantages and for underwriting an agreement on the proper distributive shares. These principles are the principles of social justice: they provide a way of assigning rights and duties in the basic institutions of society and they define the appropriate distribution of the benefits and burdens of social co-operation." (p. 4)

44 It also demands a new perspective on legal research. Such a perspective is elaborated in U. de Vries, 'Kuhn and Legal Research. A Reflexive Paradigm for Legal Research in de Second Modernity', forthcoming. The text in this paragraph draws upon some of the findings in that article.

The Global Condition

The new approach is occupied with a double problem: the continuing effort to produce and distribute wealth justly (and this time also globally!) and the new effort to manage its side effects. It does not necessitate replacing the 'old' perspective but rather seeks to incorporate this older, first modernity perspective in an encompassing perspective that can take issue with the double problem justly and legitimately. It is this aspect that forms the kernel of Beck's theory of *reflexive* modernization. As society in the second modernity is characterized by the awareness of the consequences and adverse side-effects of first modernity's successes, a confrontation with and reconsideration of the fundamental beliefs and values of first modernity will herald the transformation from a nation state-based industrial society toward a world risk society that is able to deal with the double problem. Thus, the world risk society is a society that transcends the nation state, is driven by the twin processes of globalization and forced individualization, and is, must, in respect of wealth and risks, be geared towards sustainability (rather than progress) under conditions of uncertainty.

Reflexive modernization exists in society's confrontation with its foundations and organizational structures. A national outlook alone is not sufficient but must be incorporated into an encompassing and transcending outlook, which Beck denotes as a cosmopolitan vision. In respect of the current frame of reference of modern law, it means taking issue with a structural rather than an incidental approach to risks and their manifestations, perhaps leading to a reconsideration of legal regimes, for example, the regime of civil liability; it means a more integrated approach to understanding risk, demanding interdisciplinary cooperation within the domains of law, politics and science; it means a multilateral approach that breaks through the traditional concepts of sovereignty involving other social actors that nation states and international organizations; it means taking serious issue with poverty and social risk positions – particular in those areas where one suffers the twin problem of both scarcity and risk; it demands novel categories of causality and responsibility; it demands new ways to deal with loss and damage.

Blind Spots and Limitations

As much as we are accustomed to think of law as having a problem-resolving potential so do we think of law as distributing or attributing responsibility. Luhmann already pointed to the problem-*generating* potential of law.[45] In an insightful legal analysis, Veitch shows

45 N. Luhmann, *Law as a Social System* (Tran. Klaus A. Ziegert, ed. Fatima Kastner, et al.), Oxford University Press, Oxford 2004, p. 139.

that law and legal institutions, while distributing responsibility, is also '*centrally involved in organising irresponsibility*'.[46] The kernel of the analysis is that there exists an asymmetry between the production of suffering (through violence, large scale environmental damage, etc.) and legal responsibility for it through the operation of legal mechanisms, such its modes of categorization, normalization of behaviour (lawful behaviour is deemed normal despite damage caused and, hence, remains mostly unquestioned), role differentiation (law defining the extent of my responsibility, for example, as shareholder of a major oil company destructing the environment) and as a result the fragmentation of responsibility. It is these mirror notions – law generating conflicts, law organising irresponsibility – that must become more explicit and visible in a reflexive approach to modern law.

Conclusion

The point of departure of this contribution is that we live in a world society that is characterized by world wide interdependencies and is confronted by a new, additional distribution problem. This problem is described in a convincing way by Ulrich Beck in his theory of reflexive modernization. Its essence is that modern society is now confronted with the side effects of its successes that stem from the processes of industrialization and democratization. These side effects are rubricated under the notion of modern risks. The impact of modern risks is worldwide, cutting across borders of modernized societies and beyond. It makes contemporary society a world risk society. This global aspect demands a global response. Where Western society is able to rely on knowledge, money and power to address the problem the unfortunate others are at a loss, yet again: the global poor have so far not been able to escape the problem of first modernity (scarcity) and are not also confronted with the effects of the solution: risks. It puts into focus the urgency of the new distribution problem. We are not, cannot be, merely concerned with the distribution of risks per se or their production. Rather, we are concerned with the distribution of responsibility for modern risks. The essence of the distribution key is that those who profit most in the world risk society are burdened with the heaviest responsibility for the side-effects of this profit. The distribution key is geared towards an *unequal* distribution of responsibility in order to envision a conception of global social justice. Following Rawls, the famous modern contemporary thinker of wealth distribution,[47] the key implies a just procedure. It starts of as moral imperative but must be established within a legal framework. This would involve the reconsideration of modern law's basis elements, such as the notion of for example (exclusive) property rights, contractual liability and incorporation strategies, to

46 S. Veitch, *Law and Irresponsibility. On the Legitimation of Human Suffering*, Routledge/Glass House, London 2007, p. 1.

47 Rawls 1971.

expose existing legal veils of irresponsibility. The distribution key is to stimulate debate about the formulation of such rules, who could or should formulate them and to whom these rules are applied.

List of contributors

Mariano Croce

Mariano Croce is Adjunct Professor of Philosophy of Law at 'Sapienza – Università di Roma', Department of Philosophy. His research interests include general jurisprudence, legal pluralism, and the relation between politics and law. In particular, he focuses on the role that legal thinking and discourse about law in general play in the making of the legal field and, more generally, in the ordering of society.

Costas Douzinas

Costas Douzinas is Professor of Law and Director Birkbeck Institute for the Humanities, Birkbeck College, University of London. He is a visiting Professor at the University of Athens and has held visiting posts at various universities, including the University of Paris, Thessaloniki and Prague. In 1997 he was awarded a Jean Monnet fellowship by the European University Institute, Florence. His books include *The End of Human Rights* and *Human Rights and Empire*.

Peter Fitzpatrick

Peter Fitzpatrick is currently Anniversary Professor of Law at Birkbeck, University of London. He has taught at universities in Europe, North America and Papua New Guinea and published books on legal philosophy, law and social theory, law and racism, and imperialism, recent ones being *Law as Resistance* (Ashgate, 2008) and with Ben Golder, *Foucault's Law* (Routledge, 2009).

Lyana Francot

Lyana Francot is a lecturer in the Department of Legal Theory, School of Law, Utrecht University, the Netherlands. In the *Working Group on (Reflexive) modernization & Law* she seeks to contribute to the analysis of the interdependencies between legal developments and societal evolution. Current research centres on autopoietic justice, normativity and uncertainty in current modernity and an inquiry into the possibility of an ethics of action and experience. Furthermore, she has a not yet fully explored fascination for George

Spencer Brown's calculus. She published a.o. *Normativity's Re-Entry - Niklas Luhmann's Social Systems Theory: Society and Law* (Wolf Legal Publishers 2008).

JEROEN KIEWIET

Jeroen Kiewiet is a Lecturer at Radboud University Nijmegen. He holds an LL.M from Rijksuniversiteit Groningen and is currently working on his PhD on Carl Schmitt's legal theory. His main research interests lie within the domain of legal theory and concern: general theory of law, political philosophy, and legal pluralism.

EMMANUEL LAZEGA

Emmanuel Lazega is Professor of sociology at the University of Paris – Dauphine. He is a senior member of the Institut Universitaire de France and the author of several books, among which *The Collegial Phenomenon: The Social Mechanisms of Cooperation Among Peers in a Corporate Law Partnership*, Oxford University Press, and *Conventions and Structures in Economic Organization: Markets, Networks, and Hierarchies*, Cheltenham, UK: Edward Elgar Publishing. His work focuses on the relationships between business and the State.

EUGENE MC NAMEE

Eugene Mc Namee is Lecturer in Law at School of Law, University of Ulster, Jordanstown, Belfast. He is interested in law's intersections with social theory, bio-politics, and the humanities and is currently researching on Rwandan post-conflict issues and cultural constitutionalism in Northern Ireland.

CAN ÖZTAŞ

Can Öztaş is a PhD Candidate in Law, Birkbeck College, University of London. Can completed his LL.M at King's College, London in 2009, and has previously worked as an international and national civil servant. His research interests include human rights, legal theory, race-thinking, and critical approaches to international law.

Andreas Philippopoulos-Mihalopoulos

Andreas Philippopoulos-Mihalopoulos is Professor of Law & Theory at the University of Westminster and Director of The Westminster International Law & Theory Centre. His research is interdisciplinary and includes phenomenology, autopoiesis, law and literature, geography, art, corporeality, environmental studies. His edited volumes *Law and the City* and *Law and Ecology* and his monographs *Absent Environments* and *Niklas Luhmann: Law, Justice, Society* are published by Routledge.

Ubaldus de Vries

Ubaldus de Vries is lecturer in the Department of Legal Theory at the School of Law of Utrecht University, the Netherlands and fellow of the Center for the Humanities, Utrecht Universities. In the *Working Group on (Reflexive) modernization & Law* he is engaged in conceptualizing a contextual approach towards understanding law and legal developments in the new modernity. Of special interest are issues of autonomy, responsibility and self-determination as well as the structure and pedagogy of legal education and legal research, seeking to bridge the gap between legal theory and social theory.

Marc de Wilde

Marc de Wilde is Assistant Professor of Legal History at the University of Amsterdam. He wrote a dissertation on the political theologies of Walter Benjamin and Carl Schmitt. His recent publications include: 'Locke and the State of Exception: Towards a Modern Understanding of Emergency Government', *European Constitutional Law Review*, Vol. 6, No. 2, 2010, p. 249-267 and 'The State of Emergency in the Weimar Republic: Legal Disputes over Article 48 of the Weimar Constitution', *Legal History Review*, Vol. 78, 2010, p. 135-158.